Praise from Experts for *The Grandfamily Guidebook*

"Grandparents who take on parenting will find much-needed encouragement and a wealth of practical information in this clear, authoritative book. It ought to be required reading, both for parenting grandparents and for the professionals—pediatricians and family doctors in particular—whose job it is to support them."

—Robert Needlman, MD
Author of *Dr. Spock's Baby Basics*

"In times when families and generations are blending, we are seeing more and more grandparents taking on parental roles. *The Grandfamily Guidebook* adeptly provides invaluable information and helpful tips to navigate the increasingly common scenario of grandparents raising their children's children. As a surgeon who treats countless permutations of what composes a family unit, I see that now more so than ever the grandparent assumes a parental role. This book is a must-have guide to better navigate the territory of parenting as grandparents."

—Nina L. Shapiro, MD
Director of Pediatric Otolaryngology
Professor of Head and Neck Surgery at UCLA School of Medicine
Author of *Hype: A Doctor's Guide to Medical Myths,
Exaggerated Claims, and Bad Advice*

"Few of us grow up expecting to be raising toddlers when we're on the eve of our own retirement. But for millions of American children, their parents are no longer part of traditional family structure. Is this reliance on grandparents to step in for round two of parenting the new normal? For too many families it is. *The Grandfamily Guidebook* is an indispensable part of modern child rearing and lends a parent/grandparent a right hand when we all need it the most."

—Nancy Snyderman, MD
Professor of Global Health at Stanford University
Former medical correspondent for ABC and NBC News

"This is the book you need when you become a parent all over again for your grandchild. While no one plans for this to happen, you need a plan when it does! And while children have not changed in the past thirty years, what we have learned about them has. This is the guide for navigating the challenges and joys of raising your grandchild."

—**Ari Brown, MD**
Pediatrician and author of *Baby 411* and *Toddler 411*

"*The Grandfamily Guidebook* is a must-read for grandparents raising their grandchildren, as well as for the providers taking care of the entire family. With easy-to-understand medical, psychological, and legal information and resources, this book provides the essentials for healthy "grandfamilies" that include healthy children as well as healthy grandparents. Well written and well researched, this book is sure to become a classic "must-have" on providers' as well as grandparents' and parent's book shelves."

—**Robin Miller, MD**
Co-author of *Healed: Health & Wellness for the 21st Century*

"Dr. Adesman's latest book written in partnership with Christine Adamec, a grandmother parenting her grandson, is an invaluable handbook for grandparents raising their grandchildren. It describes many of the common but often complex and even wrenching challenges grandparents may face, along with practical strategies and information. The book includes real-world cases, along with data from Dr. Adesman's original research, which makes for a very readable, engaging, and valuable book. It is an important new resource for all grandfamilies."

—**Carol Cohen Weitzman, MD**
Director of the Yale Adoption/Foster Clinic
Professor of Pediatrics and Child Study Center at Yale University

"Grandfamilies are usually formed at a time of crisis. Over the past decade, several million grandparents have taken on the parenting role for one or more of their grandchildren. Once the initial shock has subsided, *The Grandfamily Guidebook* can support grandparents as they cope with, adjust to, and thrive in their new role. In plain language, Adesman and Adamec describe ways of identifying and dealing with grandparents' feelings and ways of managing the middle generation of birth parents. They use meaningful vignettes to illustrate how to understand children's reactions and emotional needs, how to effectively guide and encourage children at home and in school, and how to set reasonable limits on their behaviors. This very practical and readable guide offers up-to-date psychological, medical, and even a little legal advice and resources. It is positive in its approach and provides both understanding and encouragement to grandparents raising grandchildren."

—Pamela High, MD
Professor of Pediatrics at W. Alpert Medical School of Brown University
Director of Developmental-Behavioral Pediatrics
at Hasbro Children's Hospital, Providence, Rhode Island

"Recognizing the large numbers of grandparents now raising grandchildren, Dr. Adesman and his colleague provide vast amounts of helpful advice, from the initial phases of taking on the parenting role through interacting with birth parents, managing illness and behavior, and interacting with schools. Much helpful advice relates to talking with children in ways that recognize their developmental abilities. And it provides good guidance on connecting with various public programs that can help support grandparents in their expanded roles. *The Grandfamily Guidebook* will be indispensable to the many grandparents entering this new phase in their lives."

—James M. Perrin, MD
Professor of Pediatrics, Harvard Medical School
John C. Robinson Chair in Pediatrics
at Massachusetts General Hospital for Children

"*The Grandfamily Guidebook* is an excellent resource for navigating the challenges of raising grandchildren when your children—their parents—can't or aren't adequately caring for them. More and more families are facing this painful situation because of our national epidemic of opioid addiction. The authors share their expertise and insights gained from interviews with many grandparents who've stepped up in a crisis. They offer detailed practical advice for handling distressing decisions and conflicts that commonly arise. And they address, with considerable empathy, the roller coaster of emotions—stress, worry, resentment, joy—that come with finding yourself called to parent again. The authors offer not only emotional support but specific scripts to guide grandparents in difficult interactions."

—Harold S. Koplewicz, MD
Child and Adolescent Psychiatrist
Author of *It's Nobody's Fault: New Hope*
and *Help for Difficult Children and Their Parents*

"*The Grandfamily Guidebook* is a timely and comprehensive resource that addresses the complexities of reality for this growing community of families, in an easy-to-read, thoughtful manner."

—Elaine Schulte, MD, MPH
Medical Director, Adoption Program
Children's Hospital at Montefiore, Bronx, New York
Professor of Pediatrics at Albert Einstein College of Medicine

"Dr. Adesman and Ms. Adamec provide excellent, clear, and practical guidance that will be useful to grandparents facing the challenging child behaviors, difficult discussions, and complicated legal, financial, and life decisions that accompany becoming a parent again."

—Nathan Blum, MD
Chief of Developmental and Behavioral Pediatrics
at Children's Hospital of Philadelphia
Professor of Pediatrics, Perelman School of Medicine
at the University of Pennsylvania

"The challenges of parenting a grandchild can be daunting: economic, social, emotional, legal, and behavioral. Based on their pioneering research and practical experience, the authors of *The Grandfamily Guidebook* offer grandparents valuable information to overcome each of these hurdles. With this expert help and support at their fingertips, grandparents will realize they are no longer alone."

—Irene S. Levine, PhD
Professor of Psychiatry at the NYU Langone School of Medicine
Award-winning journalist and author who has held senior management and policymaking roles at the National Institute of Mental Health (NIMH) and the Center for Mental Health Services in Rockville, Maryland

"*The Grandfamily Guidebook* offers comprehensive, tangible, useful information about topics as varied as parenting strategies, school and education, finances, legal rights, and more—all in a practical and easy-to-read format. Of special interest are the many sample conversations that offer grandparents words to use with children, teachers, birthfamily, and others as they navigate the unexpected but often joyful journey through parenting at older ages. This book is a must-read for all who find themselves raising grandchildren in the golden years."

—Susan Caughman
Co-author of *You Can Adopt: An Adoptive Families Guide*
Editor and publisher of *of Adoptive Families* magazine

Praise from Grandparents for *The Grandfamily Guidebook*

"I feel like I just read a whole set of encyclopedias about grandparents raising grandchildren, condensed into one book. I asked myself when I was done, "What did they miss?" and I couldn't think of a single thing. This book is cover-to-cover valuable straightforward information that is easy to read. Sixteen years into my journey as a grandparent raising her grandchildren and I still learned new things that will be helpful to me as I take on a second, younger grandchild. I so appreciate the effort and knowledge that created this book. I'll be reading it a second time, and I am sure I will be referring to it again and again over the years."

—DeeDee Sinatra
Founder of United GrandFamilies Worldwide Facebook Group

"Relatives stepping up to care for family is not new, but the numbers and the seriousness of the issues seem to have accelerated. *The Grandfamily Guidebook* is a nice blend of stories from real families together with information and resources to help caregivers on their journey."

—Sharon Howell Olson
Grandparent who has been raising "grands" for twenty-four years
Advocate with Generations United GrAND Voices
Administrator for GrandFamilies of America, GrandFamilies
of Minnesota, and GrandsPlace Facebook groups

"Thank you so much for the guidebook. I'm sure I will refer back to it for many years to come. It covered the major impacts raising our grandchildren have. I have previously researched a lot of information on this so it is nice to have it all in one place. Most helpful to me was how to respond to questions by my grands or strangers."

—Cynthia Hallinger
Grandparent raising grandchildren, Virginia

The Grandfamily Guidebook

The Grandfamily Guidebook

Wisdom and Support
for Grandparents
Raising Grandchildren

ANDREW ADESMAN, MD, AND CHRISTINE ADAMEC
with a foreword by William Sears, MD, author of *The Baby Book*

 Hazelden
Publishing

Hazelden Betty Ford Foundation
Center City, Minnesota 55012
hazelden.org/bookstore

Library of Congress Cataloging-in-Publication Data
Names: Adesman, Andrew, author. | Adamec, Christine A., 1949- author.
Title: The grandfamily guidebook : wisdom and support for grandparents raising
    grandchildren / Andrew Adesman, MD, and Christine Adamec.
Description: Center City, Minnesota : Hazelden Publishing, [2018] | Includes
    bibliographical references.
Identifiers: LCCN 2018017233 (print) | LCCN 2018019657 (ebook) |
    ISBN 9781616497828 (ebook) | ISBN 9781616497576 (pbk.)
Subjects: LCSH: Grandparents as parents. | Grandparent and child. |
    Grandchildren. | Parenting.
Classification: LCC HQ759.9 (ebook) | LCC HQ759.9 .A34 2018 (print) | DDC
    306.874/5--dc23
LC record available at https://lccn.loc.gov/2018017233

Editor's note

Except where noted otherwise, the families depicted in this book are composites,
based on the authors' professional research and experience. Names and details have
been changed to protect the privacy of those involved. In chapter 7, Janice Ausburn's
name and story are used with her permission. Quotes from Kathy Reynolds, late
founder and moderator of GrandsPlace, used with permission.

This book provides general guidance, not medical, financial, or legal advice.
Consult directly with professionals for advice on your situation.

Throughout this book, the featured brief quotations are actual statements from
respondents to the 2016 Adesman Grandfamily Study.

Readers should be aware that websites listed in this work may have changed or
disappeared between when this work was written and when it is read.

Cover and Interior Designer: Terri Kinne
Acquisition Editor: Vanessa Torrado
Development Editor: Mindy Keskinen
Managing Editor: Don Freeman
Production Editor: Jean Cook

Contents

PART 1
Ready or Not, You're Raising Your Grandchildren

PART 2
Adjusting to the New Normal

PART 3
Legal and Financial Resources:
Using Them to Your Grandfamily's Advantage

PART 4
Healthy in Body and Mind

Glossary of Abbreviations and Acronyms

If you're raising a grandchild, you'll see lots of abbreviations as you navigate social services, health care (including disorders and other diagnoses), education and learning disabilities, courts and other legal settings, and government agencies, programs, and benefits. This list offers a quick reference.

Numbers refer to the chapters in this book where the term is mentioned and the related topic is discussed.

AA   Alcoholics Anonymous: 3, 4

ADA AA   Americans with Disabilities Act Amendments Act
          (also called the Rehabilitation Act; section 504 is key): 6

ADHD   attention-deficit/hyperactivity disorder: 6, 9

AFDC   Aid to Families with Dependent Children, 8

ASD   autism spectrum disorder: 5, 6, 9

BMI   body-mass index: 5, 10, 11

CBT   cognitive-behavioral therapy: 2, 9

CD   conduct disorder: 9

CDC   Centers for Disease Control and Prevention
          (US federal agency): 1

CHIP   Children's Health Insurance Program: 10

CMA   Crystal Meth Anonymous: 3

CPS   child protective services (usually a county or state agency,
          sometimes known by a different name and with varying
          scopes of responsibility): 1, 3, 7, 9

DRA   Dual Recovery Anonymous: 3

DTaP   diphtheria, tetanus, and pertussis vaccine: 10

EIC   earned income credit (tax credit): 8

ESSA   Every Student Succeeds Act: 6

FAPE   free appropriate public education: 6

FASD   fetal alcohol spectrum disorder: 9

FDA   Food and Drug Administration (US federal agency): 9

GAP   Guardian Assistance Program: 8

HHS   Health and Human Services (US federal agency): 8

IAP   Individualized Accommodation Plan (also called Section 504 Accommodation Plan): 6

ICPC   Interstate Compact on the Placement of Children: 7

IDEA   Individuals with Disabilities Education Act: 6

IEP   Individualized Education Program: 6

IPV   inactivated polio vaccine: 10

IRS   Internal Revenue Service (US federal agency): 8

LD   learning disability: 6

LIHEAP   Low-Income Home Energy Assistance Program: 8

MAGI   modified adjusted gross income: 8

MMR   measles, mumps, and rubella vaccine: 10

NA   Narcotics Anonymous: 3

NICU   neonatal intensive care unit: 1

NIH   National Institutes of Health (US federal agency; serves as umbrella): 11

NIMH   National Institute of Mental Health (US federal agency): 9

ODD   oppositional defiant disorder: 9

PACA   postadoption contact agreement: 7

POA   power of attorney: 7

PTSD   post-traumatic stress disorder: 9

RAD   reactive attachment disorder: 9

REM   rapid eye movement (stage of sleep): 5

SNAP   Supplemental Nutrition Assistance Program, formerly known as the Food Stamp Program (FSP): 8

SPF	sun protection factor: 10
SSA	Social Security Administration (US federal agency): 8
SSI	Supplemental Security Insurance: 8
TANF	Temporary Assistance for Needy Families (formerly "welfare to work"): 8
TPR	termination of parental rights: 7
USP	United States Pharmacopeia (designation for pharmaceutical-grade quality): 10
WIC	Women, Infants, and Children (US federal program for nutrition assistance): 8

FOREWORD

Wow, what a needed book! It brought tears to my eyes as I replayed memories of my *grand*parents and how I am a wiser person because of the seeds of healthy living they planted in me during those early windows of opportunity. No other title encompasses so many roles as grandparent: mentor, teacher, therapist, provider, nurturer, and sometimes rescuer.

When I was a newborn, my dad took off, leaving my hard-working mom and me with the opportunity to live with my grandparents until I entered college. Growing up cared-for and mentored by grandparents taught me why they deserve to be called "grand" parents. First, they are wiser, an upgrade from "smarter," because they've lived longer and made more mistakes and learned from them.

Grandparents are also motivated by their gut instinct and soul to share their wisdom with us not-so-wise kids. As a child who often acted impulsively—my grandma and grandpa called them my "brain storms," which today would be labeled "ADHD"—I learned early on from them to "think through what you're about to do."

They also instilled in me the roots of empathy, to imagine how my words and actions would affect another person. In my experience of fifty years as a pediatrician, imparting empathy in their grandchildren is one of the richest inheritances grandparents can give, resulting in more compassionate grandfamilies.

In my pediatric practice, as the authors so rightfully relate, an increasing number of children are being primarily reared or co-reared by grandparents. I see this in my office every day, and I love listening to the grandparents' tales. My favorite was a grandmother who had raised her grandson and poured her heart out to him in so many loving ways. With tears in her eyes, she told me, "My new granddaughter-in-law just gave me the supreme compliment as a grandparent: 'Thank you for raising such a sensitive man.'"

The many practical pointers in *The Grandfamily Guidebook* come together as a toolbox with which new grandparents can tackle life's many challenging situations. As I was reading, I thought the abbreviation for *grandparents* could be GPS, because that's what grandparents do. They provide their grandkids a GPS for wiser living, which can best come from mentors who have been there, lived that, and instill their lifelong lessons to their precious legacy—their grandkids.

Yes, our fourteen grandchildren have given us more gray hairs, yet they also are teaching us what our purpose is in life.

I love the book's title, *Grandfamily*. That says it all. The authors' insightful information is based not only on personal experience, but also on the largest survey of grandfamily practices: the Adesman Grandfamily Study. If grandkids came with a guidebook, this book would be it.

As a pediatrician and grandfather, I am honored to highly recommend this grand resource for grandfamilies.

William Sears, MD
Author of *The Baby Book*

You're a Grandfamily Now

If you find yourself raising your grandchildren—perhaps with very little notice—you might feel disoriented at first. *This isn't what I expected to be doing at this stage of my life! Do I have the energy for this?* And you might feel alone, perhaps out of step with the much-younger parents around you. But in fact, you're not alone. Far from it: millions of children around the world are currently being raised by their grandparents. Although grandfamilies are often formed in crisis situations, they are also built and strengthened over time.

Let this book be your companion and guide through the whole grandfamily process—from crisis to the "new normal," from the stresses of shifting dynamics to the everyday joys shared with your grandchild. With *The Grandfamily Guidebook*, you can help your grandchild adjust and thrive in a new family setting—and discover how to flourish in your new role as well.

What is a grandfamily? It's a family unit in which a grandparent (or sometimes two grandparents) is the head of household and is also actively parenting one or more grandchildren. It's a form of kinship care, in which a relative of a child takes over the parenting responsibilities. (Specifically, the term "kinship care" is often used in the foster care system when a state or county agency places a child to live with relatives.) Sometimes aunts, uncles, cousins, or other relatives assume this role, but by and large grandparents are the individuals most likely to parent children born to someone else in the family.

Another name for these households is "skip-generation families." And they are increasingly common.

One main reason for the rise in grandfamilies: substance use disorders, more commonly known as alcohol or drug addiction. Since about 2010, the opioid crisis has made many young parents unfit for the job, as opioid use and addiction has taken precedence over their other priorities. It has also claimed lives. Their children, sometimes known as "opioid orphans," are often left in their grandparents' care. But it's not just opioids: many other drugs, as well as alcohol, claim lives and turn families upside down as children are neglected or abused by their drug-using parents. Another factor is incarceration. Whether for the short or long term, grandparents often step in when an adult child goes to prison, leaving a young child in need. A mental health disorder, too, can play a role, especially when it goes untreated or undertreated.

In all of these scenarios, children can wind up on their grandparents' doorstep, often with little warning. When grandparents assume the role of primary caretaker for a child, they may feel initially unsure of themselves. Yet throughout human history, an extended family playing an active role in a child's upbringing has been the norm; the nuclear family of just Mom and Dad raising the kids is a relatively recent development. Grandparents have guided and nurtured children for millennia. So you have lots of history behind you and so much to offer. This is a new role, though. It may mean shedding your indulgent-grandma role and taking on the more demanding task of daily parenting. Rest assured: with time, you'll work through the issues, and this book can help. The rewards can be rich for all of you.

You're a grandfamily now.

Who We Are

As coauthors of *The Grandfamily Guidebook*, we—Andrew Adesman, MD, and Christine Adamec—bring both professional and personal experience to this subject. Dr. Adesman is a pediatrician with extensive expertise in diagnosing and treating children's developmental and behavioral disorders. For this book, he conducted a nationwide survey of grandfamilies in 2016. The Adesman Grandfamily Study involved more than seven hundred grandparents raising their grandchildren, making his survey one of the largest and most comprehensive on this topic. Christine Adamec is a writer specializing in behavioral health and parenting topics. She has also been raising her grandson, now eleven years old, since infancy. Dr. Adesman and Adamec have collaborated previously on *Parenting Your Adopted Child: A Positive Approach to Building a Strong Family*.

As coauthors, we write primarily in one voice. (When the pronoun "I" is used, it refers to Dr. Adesman.) But you will also meet many other people in the book, through the stories of grandfamilies from varied backgrounds. Many of these are composite stories; key details and names have been changed to protect the privacy of the people involved. Yet they are true to life, and these grandparents speak straight from the heart. Throughout the book, you'll also see featured brief quotations from respondents to the Adesman Grandfamily Study. The speakers aren't named, but they are all grandparents who have walked the path you're on right now.

How to Use This Book

The Grandfamily Guidebook has four parts. You may find it valuable to read the entire book, then use it as a reference over time, as your grandfamily life settles—and changes.

Part 1, *Ready or Not, You're Raising Your Grandchildren,* is of special value during the often-stressful time when the grandfamily is first forming, usually in a crisis. In chapter 1, we discuss the reasons so many children now need their grandparents to raise them and take a look at who grandfamilies are, drawing on the Adesman Grandfamily Study and other key sources. In chapter 2, we look at the emotions grandparents are likely to experience and talk about how family relationships may shift as everyone adjusts to the new situation. Chapter 3 offers strategies for dealing with your adult child or the other birth parent of your grandchild (or both), if they're in the picture and the dynamics are difficult.

In part 2, we're *Adjusting to the New Normal.* No matter your grandchild's age, you can anticipate questions about how your grandfamily came to be: chapter 4 offers some age-appropriate ways to explain your current circumstances and other issues. Chapter 5 helps address some common behavior problems (with sleeping and eating, for example), and handling regressive and aggressive behaviors. At school, your grandchild may struggle with adjustment, academics, and social problems such as bullying. Chapter 6 addresses these issues and helps you discern whether learning disabilities or other challenges may be part of the picture—with special attention to Individualized Education Program (IEP) plans and advocating for your grandchild.

In part 3, we focus on *Legal and Financial Resources: Using Them to Your Grandfamily's Advantage.* What legal role should you consider in relation to your grandchild? Chapter 7 will help you untangle the issues and the options: physical and legal custody, guardianship, adoption, and the usefulness and limitations of power of attorney. Chapter 8, "Grandfamily Finance," covers the many sources of practical help at the federal, state, and county levels. Direct monthly financial payments, child-only Medicaid, tax benefits, programs offering free school lunch and home energy assistance, and more: you may be surprised at the variety of programs that can support your grandfamily's well-being.

Last, in part 4, *Healthy in Body and Mind*, we zero in on health issues—your grandchild's and your own. In chapter 9, we cover behavioral disorders and mental health issues common in children, with symptoms and signs to watch for and options for diagnosis and treatment. Chapter 10 covers everyday child health issues, with some updated tips for grandparents who may remember different practices when they were parents the first time around. Chapter 11 helps you stay alert to your own potential health problems that may occur among middle-aged and older adults, such as hypertension, arthritis, and weight challenges, as well as cancer and heart disease. You want to stay healthy for yourself—and now for your grandkids too.

■

It can be challenging and even daunting to start the parenting job all over again, whether you are forty, fifty, or sixty, or older. But in the Adesman Grandfamily Study, nearly all the grandparents surveyed said that, knowing what they know now, they would do it all over again. "When your grandchildren need you, you may have some initial hesitation," said one grandparent. "But you are also strongly pulled to respond. They're family! They need you and you love them. So, you take a giant leap of faith and you plunge into the deep water . . . for them. And it's okay. You've got this!"

PART 1

READY OR NOT, YOU'RE RAISING YOUR GRANDCHILDREN

My last option, the one I chose, was to take Dani home and parent her myself. It was to make a lifelong commitment to another child. I chose that option because it was the only one that fit my needs. I needed to know that this child was cherished and given the best chance at a good life. We often say, "But I had no choice." The truth is I had a choice and I made it.

—*Kathy Reynolds, late founder and moderator of the Facebook group GrandsPlace—Grandparents Raising Grandchildren*

CHAPTER 1

A Family, Reinvented

Who Grandfamilies Are—and How We Got Here

For Gail and Terry, the life-changing phone call came on a quiet Sunday afternoon. They hadn't seen their twenty-six-year-old daughter Amber for months. The last they'd heard, she was using marijuana daily and probably using other drugs too. They worried about her constantly, but Amber was an adult. And after trying to help her find recovery with no success, Gail and Terry had backed off, simply letting her face the consequences of her choices.

What they didn't know—and what the hospital social worker now told them—was that Amber had just delivered a baby girl born addicted to heroin. Gail and Terry were stunned. They had no idea their daughter had been pregnant, let alone addicted to heroin. Amber needed rehab for her addiction, said the worker, so would they take the baby and serve as foster parents? Amber had fervently told the worker that she didn't want her baby to go into foster care with strangers. Later that day, Amber called her parents herself and begged them to take her child.

Both in their late fifties, Gail and Terry had thought diapers and cribs were years behind them. But a decision had to be made. Baby Erica came home to them upon her hospital discharge, and Amber checked into a treatment facility. Now, two years later, Amber has ten months of solid recovery. After several relapses in the first year, she thinks this time, she's really going to make it. Gail and Terry are cautiously optimistic and are taking a wait-and-see approach.

• • •

Grandfamilies are often formed in crisis. Suddenly you're facing an emergency, and a child's well-being is at stake. That moment may come as a surprise, as it did for Gail and Terry. But in some families, the grandparents may have seen a potential crisis looming for a while, as the result of a long, sad decline. They may have watched their adult child slowly lose the ability to be an adequate parent—perhaps because of substance use or addiction. The grandparents may have even suspected they'd one day step into the parental role.

But either way, when you find yourself raising a family for the second time around, you may feel all alone in the world and seriously out of step. The truth is, you have lots of company. In 2016, 2.6 million grandparents in the United States were responsible for raising their own grandchildren under age eighteen, according to the US Census Bureau.[1] Surprising to note, the Census Bureau doesn't collect data on how many grandchildren these grandparents are raising. However, we do know, based on reports from many researchers and from Dr. Adesman's own study, that some grandfamilies include one grandchild while many others have two, three, four, or more grandchildren. There are also concerns that this number may be increasing, given the opioid epidemic upward trend. As a result, we believe that perhaps as many as 5 million grandchildren are being raised by their grandparents.

This chapter is about how and why children need their grandparents to parent them. It's about reinventing family roles. It's about becoming a grandfamily—ready or not. In this chapter, you'll learn about these families, in all their variety. We'll draw on the results of Dr. Adesman's extensive 2016 Grandfamily Study, which surveyed more than seven hundred grandparents who have taken on the parenting role, as well as findings from the US Census Bureau and Centers for Disease Control (CDC).

Like Gail and Terry, many grandparents are initially stunned to be heading up a grandfamily. It was not part of their life plan. At a time when they thought they'd be focusing on their careers and planning for retirement, they're preparing bottles and taking the baby to the pediatrician's office for checkups. Or cheering their school-age grandchild at basketball games, alongside parents twenty years younger. Or dealing with adolescent angst in a social-media-driven world. Some may wonder how they'll keep up with all the tech devices. Younger grandparents, in their forties or even thirties, may be at ease with the technology, but they still have lots of other questions and concerns.

With all of these situations, grandparents are rising to a difficult task, and we commend them. Like anyone in the parenting role, they may make some mistakes along the way, but they're doing a lot of things right too. (After all, they're experienced!) They're making the best of a tough situation. And we view them as heroic.

Kinship Care Is Better for Children

What is "kinship care"? It's the term used when children are removed from their parents by a state or county agency because of abuse or neglect and then placed in foster care with grandparents or other relatives, their kin. And research has shown that such children fare better than those placed with nonrelative foster parents. One large study focused on behavioral problems in abused and neglected children. Half of them had been placed in kinship care immediately after leaving the problem situation. The others were placed in

continued

nonrelative foster care and, of that group, 17 percent were later moved to kinship care. The rest remained in nonrelative foster care through the study.

Three years later, the researchers looked at behavioral problems in the entire group. Of the children immediately placed into kinship care, about a third (32 percent) had behavioral problems, compared to nearly half (45 percent) of the others. The researchers also found that children moved belatedly to kinship care had worse outcomes than children placed directly with their family members.[2] Of course, many other factors influence behavior problems, but this study suggests that immediate placement with family is preferable.

How *Did* You Get Here?

Let's take a look at the most common situations that lead grandparents to step up to the parental role—again. Substance use or addiction is often involved. When a parent abuses alcohol or drugs—prescription drugs, heroin, methamphetamine, or others—the substance can become that person's primary focus in life, even at the expense of family, children, job, and home. Child abuse and neglect are also key reasons that grandparents sometimes assume control, saving a child from a life of misery or even death at a young age. Sometimes parents face incarceration, upending their family life. In other cases, the parents have a severe mental disorder that hasn't been adequately treated or controlled. Schizophrenia, bipolar disorder, psychotic depression, or other psychiatric illnesses can seriously undermine parenting abilities. Or a parent's death—due to drug overdose, accident, illness, military service, or other causes—leaves behind one or more children who urgently need love and care and comfort. In other cases, it's a matter of a birth parent's immaturity or disinterest in providing adequate care to the child. People may "grow up" in terms of their maturity, or they may not. Parenting a child is a huge commitment. Or it should be.

On top of these factors, money problems can trigger more family troubles. As their parents are busy working multiple low-paying jobs, children may lack supervision. Health insurance may be inadequate or missing altogether. Some families face homelessness or a sense of rootlessness as they double up at the homes of relatives or friends. Money problems can complicate other problems—although rarely is it the *only* reason birth parents lose their parental role. Even for families who make use of government programs, raising kids takes money and time. (See chapter 8 for more on the programs that can help.) Financial stresses often intertwine with other problems to make good parenting difficult.

And these different factors interact at all socioeconomic levels: what starts as a substance problem could lead to child neglect. What starts as a mental health condition could lead to job loss, poverty, and homelessness. Financial stress might drive a parent to crime and perhaps result in incarceration. The sudden death of a spouse could, for some, lead to substance use and addiction.

Whatever the reason, grandfamilies are often formed under stress. Grandparents step in as the result of a crisis. Someone must immediately take charge of the children, and so the grandparents decide they will now assume this role. It's very scary and very stressful.

Substance Use and Addiction

Parents' alcohol and drug use can have far-reaching effects on their family life and their children's future. Alcohol addiction, illegal drug use, and prescription drug abuse are heartbreakingly common, and many people use more than one of these substances.

In the past decade, opioid abuse has become an epidemic of such magnitude that in 2016 the Centers for Disease Control and Prevention created its own guidelines for doctors, aiming to reduce the rampant overprescription of opioids for pain control.[3] Meanwhile, these prescription painkillers are still flooding the market, and some of them end up on the street. Users may buy them from friends or from drug dealers, and many who begin using prescription painkillers eventually switch to heroin, which is also an opioid. In fact, heroin use by young people ages eighteen to twenty-five more than doubled in the United States between 2004 and 2014, affecting people across the economic spectrum.[4] Heroin is an illegal drug and thus no one checks for its purity. That's one reason overdose is common—users have no idea how pure or concentrated it is. Or they simultaneously use alcohol or other drugs, such as methamphetamine, a stimulant, with harmful results up to and including death. Overdose is also common for opioid users who have abstained for a time and then relapsed: their tolerance has dropped, and a previously survivable dose is now a lethal one.

• • •

"The most important thing is for the children to know they are wanted, loved, and safe. Be firm and consistent and let them know that, no matter what, you are always there for them."

— A GRANDPARENT FROM THE ADESMAN GRANDFAMILY STUDY

For the children of these users—the "opioid orphans"—the results are the same whether the parent is buying heroin from a dealer or stealing prescription painkillers from family members. These children are ignored and neglected. Sometimes they are physically and sexually abused by the parents or others in their circle. And they truly become orphans if the parents die from overdose.

Opioid addiction also can be passed on to unborn children. When the mother gives birth, the infant may need to undergo withdrawal under medical care. On top of that, pregnant women who are addicted are also at risk of endangering their unborn children through other behaviors: smoking, alcohol or other drug use, poor nutrition, lack of prenatal care. These babies may have later developmental problems, further complicating the task for those in the parental role.

If drug addiction or alcoholism has played a part in your grandfamily's history, you're not alone. In 2016, 40 percent of all children removed from their homes because of abuse or neglect had parents with substance use or addiction problems, including 34 percent removed because of parental drug abuse and 6 percent removed because of parental alcohol abuse.[5] Other studies have suggested the rate is even higher. In a study published in 2000, the most common reasons children were removed from their homes were substance abuse on a parent's part (70 percent), followed by the parent's inability to care for the child (60 percent), and child neglect (59 percent)—with frequent overlap in those factors.[6]

In the Adesman Grandfamily Study, grandparents reported on the problems they were aware of in the child's home of origin and which parent was involved. By far the most common was alcohol or other drug use, often associated with other dangers.

Here's what the study found:

SUBSTANCE ABUSE RATE:
74 percent for mothers, 61 percent for fathers

CHILD NEGLECT RATE:
65 percent for mothers, 47 percent for fathers

CHILD ABANDONMENT RATE:
35 percent for mothers, 6 percent for fathers

DOMESTIC VIOLENCE RATE:
28 percent of mothers had been victims, 7 percent of fathers

CHILD ABUSE:
23 percent for mothers, 15 percent for fathers

Why do these numbers skew higher for mothers than fathers? In many cases, the mothers may be single parents with custody of their children and the fathers are not present in the household. In cases of two-parent families, birth mothers are more likely to be the victims of domestic violence than birth fathers. If the primary problem lies with the mother, the father may be missing, unknown, or not wish to have custody of the child. Substance-using mothers often delay getting help longer than fathers do, all other things being equal. Fair or not, women often feel that they are the glue holding the family together, while men might be more willing to separate from the children long enough to seek treatment. Ironically, though, a mother's refusal to seek help only makes the dysfunction worse. A perception bias may also be at work: when the chips are down, grandparents may hold the mother more responsible for the children's well-being, pinning more of the blame for neglect, abandonment, or abuse on Mom rather than Dad.

Treatment Can Work: Finding a New Family Balance

Looking back, Grandpa Jimmy knows his family is fortunate. When he and his wife, Carol, gained permanent guardianship of their grandchildren five years ago, they were fearing the worst for their daughter Sue, recently divorced. A heavy drinker, jobless, with multiple DUIs, she seemed bent on self-destruction, said Jimmy. But in Sue's case, the shock of losing her children, combined with the stark realization that her life was circling the drain, pushed her to seek rehab—and succeed in a solid recovery program.

"I'm so proud of Sue," said Jimmy. "Recovering from alcoholism is a lifelong process. But she's doing it!" She changed her friends and her lifestyle, and now, at four years in recovery, she's stayed alcohol-free. Jimmy said that Sue still regards herself as a recovering addict, and she realizes there's always a risk of relapse.

She has also decided to not seek to overturn the custody order, because her children are healthy and happy with Jimmy and Carol. This grandfamily is the only one the children remember, and she doesn't want to pull the rug out. Sue has a job now, lives in an apartment nearby, and she visits her children and her supportive parents regularly. She even pays child support, which Jimmy deposits in a special account for the children's future. "We're really lucky," said Jimmy, "and we know it. So far, and by the grace of God, our story has a happy ending."

Opioid Orphans

As the opioid epidemic unfolds, more and more grand-parents are facing down the death of an adult child by overdose. It might be prescription painkillers; it might be heroin—either way, the addicted person's decline is often swift and devastating.

"I really thought Scott was going to get off heroin, and he tried—but it just did not happen," said Amanda, his mother. Scott died several months ago from an overdose at age thirty. The emotional pain is still searing to Amanda, who isn't sure anyone ever gets over a child's death. But through the pain, she is finding joy—and exhaustion, she admits—in her grandfamily: Scott's two children, now ages seven and five. When Matt and Tina were first placed with her by the state's child services agency five years ago, Amanda thought that Scott would kick his drug problem if only he tried hard enough. But even after multiple times in treatment, the lure of heroin was too powerful for Scott, stronger than the pull of his children's needs—or the needs or wishes of anyone else. The children's mother was also addicted to heroin. Amanda hopes she's still alive, but she hasn't been heard from in years.

How could this tragedy have happened? Amanda admitted that she just doesn't get it. She used to think of drugs as an inner-city problem, often linked with gangs, but now she knows better. A single mom, she raised Scott in a middle-class suburb, and he showed no early signs of drug use. But in his senior year of high school, Scott tried prescription narcotics at a party. Soon he was hooked, and within months he had moved on to heroin, which was cheaper and just as easy to get. For a decade, through college, marriage, and fatherhood, Scott had tried to break his addiction. But months of recovery would be followed by a heartbreaking relapse. If Amanda could go back in time and somehow change the story, she would. But she can't.

Both of the babies had been born addicted to heroin, and both had gone through withdrawal in the hospital's neonatal intensive care unit. When Amanda gained custody of them, she found both legal and financial help. And now, so far, the children seem okay developmentally. Matt reads well, and Tina enjoys kindergarten. Both love to sing, as their dad did. Still, they may develop issues in the future—emotionally or behaviorally. If they do, Amanda is determined to help them as much as possible. "There's a part of Scott in each of them," said Amanda, "and that helps me keep going."

Child Abuse or Neglect

What's the difference between child abuse and neglect? "Child abuse" refers to actions taken: for example, beating a child. "Child neglect" refers to important actions not taken, such as failing to feed a child. "Abandonment" is also a form of child neglect, and often it's unclear where the birth parents have gone. They may have dropped the kids off with the grandparents, saying they'll be back soon. But now it's been six months since the grandparents have heard anything, so, where are they? No one knows.

Sometimes the children are starving and filthy when they arrive at Grandma's. The parents may have barred Grandma from seeing the kids previously, because they knew she'd be horrified and feel compelled to act. In such a case, someone else, such as a neighbor, might have seen the children and reported the problem to the state agency often known as Child

Protective Services (CPS)—the agency responsible for immediate protection of endangered children. Sometimes CPS caseworkers look for a relative, find Grandma, and go to her house with the kids in tow. In an emergency, they might even arrive without so much as a phone call. It's a shocking scene for Grandma. But often it's the beginning of a new normal life for the children.

How common is it? A recent statistic: in the United States, 437,465 children were in foster care in 2016, up from 400,911 in 2013. Most of the children were removed from their families because of neglect (61 percent), and 34 percent were removed because of parental drug addiction.[7] (There may be more than one reason why the children were removed from their families.) In 2016, and in most cases—about 91 percent—the perpetrator was one or both of their own parents.[8]

A Birth Parent's Mental Health Disorder

Any psychiatric problem can undermine a person's parenting skills. Whether it's major depression, bipolar disorder, schizophrenia, or another diagnosis, a mental health disorder can compromise a parent's ability to focus, make good judgments, and maintain the energy to care for a family. You may wish to do further research on these diagnoses, but let's take a brief look at them now.

Clinical depression is a state of extreme hopelessness, sadness, and low motivation. It is often characterized by changes in sleeping or eating habits, but it can also go unnoticed by the casual observer. Some people with depression function fairly well in daily routines, although they may feel miserable.

A person with untreated bipolar disorder may also have periods of severe depression (lows), but they are interspersed with periods of euphoria (highs). Good judgment is often absent and, instead, fleeting impulses may rule when the person is in the grips of a manic high. For example, when she's feeling up, a woman with bipolar disorder may decide to go to Atlantic City and bet all her money on "red." (In contrast, a healthy person who feels happy may decide to have lunch with a friend.) Hypersexuality, spending sprees, and other impulsive choices are common during the euphoric period of bipolar disorder.

A person with untreated schizophrenia may have periods when clear thinking and appropriate action are difficult. The person may experience paranoia, delusions, or hallucinations or hear voices.

In all of these cases, parenting abilities are compromised. And when a mental health disorder is accompanied by a substance use disorder—sometimes referred to as co-occurring disorders—the problems can multiply. Some people try to ease anxiety, depression, or other symptoms with alcohol and then find themselves hooked. Others might try to self-medicate with drugs such as methamphetamine or heroin rather than take prescribed medications to treat psychotic behavior, for example. (Some illegal drugs, such as meth, can even trigger mental illness or psychotic delusions.) Although complex, co-occurring disorders can be treated. Some inpatient and outpatient programs are particularly focused on addressing all the issues at once. Even so, solid recovery takes commitment and time.

Incarceration

Of the 1.5 million adults incarcerated in US federal or state prisons, more than half have one or more children under eighteen.[9] Add all the mothers and fathers incarcerated in local or county jails, and we have a massive parenting displacement. When incarceration leaves children without a parent to care for them, the only option generally offered by the state is foster care with strangers, unless grandparents or other relatives are willing to step up. (There are exceptions: in a few corrections programs, as well as rehab centers, mothers are allowed to keep their children with them.)

For the older generation, just having your adult child incarcerated is distressing in itself, and you're deeply concerned for their well-being. But here's the key: if you've decided to care for the grandkids, you need to concentrate on them—not on the birth parent. Of course, you still love your adult child, and if you can help, you often do so. But when you take over the parenting role, your priorities must shift. Those grandchildren will need a great deal of attention as they adjust to the "new normal." Babies won't understand why a parent is gone, but they'll sense a difference in caregiving and may show stress reactions. Older children will be confused and upset and may ask the same questions over and over, hoping for a different answer. These kids will need their grandparents' best efforts and full energy. You must focus on them—not on their parent. As one grandparent said to her daughter, "If you're in trouble and my granddaughter needs me, she will always win."

Should you tell your grandchild that a parent is in jail or prison? Some experts say you should, because if birth parents suddenly disappear with no explanation, their children will worry about them. If you agree and do tell your grandchild that the parent is incarcerated, keep it simple, such as by saying that Dad used illegal drugs or Mom hurt someone, and this is the punishment. Let the children know that their parent still loves them and that it is *not* their fault that the parent is in jail.[10] Even though it sounds ridiculous to most grandparents and other adults, children often blame themselves for what happens around them in life. For example, they may think their parent committed bad acts because he was upset with them, and thus, the crime was their fault.

Should you visit the birth parent in prison? That's an individual decision. If you decide to do so and you are thinking about bringing your young grandchild with you, ask ahead of time whether the facility has a parent-child visitation program, which provides a more relaxed environment with games and toys. How do you find out? Call the prison and ask or check its website for possible further information.

Last, remind the child from time to time about the parent's good qualities, and yes, you can find something good to say. Children identify with their parents. Perhaps the parent is musically talented, physically fit, or makes people laugh by telling funny jokes.

A Birth Parent's Death

It's an unimaginable loss: your own adult child dies—of a drug overdose, a car accident, an illness, or other reason. Now consider what it would be like to absorb that shock while trying to cope with the grief, despair, and confusion of your grandchildren, who urgently need someone in the family to take over. Even if the children are babies, such a change is hugely disruptive.

But this painful situation is, sad to say, common. The Centers for Disease Control and Prevention reported more people died of drug overdoses in 2014 than in any other year—nearly two-thirds of them from opioids—and largely among adults ages twenty-five to forty-four. The states with the highest drug overdose rates were West Virginia, New Mexico, New Hampshire, Kentucky, and Ohio.[11]

Carlos's Story: A Loss, and a New Purpose

Some grandfamilies are thrown together overnight, often as a complete surprise. Others settle in as a temporary situation that becomes permanent. That's what happened to Carlos.

When Carlos became an *abuelo*—a grandfather—at age sixty, he was thrilled with Lucia, the tiny infant in his life. He only wished his wife, Silvia, could have enjoyed the pleasure and honor of being an *abuela*; she had died of breast cancer the year before. Their only son, Roberto, loved being a dad, although he was busy with his sales career and commitment to the US Army Reserve. From the start, his wife, Inez, was overwhelmed by motherhood: the sleep loss, the mood swings, and the financial pressures. To keep her energy up and her weight down, she started using prescription amphetamines—and then overusing them and finally turning to meth. By the time Roberto learned about it, it was a full-blown addiction. Inez disappeared for days at a time, losing all interest in being a mom.

Then Roberto was called up for duty in Afghanistan. Inez was gone, perhaps for good. Where would Lucia go? The answer seemed clear: to her *abuelo*. Carlos was semiretired, and Silvia's relatives lived nearby. They could lend a hand for a year; then Roberto would be back home. Carlos rolled up his sleeves and turned his spare room into a nursery.

But six months later, the news came: Roberto had been killed in an Army maneuver. Carlos was brokenhearted. Yet in his grief, Carlos discovered a new purpose.

He would continue to raise Lucia, and if possible, he would adopt her. Carlos resolved to do everything in his power to give her the happy life she deserved, something like the life her wonderful father would have given her. Lucia would have an extended grandfamily, but Carlos would be her rock. "It's a sacred responsibility," said Carlos.

Emotional Immaturity

Sometimes the birth parents are not addicted to alcohol or other drugs, nor are they mentally ill or in prison. They are instead very emotionally immature and self-centered. Children require a lot of attention, which means the parents need the ability and desire to put the child first. Even if the birth parents are over eighteen, they may not have grown up sufficiently to emotionally handle parenting a child.

That's what happened with Jack and Lori, both twenty, who enjoyed a dramatic relationship full of extreme arguments and great makeup sex. Every couple quarrels from time to time, but these two could argue about anything—and did, meanwhile neglecting the needs of their two-month-old.

> Jack: Hey, Lori, the baby stinks! When was the last time you changed her diaper?
>
> Lori: When was the last time *you* changed her diaper, Jack? I think it's like, maybe *never*, and it's for sure your turn now!
>
> Jack: No, that's your job. I do the other stuff for the baby.
>
> Lori: Like what? Holding her? No. Bathing her? No. Taking her for a walk in the stroller? Again, no.
>
> Jack: You are such a bitch! Why don't you just take care of that baby you wanted so bad?
>
> Lori: She was an accident and you know it!
>
> Jack: Well, I don't know why you had to get yourself pregnant. Everything was better before.
>
> Lori: You had something to do with that, Jack! She's your baby too!
>
> Jack: Oh yeah, how do I really know that she's mine?
>
> Lori: What? How dare you say that!

And on and on. In the meantime, the baby screams because she's hungry or wet. And the immature parents are too wrapped up in their never-ending argument to notice. Fortunately, often other people *do* notice that the baby's needs are not fulfilled. If Jack and Lori don't grow up fast, neighbors may notice a pattern —a wailing baby left in a hot car in the driveway, a wandering toddler—and report the couple to Child Protective Services.

Think Again:
Avoiding Common Pitfalls

Every grandfamily is unique, but we've identified some common pitfalls and often-mistaken assumptions. For example, grand-parents might berate themselves, assuming they're at fault for their adult child's behavior or inability to parent. Or they might waste precious energy trying to "save" their adult child, even as they step in to care for the grandchild. For grandparents new in this role, perhaps the most common assumption is, "Surely this situation will be temporary"—so let's start there.

"It's only temporary."

Many grandparents optimistically believe it may take a few months—or maybe up to a year—for their adult children to get their act together and take over raising their own kids again. It may be a temporary situation—but also may not be. In the Adesman Grandfamily Study, nearly half (44 percent) of the grandparents had been raising the child for more than five years.

Andrea and her husband, Mike, found their infant grand-daughter, Julia, sleeping in her car carrier, abandoned in their entryway one Friday night. Julia's parents were nowhere to be found—their apartment empty, their phones out of service, all social media accounts closed. Andrea knew that her son had recently been caught driving drunk and was in trouble at his workplace. Maybe he'd had other brushes with the law too. But surely they'd come back, right? They wouldn't just *leave* their daughter!

Andrea and Mike took the six-month-old in. While they waited for word from their son, they reported the couple as missing persons, and a family services social worker was assigned to the case. At their first meeting, the worker told them, "You may need to commit to raising your granddaughter until she's eighteen." And she was right. Now a second-grader, Julia has lived continuously with Andrea and Mike, who still have no idea where Julia's parents are.

Of course, some adult children *do* overcome their problems and *are* able to take back their children and parent them successfully. But when severe problems such as alcohol, drug, or mental health disorders are involved, you can't be sure that recovery will occur soon or ever—or if it does, that it will last. Which leads us to the next assumption you might want to question.

"I don't need a new legal role with my grandchild."

When a grandparent steps into the parenting role, it's usually wise to obtain legal custody or guardianship over the child. Adoption may be an eventual option, if the parents are agreeable or if their parental rights are involuntarily terminated by the state—but that option may be years in the future, if at all. Sometimes grandparents have *not* established *any* form of legal rights, such as custody through the state protective services system, temporary or permanent guardianship, nor adoption. In the Adesman Grandfamily Study, 62 percent of grandparents reported having a formal or legal agreement about custody or guardianship, while 17 percent reported living in an informal arrangement—physical custody without legal custody. In 19 percent of the cases, they had adopted the children. Two percent were unsure of their custodial status.

Why don't these new caretakers establish custody? Often, it's because they think their role is temporary. Surely as soon as Sonja gets out of rehab or Juan gets out of jail, everything will be fine again. But meanwhile, the grandparents may encounter legal barriers to getting medical care or child care services for their children or enrolling them in school. Help is available, but grandparents may not realize this. (Part 3 of this book focuses on legal and financial resources for grandfamilies.)

At the least, you need to create a new legal relationship with the child, which often involves the state social services agency and the court. Emergency guardianship is one possibility, particularly if the parent is in jail or in a long-term rehab facility. State laws vary, but all states offer emergency provisions for situations where the parent is incapable of caring for the child. Talk to a family law attorney; many of them offer a free initial consultation (verify this first). In some cases, you may be able to file an emergency request with the court yourself. This issue is discussed in more depth in chapter 7.

"Those social service agencies are only trying to undermine us."

Many grandparents need financial help in raising a grandchild but don't seek state assistance such as Medicaid and foster care payments. Why not? They simply mistrust the social services system—the agencies that pick up where Child Protection Services leave off, managing these cases over time. Often, they worry that if they ask social service agencies for help, the child will be taken away as a sort of punishment. The reality is that, although the caseworker may not be your new best friend, it is unlikely that you should shrink from this person.

Note: The names of these agencies, and the scope of their duties, vary from state to state. For example, in a rural area, the same agency might be involved with removing children from danger, placing them in foster care, and managing their cases over time. In other areas, those tasks might be handled by two or even three agencies. In this book, we refer to these agencies as "child services," "child and family services," or simply "social services." Find out the name and the scope of the agencies where you live.

In a small study of caregiving grandparents in Montana (ages fifty-six to seventy-one),[12] most had not sought state financial assistance, and a fear of the child welfare system was one key reason. But more than two-thirds had consulted with a private attorney to create a legal relationship with the child, such as legal guardianship.

Grandparents who need health care for their grandchildren may apply for Medicaid for one person—the child. But many are afraid to do so, or, even if they do apply for such services, they may by blocked by state workers who don't understand—or don't want to understand—that the grandparents are seeking aid for the child only and not for themselves.

Some grandparents say they feel caseworkers blame them for the parenting failures of their adult children. Yes, this stigma can be real, although many people say they admire grandparents who take on the parenting role all over again. But what about child social service workers? Do they admire the grandparents? Or do they think, *The apple doesn't fall far from the tree*—a variation of the thought *It's really all your fault?*

"Many grandparents describe feeling judged or disrespected by service providers," say the authors of "Grandparents Raising Grandchildren," Megan L. Dolbin-MacNab and Burt Hayslip Jr. They go on to say:

> This judgment may stem from a larger sociocultural assumption that, if they are raising their grandchildren, grandparents must have failed in raising their own children. When compounded with cultural expectations about caregiving, racism, and other forms of discrimination, these societal attitudes can leave grandparents feeling ashamed about their family situation and further isolated from sources of support.[13]

Some grandparents may (somewhat irrationally) fear that if state workers are involved, they will take away the grandchild. They might imagine that if they did report to the state that their daughter abandoned little Brandon three months ago, then social workers would suddenly swoop in and snatch him away, saying, "Oh, what a cute baby! I think we'll give him to a nice couple to be adopted."

Yes, it's true that state agencies have a lot of power. Yet they often regard grandparents as potential assets and caregivers to children. In fact, social service agencies usually seek kinship-care foster families rather than nonrelative foster care situations.

Of course, caseworkers *could* remove a baby or older child from the grandparents' home—but not to offer for adoption. The first mission of child services agencies administering foster care is reunification, to try to reunite children with their biological parents when it is safe to do so. Moreover, most people who want to adopt healthy children apply to adoption agencies or they hire an adoption attorney; they don't apply to state social services agencies. Most don't want to adopt a child with "special needs," which describes a large portion of the children that the state controls in the child social services system. Many of these children have special needs *because* they were abused, neglected, or abandoned in their parental homes.

When Grandparents Feel Disrespected by Caseworkers

Sometimes caseworkers for child services assume that their own judgment is far superior to that of any grandparent, and this attitude may be communicated through an underlying attitude of condescension. And some grandparents may put up with this patronizing behavior, fearing that if they complain, the caseworker could punish them by recommending the child be given back to parents who are still problematic.

Emilia, age fifty and a college graduate, recently received custody of Luis, her four-year-old grandson. Because she speaks English with a Spanish accent, Emilia says some people seem to think she's not smart—people like Luis's caseworker. "She talks to me very slowly and says each word so precisely, I guess to make sure I understand her," said Emilia. She restrains herself from telling the caseworker to talk faster, because she doesn't want to offend the worker. "But it makes me mad when people act that way!" Emilia said.

What could Emilia do, rather than just put up with this treatment? She could tell the caseworker once, politely and in a friendly voice, that she understands English very well and that she doesn't need to speak slowly and take such painstaking care enunciating her words. The caseworker may have been making an error of judgment, with the best of intentions. Emilia could give her that chance. But then, if the habit continued, Emilia might have reason to feel patronized.

"It's all my fault! Where did I go wrong?"

Although the guilt and anxiety eventually subside for most people, nearly all of us worry at first that we're to blame for this family situation. Were we too strict with Johnny when he was little, so now he's acting out with criminal behavior? Is Marla hooked on methamphetamine because we were too lenient with her? What did we do to cause Debbie to lose interest in her child or to make Victor think it's okay to leave town without a trace?

Stop wracking your brain. Nobody is perfect, but most of us are plenty good enough as parents. Unless you abused or neglected your children when they were little, it's unlikely that the current parenting situation is your fault. Kids are often resilient. They're also subject to many influences besides parents—including friends, classmates, and neighbors, teachers, coworkers, bosses, and many other people who still play a role in their lives.

Fixating on your possible former faults sucks time and energy out of you—precious resources that would be better spent on your grandchildren and on yourself.

"It's up to me to save my child,
along with my grandchild."

Your child is your child for life and doesn't become your un-child at age eighteen. Or thirty-eight. But growing up means facing the consequences of our choices. Shielding adult children from those consequences does them no favors. So many people try to "fix" the immediate problem that is preventing their adult child from being a good parent. Let's say that birth parents Dylan and Chloe were just evicted and have no place to live, so Dylan's parents let them move in, along with baby Sandy. But this situation makes life a bit too easy for Dylan and Chloe.

Soon they're out partying every night, and who gets up to comfort the crying infant? *Hint:* It's not Dylan or Chloe.

It's a tricky balancing act to parent your grandchildren while also trying to help adult children solve the problems that make them unfit to parent. Often you find that you must make a choice about who is more important, and you may decide that the grandchild simply needs you more. But this choice can come with major guilt and frustration. You want to help your own child, so you offer help when you can—assuming your adult child is willing to accept help. And when you can't, you acknowledge to yourself that the grandchild, who is just a kid, needs to come first. That means if you're Dylan's parents, you'll need to decide how and where to draw the line—and soon.

Offer a reasonable level of help for your adult child, rather than taking extreme measures. What is reasonable help? For example, you could help your son find a drug treatment center and encourage him to stick with its programs. You might suggest a counseling center or parenting support group to your daughter.

But don't put yourself in financial jeopardy and spend thousands of dollars on housing for an adult child who was just evicted for nonpayment of rent. (Though if you do so anyway, always pay for rent and utilities directly, particularly if substance use is a factor.) Only your child can solve these self-created problems; you cannot solve them. On the other hand, your grandchild may truly need immediate help.

"I don't need any time for myself— and it would be impossible anyway!"

For a custodial grandparent, free time and outside interests may feel like distant memories. But try to carve out some "me" time, for the sake of your well-being and endurance.

"It's been tough to go from being free and spontaneous to being tied down," said Jean. "I have to deal with my granddaughter Cassie's emotional meltdowns. They stem from the drug addiction she was born into, and they can be unpredictable. That takes extra time." Cassie receives Medicaid, and Jean has applied for state assistance with applied behavioral therapy (ABT; expert help for severe cases is offered by some states but not all). With better techniques for preventing meltdowns and handling them consistently when they do happen, perhaps Jean can breathe easier and hover less over Cassie.

"My old life is over—and so are my old friendships."

Danette had custody of her toddler grandson when she found out that an old high school friend had died in another state. She wanted to go to the funeral, but she had no one to watch her grandson. "Can't you just put him somewhere?" said her hometown friend Tanya, sounding exasperated. Danette refrained from retorting that her grandson wasn't a dog she could board in a kennel. He was an active little toddler who was very dependent on his grandma—in fact, he hadn't been away from her in months. Danette had to miss her friend's funeral. But she resolved to identify some backup help in case of unplanned future events—especially chances to connect meaningfully with others. Her brother could step in, and so could her neighbor's babysitter. Danette showed those people her grandson's routines at home, so they could help out in a pinch. She also called Tanya back and invited her to visit the next time she was in the area.

"I can't stand having my adult child angry at me."

Some adult children are upset or ashamed about their own parenting failure and may deflect their guilt by blaming their parents for their own flaws. "Mom, if you hadn't been so controlling, none of this would have happened," your child might say, or "Dad, why did we move all the time when I was little? I never belonged anywhere!" But it's a mistake to heed these cruel comments, although it can be hard to not take them to heart. Remember, your child made choices too. Keep in mind you are a grandfamily for at least one very good reason—your adult child's inability to be a good parent. While your adult child may lash out in anger and confusion, it's best to ignore such comments. Your focus is now on your grandfamily.

In sum, your new, "reinvented" family life may feel un-predictable—and indeed it may be. But as you stabilize the children's lives—and eventually your own—you can look ahead, anticipate possible problems, and learn from others who've been there. Keep these potential pitfalls in mind so you can give yourself a reality check. And support groups—in person or online—can help you think issues through as they arise.

Grandfamily Data: Who Are We, and What's on Our Minds?

Data may sound dry, but it can be revealing. In this case, some select data can help us see ourselves as part of a nationwide community, a community of families reinventing themselves. Data can help us envision those thousands of people who are in situations like ours. Let's look at some data from three sources: the US Census Bureau, the Centers for Disease Control, and my (Dr. Adesman's) own Grandfamily Study conducted in 2016 and discussed in this book's introduction. Together, they'll draw a group portrait of our nation's grandfamilies and also show what many of us are thinking about.

Let's look at the US national data first. The figures shown here track the features of grandfamily households, and the most recent data is provided when available. What are the children's ages and racial or ethnic backgrounds? What is the household income, and what kinds of public assistance are being used, if any? Collected by the United States Census Bureau, this data most closely reflects the actual population, although it is by no means exact. Let's summarize some main points here. (All the following figures are rounded, including percentages.)

Age of children. The age brackets these grandchildren represented in 2016:

- under six years: 39 percent
- six to eleven years: 34 percent
- twelve years and up: 27 percent

Adding the first two figures, we see that three-quarters of these children are under age twelve.[14] The reasons for this predominance of young children is unknown, although the significant rise in the opioid epidemic since about 2000 is likely one of the key factors.

Race/ethnicity of children. In the Census Bureau data on children whose grandparents were responsible for them in 2016, races and ethnicity percentages were as follows (rounded):

- **Individuals of One Race (92 percent)**
  - —white: 58 percent
  - —Hispanic (of any race): 24 percent
  - —black or African American: 24 percent
  - —Asian: 2 percent
  - —American Indian and Alaska Native: 3 percent
  - —another race: 6 percent
- **Two or More Races (8 percent)**[15]

Grandparent age, gender, and duration of caregiving.
According to information released in 2014 about 2012 data,
about two-thirds of the grandparents (63 percent) were
female, and two-thirds were under the age of sixty.[16] Overall,
the largest percentages were:

- in their fifties: 39 percent
- in their sixties: 26 percent

The duration of time spent raising their grandchildren
ranged from less than six months to five years or more. (Note
that this does not refer to the age of the child but to the amount
of time the grandparents spent in the parenting role.)

For more extensive statistical data on grandparents raising
their grandchildren, released in 2014 by the Census Bureau,
read the report by Renee R. Ellis and Tavia Simmons, *Coresident
Grandparents and Their Grandchildren: 2012* at www.census.gov
/content/dam/Census/library/publications/2014/demo/p20
-576.pdf.

In 2013, a small survey by the US Centers for Disease Control and Prevention yielded some more data on grandfamilies.
With just 558 respondents, it showed some different demo-
graphic proportions: for example, racial data showed white and
black children at 59 and 21 percent respectively, compared to
41 and 25 percent reported by the Census Bureau for that year.
But because of its focus, the CDC survey had some interesting
findings:

- Of parenting grandparents, 88 percent believed that the
  child would stay with them until adulthood.
- About 75 percent reported that they had a legal relationship with the child, such as custody or guardianship.[17]

*Beyond the Demographics: Dr. Adesman Interprets
His Grandfamily Study Results*

For the Adesman Grandfamily Study conducted in 2016,
Dr. Adesman explained:

> "I gathered responses from 747 grandparents nation-
> wide through my survey website, promoted through
> national organizations and online grandfamily support
> groups. As such, it was a self-selected group: respon-
> dents were those with a computer or device, internet
> access, and extra time to fill out a survey, and perhaps
> those who had already tapped into grandparenting
> resources online. Therefore, it's no surprise that they
> were an educated group of grandparents: about 80
> percent had at least some college education or higher,
> much greater than the national average of 59 percent,
> according to the Census Bureau.[18] We can guess, then,
> that most respondents were in relatively comfortable
> circumstances, with the other demographic features
> that go along with that. In contrast, US Census sur-
> veys are done at least partly door-to-door, and CDC
> surveys are done by phone. Both of those approaches
> are likely to capture a broader range of socioeconomic
> circumstances."

Some notable findings from the Adesman Grandfamily Study
follow here.

Gender and marital/cohabiting status. The majority
(93 percent) who responded to Dr. Adesman's study were
female grandparents, while 7 percent were grandfathers.
Sixty-five percent lived with a spouse or partner. Of the
total 747 respondents the marital statuses divided like this:

- married: 60 percent
- divorced: 21 percent

- widowed: 8 percent
- living with a partner: 5 percent
- never married: 5 percent
- separated: 3 percent

Age. Our respondents skewed a little older than the Census Bureau study, but the proportions were about the same, with the largest group aged fifty through fifty-nine. Ages of parenting grandparents:

- less than age fifty: 18 percent
- in their fifties: Almost half (44 percent)
- in their sixties: About a third (31 percent)
- in their seventies: 7 percent

No respondents were in their thirties, but plenty of these young grandparents are to be found. (One notable example: Actor Whoopi Goldberg was a grandmother at thirty-three, as Lesley Stahl points out in her 2017 book *Becoming Grandma.*)[19]

Race/ethnicity. The study's racial diversity doesn't reflect the United States as a whole, probably because of the self-selection factors noted earlier. (Note that more than one race or ethnicity could be chosen in the study. For example, a person may identify as both "white" or "black" and also "Hispanic.") Respondents self-identified this way:

- white: 85 percent
- black: 10 percent
- Hispanic: 7 percent
- other: 4 percent
- American Indian: 3 percent

Employment status of grandparents. Grandparents aren't all retirees: in this survey, only a quarter of them were retired. Note that some of these individuals fit more than one category, such as being employed full time and owning their own business or other combinations. According to the Census Bureau, nearly 1.5 million grandparents work to support their grandchildren. About 370,000 are ages 60 years and older.[20] In my study, I found the following was true of grandparents:

- employed full time: 32 percent
- retired: 25 percent
- self-identified as homemakers: 16 percent
- disabled or otherwise unable to work: 12 percent
- employed part time: 11 percent
- self-employed: 10 percent

Numbers of grandchildren being raised. Some grandfamilies had more than one grandchild:

- one grandchild: 54 percent
- two grandchildren: 28 percent
- three grandchildren: 12 percent
- four grandchildren: 4 percent
- five or more grandchildren: 2 percent

Years raising their grandchildren. In the Grandfamily Study, nearly half of grandparents had been raising their grandchildren for five or more years:

- five or more years: 44 percent
- three to five years: 25 percent
- one to two years: 23 percent
- less than one year: 8 percent

Custodial status of the grandparents. Most grandparents had taken legal steps: they had legal custody or guardianship, or they had adopted the child. This contrasts with what some researchers have believed, which is that most of the grandparent caregivers had no legal relationship to the grandchild. (Read more on these custodial relationships in chapter 7.) Respondents said they had

- legal custody or guardianship of the grandchild: 62 percent,
- adopted the child: 19 percent,
- informal custody (that is, physical custody with no legal custody): 17 percent,
- uncertainty about their custodial status: 2 percent.

Biological parents living with grandparents and child. In most cases (97 percent) of my study, the biological mothers did *not* live with the grandparents and children, and this was also true of 97 percent of the biological fathers. Sad to say, 7 percent of the biological mothers had died, as had 4 percent of the biological fathers.

Beyond the demographics. How are grandparents managing, and what are they learning? Grandparents reported on the quality of their lives, their concerns, their needs, and their relationships. On a scale ranging from "strongly disagree" to "strongly agree," they rated how closely given statements applied to them. As a group, here's the percentage that agreed (either "strongly" or "somewhat") with these statements on a variety of topics:

- 72 percent: "I worry about who will care for my grandchild if I am not able to."

- 72 percent: "I am less able to socialize with friends because I am raising my grandchild."
- 30 percent: "I would like to receive counseling services."

Some grandparents also commented on what they know now that they wish they'd known before they started parenting their grandchildren. Some samples:

- "I wish I had known how challenging it is but also how very rewarding it can be."
- "I wish I had known the kids did not know to ask for help. . . . They believed abuse was normal."
- "Be more patient and understand the impact their past has on the children."
- "Set boundaries early and stick to them, no matter how much they push."
- "Take each day as a blessing, and stress out less."
- "There are more people out there going through the same thing. . . . You are not alone."
- "Life is not perfect. It is messy, frustrating, funny, emotional, a hilarious roller-coaster ride. Buckle up!"

Buckle up indeed! You may already be riding that roller coaster. In the next chapter, we'll cover the emotions you may experience and how to handle them.

〉〉

CHAPTER 2

From Shock to Joy— and Everything in Between

Laurie stood in her living room sobbing. At age fifty-four, she was in a tailspin: a few days ago, she had received custody of her twin three-year-old grandsons, and her life changed from calm to chaotic. This afternoon, while Laurie was attending to David, Danny had discovered and eaten an entire box of cookies, after which he threw up all over the carpet. Laurie cleaned up the mess while Danny was now happily banging a wooden spoon on pots and pans on the kitchen floor. David was napping, having fallen asleep after a temper tantrum because Laurie had no idea where his favorite "blankie" was. Now, during a calm moment, Laurie asked herself how she, a single parent, could hope to handle two active boys.

• • •

Laurie's story may sound familiar. Your life, as you knew it, is not completely over, but it's drastically different now that you have a grandfamily. For many grandparents in this role, becoming a parent again was a jaw-dropping shock; for others, it might have seemed inevitable because of their adult children's parenting problems, whether due to substance use, incarceration, child neglect, or something else.

Either way, your life may suddenly feel like an emotional battleground—especially when you're new to the role. Over time, you will adjust to this "new normal," but new feelings emerge as the children grow up and as you age too. So let's talk about identifying and dealing with these emotions and when to seek help from others.

Notice Your Feelings: Some Common Emotions

Grandparents describe a dizzying range of feelings as they take on the role of parenting again, sometimes decades after raising their own children. With so many stressors at the same time, they may feel many emotions. Relief, for the children's sake, but also shock and role confusion as their own lives are upended. Over time, they may feel not only depression, loneliness, and isolation but also periods of great joy and satisfaction. Anger and resentment, often at the adult children's inability to parent. And likely anxiety, grief, perhaps guilt. How will you handle it all? Let's hear from some grandparents who have been there.

Relief: The Child Is Finally Safe

You may have been worrying and mentally wringing your hands over potentially dangerous (or certainly dangerous) situations that your grandchild has been facing, such as being alone with parents who are abusing alcohol or other drugs or who are mentally ill and untreated and therefore unpredictable. Despite the challenges of forming a grandfamily, many people report experiencing profound relief when a grandchild comes to live with them, because now they know the child is safe.

Some of the respondents to the Adesman Grandfamily Study expressed relief at securing custody:

- "I saved two children from lives of hell."
- "I sleep at night now, knowing that she is cared for and loved!"
- "She was out in the streets with her mother, a meth addict. Now she is safe."

- "He would have been seriously injured or killed in his parents' care."
- "A child should never have to live in a car."

Shock: You're a Parent Again

Surprise! For many grandparents, shock is an initial response to becoming a parent again. These grandparents didn't realize that as parents their adult children were inadequate or worse: abusive, neglectful, or dangerous. Maybe the birth parents lived far away or didn't visit for a variety of reasons. Perhaps they discouraged the grandparents from visiting them, knowing that if the grandparents *had* entered the home, they'd have been shocked by the chaotic environment and the dirty child and called them on it. Some grandparents say that when they later saw the birth parents' home conditions, it was like a scene from the television show *Hoarders* with filth and debris everywhere, rotting food, and even animal excrement from confined pets. This situation would appall anyone. But even if your grandchild came from a safer setting, the swiftness of the transfer can be a shock to your system.

Depression: When Your Spirit Feels Drained

Some research studies show that depressive symptoms are more likely for parenting grandparents than for "traditional" grandparents, who can spoil the children and send them home. However, depression doesn't necessarily come with the role. It simply occurs at a higher rate; for example, one large study showed that custodial grandparents were nearly twice as likely to have depressive symptoms as were traditional grandparents.[1] But the researchers also found some good news: the situation often improves over time. After acting as parents for five or more years, grandparents were significantly less likely to be depressed than those who were newer to the role. Why? The researchers speculated that as the crisis recedes and routines become more settled, the stress eases for everyone. And, as children grow from infant to toddler to school-age, the job of caring for them gradually becomes less demanding.

The researchers also found that grandparents who were in good health were less likely to be depressed,[2] which makes sense—health and exercise build our resilience and well-being.

One risk factor for depression: parenting a child with developmental disorders or chronic medical conditions. Even when the caregiver is fully and lovingly committed, children with special needs require more assistance than other children and may need multiple therapies, which can be taxing on families. It's a more challenging parenting experience, perhaps with milestones fewer and further between. In a study of seventy-four Latino grandparents (average age sixty-three), researcher Denise Burnette found them more subject to depression when raising a child with special needs. Other risk factors were the poor health of the caregiver and higher levels of life stressors, such as the death of a family member, the loss of a close friend, or the end of a job.[3]

Loneliness and Isolation

Many parenting grandparents report feeling like they're the only individuals who are in this situation, and this perception could lead to feelings of loneliness and isolation. In the Adesman Grandfamily Study, most of the grandparents (69 percent) said they strongly or somewhat agreed with this statement: "I am less able to socialize with friends because I am raising my grandchild."

Parenting your grandchildren limits your free time, and sometimes your former friends and relatives don't want to deal

with a crying baby or an active small child. Here's how researchers Deborah Sampson and Katherine Hertlein described the
situation in their 2015 article in *Grandfamilies: The Contemporary Journal of Research, Practice and Policy*:

> Custodial grandparents can also become isolated from
> their peers due to caregiving responsibilities. Such
> responsibilities may put them out of step with their
> peer group. The social isolation that grandparents ex-
> perience may make management of their physical and
> emotional issues more difficult.[4]

Reach Out to Young Parents—and to Old Friends

Ever since Doreen began raising her three grandchildren, she
has been unable to see her friends as often as she'd like—
and she doesn't feel as comfortable with them anymore,
either. Most are in their late forties, like Doreen, but many are
empty-nesters. She also feels she has nothing in common
with younger parents who are the age of her own adult
children—or younger. So Doreen feels isolated, not fully
belonging to either circle.

Some younger parents may become your friends, while
others may not. And sometimes older friends drift away,
whether you're raising a grandfamily or not. In both circles,
you may need to make extra effort to find people you truly
connect with. Here are a few suggestions for Doreen and
others in similar situations.

Find Common Ground with Younger Parents

You may need to take the initiative, because younger parents
may feel initially reticent around a person their mom's age.
And in public places, they're likely to be absorbed with their
smartphones or other devices too; that trend is becoming

continued

more and more noticeable. But when they take a breather, consider these suggestions, whether you're at a birthday party, the local playground, or even in the pediatrician's waiting room.

Say something nice about their child. Who isn't pleased by that? If you know the child even slightly, use what you know—you could say she's a fast runner at the T-ball games. If you don't know the child, you could notice that he's polite or shares his toys well, or wow, he's only four and he's tying his own shoelaces. You can add that the parent is obviously doing a great job. This gives other parents the opportunity to be proud of their children and feel good about themselves. It's hard to not respond when someone compliments your children.

Compliment the parent. Doreen and another mom, Lisa, took their children to the same playground and often saw each other there. One day, Doreen told Lisa that she'd noticed how carefully Lisa listened to her daughter, Kira—she admired that. Lisa thanked her and added that she hadn't been close to her own parents, so she'd decided to really get to know her daughter. Doreen said, "You're doing a great job! I can tell that you really communicate." She might go on to ask Lisa, "Did you grow up around here?" and let the conversation evolve from there.

Think of some icebreaker topics. Movies, YouTube videos, online games—now more than ever, kids share these media experiences. You could mention that you and your grandchild recently saw a movie and wonder what others think about it. Wendy, age forty-five, started a lively conversation with a roomful of parents in the dentist's waiting room about a popular Minecraft YouTube video series. Some of the parents couldn't understand the appeal, while others thought the videos were humorous. The conversation became so engaging that some of the parents, including Wendy, decided to meet for coffee later.

Homework can be a good topic. How do other parents structure homework time? What do they think of the school's approach to teaching math? If you're struggling to help with homework, you're not alone. You may learn some helpful hints by bringing up this topic casually with other parents— maybe during a basketball game or at a birthday party.

Listen to what younger parents say. Yes, you're more experienced than they are. But rather than rushing in to share your own stories, listen to them. They may have just the perspective you need. Draw them out; avoid being dismissive or judgmental. For example, if the younger parent responds to your positive comment about her energetic child by saying, "She's high energy all right! Sometimes she makes me crazy!" avoid giving a lecture on ADHD or saying she's lucky the child isn't disabled. Instead, you can laugh at her comment and empathize, perhaps adding something like, "Yes, it can be hard to keep up!" or even "How do you calm her down at bedtime? I have trouble with that myself."

Connecting with Your Same-Age Peers

If you're raising a toddler, then potty training and bedtime rituals are interesting topics for you—but not so much for your same-age friends. So, when you have a chance to see your older friends, it's okay to talk about some grandfamily topics, but hey, now's your chance for a break! Listen to what they're discussing. Books, TV shows, neighborhood issues, fitness, gossip? Listen, learn, and speak up. If you're sixty something, your friends might be talking about retirement decisions and health issues too. As with your new, younger friends, use positive (but sincere) comments to reconnect with your older friends.

continued

You can also ask about their adult children and respond supportively. Be noncommittal about your own adult children if they are having serious problems. Your friends don't need to know that Samantha is on probation for eighteen months for using drugs. Instead, simply say that she has some issues. Use your judgment. You may want to confide in close, trustworthy friends who seem concerned about what you are dealing with and want to offer support. Even then, be careful to not overshare.

Call your old friends occasionally to check in. They may miss you and be very happy to hear from you. But show them that you're interested in topics other than raising children!

Joy in Raising Your Grandchild

Of course, there are many positive emotions associated with parenting your grandchildren. Relief is one of the already discussed positive emotions, but here are a few more related to the joys of parenting:

The love you and your grandchild feel for each other. Parenting is an opportunity to give and receive an enormous amount of love and affection. Depending on how old the children are when they come to you and their past experiences, it may take time to develop a bond. But when it does, it's a wonderful feeling. "There are lots of hugs and kisses, tickles, and play-time. It's also fun going to the park and doing things together," said one grandparent in the Adesman Grandfamily Study. Another explained it this way: "Watching him blossom from a shy little boy who wouldn't look at anybody into an outgoing social butterfly has been a joy for us." And another remarked, "Seeing this heartbroken child start to laugh and enjoy life again has been wonderful."

The joy of seeing your grandchild achieve new milestones. The radiant face of a child upon learning how to ride a bike or how to swim is one of life's great pleasures. Later, it might be seeing the child learn to play a musical instrument or score points on the soccer field that will fill your heart with joy. "Look at me, look at me!" is often heard, and don't worry, Grandma or Grandpa (or both) *are* watching. Exceptional talent is not required. What matters is that the child is mastering skills that previously were too difficult and you share that joy with your grandchild.

The fun you enjoy together. Children enjoy life much of the time, and they can be wonderful companions. "When we started parenting our granddaughter, at first I was surprised by how much fun we have together," said a grandfather. "She marvels at things that most of us take for granted. Beautiful flowers, the sunset, a rainbow—it's all special to her, and it makes me realize that these really *are* wonderful aspects of life we can enjoy together."

When Being a "Beast" Is a Good Thing

On the soccer field sidelines, Stacy was cheering for her ten-year-old grandson Brian. It was a close game, and Brian was getting a workout. The man standing next to her suddenly turned and said, "Your boy is a *beast* on the field!" This did *not* sound good to Stacy, but as she looked at the dad's smiling face and his welcoming and open posture, she realized being a beast is a good thing. This wasn't an insult—it was a great compliment. So Stacy said, "You're right! He is a total beast!" and the two of them high-fived. (Soccer parents do a lot of high-fiving.) And Stacy made sure to tell Brian about the compliment later.

continued

Slang words ("slanguage") is constantly changing. If someone makes a comment and you wonder if it's good or bad, you may be able to read the meaning from the person's face and/or the context, as Stacy did. Of course, you can always ask what he means—perhaps joking about the new vocabulary you're learning. For example, "chill" means relaxed, while "sick" is excellent. Don't worry about being totally up to date on it.

Stressing Out: Can You Really Handle Parenting?

Stress is common among parenting grandparents, particularly in the first year or so as the situation evolves and your routines change. Sure, you've been a parent before, but now you're in new territory. It'll take time to work out how you adapt. Like Laurie with her mischievous three-year-olds, we wonder, *Can I handle this job? Am I truly up to the task?*

In the Adesman Grandfamily Study, grandparents were asked to what extent they agreed with this statement: "I am generally able to cope with the daily stressors of parenting my grandchildren." Three-quarters of them—76 percent—agreed, either strongly or somewhat, that they could generally cope. Approximately 12 percent were neutral; 10 percent somewhat disagreed; and 1 percent strongly disagreed. (Figures are rounded to the nearest percentage point.)

Clearly, for a minority of respondents, the stress is hard to handle. And, as noted earlier, this study group was self-selected, skewing toward people in comfortable circumstances. A more representative group might have fewer resources for coping with stress.

Some researchers have found that perceived stress is heaviest in the early years of parenting one's grandchildren.[5] When the child or children first arrive, nobody really knows what to expect, making for some difficult times ahead. So it's a very good time to get help from support groups and others on how to proceed from here on out. Although times may be difficult later on as the children grow up, in later years the needs and demands of older kids may be more predictable, grandparents will be more likely to have set schedules in place, and the children will have learned what's expected of them.

Not only do younger children need more care, but younger (non-retired) adults can feel stretched pretty thin. Adding parenting to their already busy lives can feel like too much. In a smaller study of custodial grandparents—92 percent of them grandmothers—the researchers found that younger grandparents, closer to age fifty, were more likely to be stressed out than older ones, and a lack of support also increased stress levels.[6] Other researchers, too, have found that parenting grandparents who are younger face more stress. The reasons are unknown but may be related to the demands of a full-time job, other children still in the home, possible loss of income, increased expenses, and the adverse impact on the grandparents' social life because young children require more supervision.

Anger and Resentment: Why Can't the Birth Parents Raise Their Own Kids?

Often grandparents feel angry and resentful that they "have to" take over parenting their grandchildren. They may feel like they have earned their retirement, and *how dare their adult children do such a poor job of parenting that someone else must take over!* They often believed their parenting days were over or should be. And now they think it isn't "fair" they must spend years, sometimes the rest of their lives, being hands-on parents again.

It's also true that sometimes the children have special needs stemming from prenatal exposure to alcohol and other drugs or from abuse and neglect they experienced after they were born. The children may need special education services, counseling, behavioral therapy, and other types of services that require a great deal of time, and these issues make the parenting job even more difficult. Grandparents may feel outraged, knowing these issues were inflicted on the children by their substance-using adult children.

Other people in the grandparents' lives may feel resentful too. Sometimes other adult children resent that Mom and Dad don't spend much time with *their* children. Of course, Mom and Dad would love to be "regular" grandparents—but they are raising one or more children as the primary parents—and may no longer have the time or money to be the storybook indulgent grandparents.

Needless Guilt

Many grandparents report experiencing feelings of guilt over how their adult children have turned out, whether the problem is drug or alcohol use, criminal behavior, or other dangerous habits that have prevented them from being good parents. But unless you were criminally abusive or neglectful to your children as kids—and if you were, you probably wouldn't be parenting the grandchildren—then your adult child's parenting problems are not your fault.

Also in the guilt domain is the feeling that parenting grandparents should now try to "help" their adult children by paying their bills for rent and utilities or bailing them out of jail for the third time. Though well-intentioned, this thinking may be counterproductive, because if you are always saving your adult children, they will never grow up. It also takes time and energy away from parenting your grandchild.

Anxiety and Worry about the Future

Anxiety and worry are common—probably even universal—feelings among parenting grandparents. If you're older or have health problems, you may worry about your capacity to provide for the long haul. If you don't have permanent custody, you might worry about that. And you may be anxious about the long-term effects of past abuse and neglect on your grandchildren.

These worries are normal. This job is demanding, and you need support. Grief, shock, and a massive lifestyle adjustment that may also seem ambiguous—who wouldn't be anxious in your position? So first, an invitation: even if you've never sought professional help for anxiety or any other persistent mood problems, please consider it now. It doesn't reflect poorly on you. Quite the opposite—it takes wisdom and self-knowledge to realize you need more support. Consider support groups too; resources are found in appendix 1.

Meanwhile, let's look at some of the most common worries and how we can help ease them in practical terms.

WORRY ABOUT FUTURE INCAPACITY OR DEATH

Grandparents may wonder whether they can expect to parent their grandchildren to adulthood. "My biggest worry is that we won't be alive long enough for when she can be on her own," one grandparent said, adding, "I will be seventy-five when he is twenty years old." In the Adesman Grandfamily Study, 72 percent of respondents strongly or somewhat agreed that "I worry about who will care for my grandchild if I am not able to." To allay such fears, it's a good idea to create a backup plan for who will raise the child if you can't—and make sure that person agrees to it. This kind of information can be included in your will. See chapter 7 for more discussion of legal issues.

WORRY ABOUT PAYING FOR EVERYTHING THE CHILD NEEDS

Grandparents may be anxious about meeting the child's financial needs, now and in the future. Joining the soccer team costs money, birthday gifts for parties must be bought, and many other expenses are involved in raising a child. Some grandparents might even feel compelled to draw down on their retirement funds now, rather than using them later—but resist that instinct until you've researched the issue. Read more about money matters in chapter 8.

WORRIES OVER CUSTODY ISSUES IN THE FUTURE

Another worry is that the parent may demand the child back at some future date. "They've left, but I still worry about them returning and kidnapping him," said one respondent to the Adesman Grandfamily Study. That's a valid fear when the grandparents lack any form of legal custody of the child, such as legal guardianship or temporary custody granted by the courts. You can ease your mind by learning your options and taking appropriate action. Read more about custodial arrangements in chapter 7.

CONCERNS ABOUT THE FUTURE IMPACT
OF PAST ABUSE AND NEGLECT

Grandparents may worry about the continuing effects of past abuse and neglect on the child, wondering whether the child can ever fully recover from this early damage. "He has abandonment issues and I can't leave him with others for very long," said one grandmother. "He also suffers from nightmares and sleepwalking, and it's a constant worry for us."

Money Can Be Tight Sometimes

Nine-year-old Ashley and her best friend, Brianna, had an idea one Saturday afternoon while they were riding bikes. They both wanted to see the latest Disney movie at the multiplex. Why not today? They just needed Ashley's Grandpa Bill to take them there and maybe sit a few rows away.

But when she asked him, Bill told Ashley, "I'm sorry, sweetie. We just can't afford the movies this week—it costs almost ten dollars a ticket."

Ashley's face fell. Then she flushed and clenched her teeth. "I hate you, Grandpa! You ruin everything," she said, bursting into tears and running off to her room.

Ouch! In fact, Bill would have enjoyed taking the girls to the movies. But he was low on cash right now, or, as he sometimes put it, "There's too much month at the end of the money." Bill was close to retirement age, and he used his credit card only if absolutely necessary. *Was this one of those absolutely necessary times?* he wondered. Back when he was raising Ashley's mom, a trip to the movies was a big treat—you didn't just go on a whim. *Have times changed that much?* Bill asked himself.

Suddenly, Ashley reappeared. "I'm sorry, Grandpa," she said. "It's okay. It's not your fault. Can we play dress-up instead? Can I show Brianna the clothes in that old trunk in the attic?" Bill said sure, and a newly excited Ashley clapped her hands. She loved trying on the old grown-up clothes in the trunk and knew Brianna would like it too.

To help ease your worries, it's a very good idea to join a local support group or an online support group of grandparents raising grandchildren. You can compare notes with others and often find solutions that had never occurred to you before. Keep in mind, however, that state laws vary, and you should not assume that a situation in Utah could be resolved in the same way as it was in Vermont. More advice: ask for help from others. Some grandparents complain that many people *say* they will help, but these same people disappear when you need them. In that case, seek out others, such as people in your religious organization, clubs, or your other affiliations. Also, be sure to make some "me" time for you, whether what you really need is a long, relaxing bath or a brisk walk by yourself. Don't feel like you are chained to the children 24/7. Support may be hard to find sometimes, but it's often out there.

An Olympic Athlete Raised by Her Grandparents

Gymnast Simone Biles, who won four Olympic gold medals in 2016, was raised by her grandparents. Born to a drug-addicted and alcoholic mother and put in foster care at age two, she was placed with her biological grandfather and his second wife, who later adopted both Simone and her younger sister. She calls them Mom and Dad, and they have always strongly encouraged her in her athletic pursuits. Biles was home-schooled from age thirteen and is a high school graduate.[7] When she appeared on *Dancing with the Stars* in 2017, she honored her parents for their sustained love and encouragement, saying, "My parents saved me. . . . There's nothing I could say to them to thank them enough. Even though there's no right words, maybe dance will say it for me."[8]

Grief

It's sad to think that your grandchild has suffered because of your adult child's actions and, from another perspective, it's sad that your adult child won't see what you're seeing: a child's first steps, first day of kindergarten, and other important milestones.

How do caretaking grandparents experience grief and loss? That was the focus of a small study in Australia. Researchers studied thirty-four grandparents caring for forty-five grandchildren, most of whom had been placed with them by social services because of parental substance use or addiction, mental health disorder, or both. The grandparents expressed feelings of grief and loss related to conflict with the birth parents, legal battles, social isolation, and other issues. They were also grieving about the background circumstances. Some said that even before their grandchild was placed with them, just observing the child's attempts to adjust to a troubled home life caused them significant grief.[9]

Grandparents might also grieve over giving up cherished retirement plans. "We always planned to move to Florida when we retired," said a grandmother. "Now that is all on hold because of our grandchild."

Role Confusion: Am I a "Regular" Grandparent Now?

Many grandparents say they enjoyed their past role of a "normal" grandparent, someone who said yes to nearly everything, from an extra cookie to a spontaneous trip to the zoo. Yet this is not a role you can maintain when you step up to take on the role of parenthood all over again. "I miss being the fun grandma. I'm the one doling out homework, chores, and responsibilities," said a grandparent. Another added, "I have to be the disciplinarian. I can't spoil them and send them home to their parents."

"Aren't You Too Old for This?"

Many people will be curious about why you are constantly with the child. Are you raising the child yourself? One simple answer is, "Yes, I am." But the questioning is unlikely to stop there. There may be a range of follow-up questions, from amusing to annoying, that can be tough to answer. This chart offers you a few suggestions.

Comments You Might Hear—and How You Might Respond

Comment	What a Grandparent May Think	What a Grandparent Could Say Instead
"It must keep you so young, raising a child again!"	Yes, tell that to my arthritic knees and my aching back.	"It's a challenge, but I do my best."
"You must be a saint! I'd never want to be a parent again."	I really didn't want to either, but my son's heroin addiction made it an urgent priority.	"Many people step up to do what's needed, and I am one of them."
"Why aren't his parents raising him?"	Why don't you mind your own business?	"That's a private matter."
"Who's going to raise her if you die before she's grown up?"	Are you really asking me this question?	"We have a plan for that."
"Maybe his parents will straighten out and take over the parenting again."	Sure, when pigs fly.	"We've adopted Joey, so we are now his parents."
"Do you take him to basketball practice and do all that other stuff?"	What do you think we do, read AARP magazines to him and play shuffleboard?	"Yes, we do. And we cheer as loud as the other parents."

"I could never do what you do."	I'm not entirely sure how I am doing it!	"Sure, you could, if it were your grandchild."
"Does she miss her mother?"	That question is so out of line.	"I imagine so."
"Why don't you adopt him?"	We would if we could.	"Maybe someday we will."
"Does it feel weird to be your age and raising a child again?"	It feels sad, stressful, and often very joyous.	"It feels like we're doing the right thing."
"If you die, will his parents get him back again?"	Considering their history of child abuse and drug addiction, I'd say no.	"It's hard to tell."

Dealing with Your Own Emotions

A little sadness, loneliness, or anxiety is common, but sometimes sadness escalates to depression, and nervous anxiety can increase to an anxiety disorder. These are important conditions you need to cope with. Whether your grandchildren understand what you are feeling—and they probably won't—they will likely be affected negatively by your chronic emotional struggles. For this reason and many others, it's important to get help with overwhelming emotions, because when you feel better, you'll also be a better parent.

Do I Need Help? Some Signs

You might think people would just know if they needed professional help from a psychiatrist, psychologist, or other mental health provider: they'd feel some urgency about their mental health. But sometimes people *don't* know because they're so entrenched in their current situation. They might feel helpless and hopeless, but they are nonetheless functioning and may not realize how far they have slipped. Sometimes they have felt that way for so long that it seems normal. In the Adesman Grandfamily Study, about a third of respondents (30 percent) said they strongly agreed or somewhat agreed that they would like to receive counseling services. In addition, 28 percent said they were currently receiving counseling services.

Let's look at some of the behaviors and symptoms that indicate a visit to the doctor, and perhaps a counselor, is in order: excessive fatigue, obsessive worrying, changes in eating or sleeping habits, and irritability.

FATIGUE OR SIGNIFICANT LOSS OF ENERGY

Do you feel extremely tired or even exhausted just about every day? That's a sign that you're overdoing things and you need to regroup. Check your priorities. For example, is it necessary or even possible to keep a perfectly tidy home when you have a curious toddler running about? What other household or volunteer tasks could you eliminate? If you cut back on some of your commitments and the severe fatigue does not abate, be sure to see your doctor. And please strongly consider joining a support group for grandparents. The sense of camaraderie can be a real energy boost. If you can't get out, then join an online group (see appendix 1 for some resources).

OBSESSIVE WORRYING

Some grandparents find they cannot concentrate during the day because they are so anxious, and they cannot sleep at night either. Either way, obsessive worrying is a debilitating symptom that can signal depression, anxiety, or other disorders. You need to seek help, and the first stop is to your physician to verify that you don't have any serious illnesses. If your daytime or night-time symptoms suggest depression, anxiety, or both—which is common—your doctor may wish to prescribe a low dosage of an antidepressant or antianxiety medication. (Always insist on starting at a low dose.) It can take several weeks to gain the full effect, so be patient.

Unfortunately, when we hear about these medications, some of us automatically think, *I'll never take those! They're for crazy people, and I'm not that bad off.* The fact is, antidepressant and antianxiety medications are widely used, and many people lead much richer, more manageable lives because of them. The stigma is slowly fading, which is a good thing. Just as a person with diabetes needs medicine, people with depression and/or anxiety find they function much better with the help of these drugs.

EMOTIONAL DISTRESS, ESPECIALLY AT NIGHT
Some new grandparents, generally grandmothers, say they cry themselves to sleep each night, upset about their adult children as well as their grandchildren and unsettled about the future. When it's severe, this fear and distress can signal depression, anxiety, or other disorders. Ask your doctor for help, and again, rule out a medical problem before considering a psychological problem. It's best to make sure you're not experiencing symp-toms of menopause, thyroid disease, or another medical issue. Some doctors may be a little quick with the prescription pad for treatment of emotional problems, so keep in mind that counseling or therapy is often helpful, and there are other non-pharmaceutical means to help elevate a depressed mood, such as exercise, which naturally boosts mood for many people.

A healthy diet, daily meditation, and satisfying social contacts can all help with these symptoms in many cases.

If you do seek therapy or counseling, welcome to the club! It can be highly effective in helping you overcome the issues discussed in this section, as can joining a grandparent support group, either in person or online. There's a lot to be gained through the sharing of information and opinions from people in such a group. Knowledge is power! You may be worrying over something minor. Or it could be a valid worry, and others will have suggestions on ways to overcome the problem. See appendix 1 for group resources.

EATING TOO MUCH OR TOO LITTLE

Have your eating habits changed? If you've lost or gained more than 5 percent of your weight without trying to, you may be depressed. Consult with your physician to make sure you don't have a health problem that causes weight loss or gain, such as a thyroid disease. If you are depressed, the doctor may recommend a low dosage of an antidepressant or suggest other strategies.

SLEEPING TOO MUCH OR TOO LITTLE

It's hard to sleep too much when you are parenting a small child, but if you sleep all day while the child is in school, that's a problem. It's more likely for parenting grandparents to sleep too little—perhaps because of nighttime worry. Either way, if your sleep habits are unhealthy, consult with your physician, checking first for medical problems, then for mental health issues such as depression. Again, antidepressants or lifestyle changes can be a big help.

Beyond Resentment: "I Chose This Life"

An activist and advocate for grandfamilies, the late Kathy Reynolds founded the popular Facebook group GrandsPlace —Grandparents Raising Grandchildren. She spoke about a feeling common among grandparents at this transitional time:

Resentment is a natural expected stage we all go through in parenting grandchildren. Most of us never planned to spend our older years changing diapers, joining carpools, and watching *Paw Patrol.* We spend our time, our energy, and our money fulfilling someone else's responsibilities. We think that the bios are out there having the time of their lives while we do all the work. We hate the things our wee ones have been through. Yes, some days, resentment is a mild word. . . .

What helped me get past the resentment stage was realizing that I chose this life. I was presented with a mandatory choice where I didn't like any of the options, but I did choose to parent Dani. I could have ignored the problem and let nature take its course. That was unacceptable. I could have let CPS [child protective services] do its thing and allowed my grandchild to go to foster care. That too was unacceptable. My last option, the one I chose, was to take Dani home and parent her myself. It was to make a lifelong commitment to another child. I chose that option because it was the only one that fit my needs. I needed to know that this child was cherished and given the best chance at a good life. We often say, "But I had no choice." The truth is I had a choice and I made it.

LOSING YOUR TEMPER OVER EVERYDAY IRRITATIONS

Everyone gets angry occasionally, but if you are getting distraught over minor mishaps, like yet another cup of spilled juice, you may have a problem with depression, anxiety, or another issue. Again, consult with your doctor to rule out medical problems before you consider if you may have a psychological problem.

What Kind of Help Is Available?

You might be surprised by the variety of help at hand—not only from mental health professionals but also from a thriving number of local and national support groups, both in person and online.

Support Groups

Support groups can help you get through the bumpy times of parenting. Parenting grandparents can find local, regional, and even national support groups in the United States, Canada, and other countries worldwide. There are groups available online too: find them by using simple search terms such as "grandparents raising grandchildren support group." Local groups can provide information about additional resources and financial support in your area. For example, you may have thought that you had to pay all the medical expenses for your grandchild and not known about child-only Medicaid, which considers only the income and assets of the child. You might also be eligible for reduced fees for child care.

You'll find some support groups listed in appendix 1, but do your own search, too, to find the latest groups. (You may also wish to check the AARP's website, which offers many resources for grandfamilies.) One caveat: Sometimes support groups can become complaint sessions that focus on the adult children's problems, rather than discussing how situations can improve. A little complaining is normal, but if 50 percent or more of the time is spent on deriding the adult children, this is usually not a helpful group. How do you know if a group is right for you? Attend some meetings or read its online discussions to see if you learn new information and can feel supported by the members.

Working with Mental Health Professionals

If you are struggling with depression, anxiety, or another psychological issue, sometimes it's best to consult a mental health professional and consider counseling or therapy. You don't have to have a diagnosed problem to benefit greatly from at least a few sessions. In fact, most people who seek such help simply have life problems that are temporary and don't constitute a mental illness. Instead they're just people going through difficult times, people who are sometimes called the "worried well." Any of these professionals may refer to you as a "patient" or a "client." Either way, you have lots of company. We all have problems from time to time, and being a custodial grandparent is a tall order. Take all the help you can get.

So, should you choose to see a psychiatrist, psychologist, therapist, or social worker? Let's look at the factors to consider.

THE PSYCHIATRIST

A psychiatrist is a medical doctor who specializes in mental health issues, and, as such, can prescribe medications. A psychiatrist will listen to your problems, assess what you say, and make a diagnosis, if appropriate. The psychiatrist may recommend that you see a therapist for counseling, prescribe a medication, or both.

Of course, any medical doctor, as well as nurse practitioners and physician assistants, may prescribe medication, and you may not have to see a psychiatrist to receive a prescription for an antidepressant or other psychiatric drug. Still, psychiatrists are the professionals most knowledgeable about these medications.

You can also see a psychiatrist for treatment with medication and periodic follow-ups for prescription renewals and adjustments, while also seeing another mental health professional for "talk therapy." Keep in mind that today, psychiatric consultation is often covered by insurance companies, in contrast to years ago when it was rarely covered. That change is largely thanks to state and federal mental health parity laws passed in 2008 and thereafter.

THE PSYCHOLOGIST

The psychologist is not a medical doctor but does have a doctorate (PhD or PsyD) in psychology. When you see a psychologist, the first step is to undergo an assessment so a diagnosis can be made. After that, the psychologist will focus primarily on a therapeutic treatment plan. You may also be referred to a psychiatrist for medication. (Note: After additional training, psychologists may prescribe medications in some states: Idaho, Illinois, Iowa, Louisiana, and New Mexico.)[10] Many psychological problems will either improve or resolve within ten to twelve sessions of what is often called talk therapy.

What happens in this type of therapy? Many psychologists use a practical approach called cognitive-behavioral therapy (CBT). It is based on the idea that we all engage in "self-talk"—messages we tell ourselves in our mind, perhaps judging ourselves harshly or jumping to negative conclusions. With CBT, a psychologist helps you become more aware of this self-talk and then create more rational or positive thoughts to counter the irrational, negative ones. Having looked at your own cognitive process, you can then adjust your response—your behavior—

Grandparents Can Have Adjustment Disorders Too

Grandfamilies are often formed in crisis. And for some grandparents, the shock and high drama of taking on the care of one or more children to raise may trigger what is called an adjustment disorder, such as post-traumatic stress disorder (PTSD) or acute stress disorder. In some cases, an adult child has died, compounding the stress. But even if not, this is a stressful, accident-prone time for many of us. One grandmother reported that a week after the state gave her an infant granddaughter to raise, her own father was in a terrible traffic accident, dying a few weeks later. Such cascading troubles can make the adjustment especially traumatic.

Adjustment disorders can be accompanied by depression, anxiety, or both. Symptoms of an acute adjustment disorder occur within three months of the main stressful event and may include the following:

- severe distress that appears to be disproportionate to current events
- major difficulty and impairment at work, home, and in other environments
- symptoms that are different from normal symptoms of a bereavement or major loss.[11]

People with adjustment disorders should be treated with therapy by a mental health professional. If the symptoms last for more than six months, the condition is considered chronic.

accordingly. This approach is also helpful in challenging common false assumptions. For example, when life is difficult, it may seem "unfair." *It's usually easier than this—what happened? No fair!* But life isn't fair or unfair—it's just life. So focus on what you can control: your choices. Sometimes you will make mistakes, and other times the choices work out well. Most people find that they can improve their choices by making their thought processes more conscious—and psychologists can be a great help with this.

Many forms of health insurance cover psychotherapy but not all. Check your insurance card to see if you have psychological care, which may be listed separately from medical care. The headings may include words such as "psychological," "mental health," or "behavioral." You may even have a separate insurance card for mental health issues. If you are still not sure, call your health insurance company.

THE SOCIAL WORKER OR OTHER THERAPIST

A social worker who counsels people usually has a master's degree in social work (MSW), while other therapists may have a master's degree in psychology or counseling. In general, these therapists are practical problem-solvers. They often look at your ongoing struggles as problems they can advise you about or identify other resources to help you. The social worker or other therapist is generally focused on the here and now rather than looking at your long-past issues or what may happen years from now.

Some therapists specialize in marriage and family issues; others specialize in helping children. You'll find other specialties, too, such as addiction counseling. Keep these resources in mind as you continue your life journey.

A Painful Choice

Family dynamics shift, sometimes painfully. Professional help might help you find new solutions. But even if it doesn't, it can help everyone feel better about "how things are." Here's Lena's story.

Lena was in her forties when she started caring for her grandsons, ages three and five. The boys' mother, Melissa, was seriously ill. After several hospital stays, it was clear her disease was incurable. Lena did all she could to help her daughter, finally taking the boys into her own home.

Just a year earlier, Lena, a widow, had remarried. She'd met her new husband, Paul, while hiking, and they'd enjoyed an active life with lots of sports, bike treks, and weekend backpacking trips. But all that stopped now that they had youngsters under their roof. *It's a no-brainer,* thought Lena. She'd make that sacrifice, and she assumed the same for Paul. With Melissa a single mom and no other relatives nearby, it seemed like the obvious path.

Shortly before her death, Melissa begged her mother to raise the boys. She agreed, they put the plan in writing, and when Melissa died, Lena became their guardian. Paul went along with it, albeit reluctantly. For a few months, he helped with the boys and got away for a solo hike occasionally. But one day, Paul told Lena that he had to face his true feelings. He didn't want to raise a family for the next fifteen years— it's not what he'd planned when he married Lena. He said she should either find another home for the boys, or he was leaving. He was sorry, but "that's how things are."

Lena was shocked. After she'd recovered a bit, she convinced Paul to see a marriage counselor with her. But after several sessions, they were at an impasse. Lena's strongest feeling was clear: no one was going to come between her and

continued

her promise to Melissa, not even Paul. Still, both were glad they'd discussed their priorities and come to closure, with the counselor's help. She and Paul started divorce proceedings, and when they parted, they wished each other well.

How to Find Help

After you've chosen to seek help from a psychiatrist, psychologist, social worker, or other type of therapist, how do you start? There are various ways, but first, a caution: you may not like the first person you contact. Yes, these are trained professionals, but it's also a matter of having the right chemistry. And you may not immediately find that chemistry, even if friends have told you that a particular therapist is wonderful, talented, and the greatest thing since sliced bread. If you don't find the right person your first time out, don't condemn all mental health professionals as incompetent. Just keep looking; another therapist could be very helpful to you.

ASK FOR REFERRALS AND RECOMMENDATIONS

Some good options for recommendations are your primary care doctor, trusted friends, local support groups, and your health insurance company.

Ask your primary care doctor. Your family care doctor or internist may be well aware of the best local mental health counselors, or your doctor may wish to check in with colleagues for recommendations before getting back to you. Not all primary care doctors are aware of such professionals in your area, so it's best to also consider referrals from other sources.

Ask trustworthy friends. Friends who know you and your situation may be able to give you names of mental health professionals to consider. Ask your friends what they particularly like about the person who is recommended.

Ask local support groups for recommendations. Grandparents in your area who are also raising their grandchildren may know the names of good mental health professionals. Moreover, they're likely to be sympathetic, helpful, and positive. To find local support groups, see appendix 1 or ask online groups to point you to resources.

Find referrals from your health insurance company. If your insurer provides coverage for a given mental health professional, then this person meets its standards for credentials and licensing, and at least part of your costs will be covered. Remember, though, that any professional's training and experience may or may not be sufficient for your needs.

DO SOME ONLINE RESEARCH

Most credentialed health care professionals are listed online—if not through health insurance networks, then through hospitals or other health care organizations. Take advantage of these online descriptions. After you have some referrals, it's wise to look them up online to find out more. If gender is important to you, you can verify if they are male or female. Check their areas of expertise, if listed. Often you will learn where they were trained and when they graduated. If you want a therapist with many years of experience, then don't consider someone who earned an MD or PhD only a couple of years ago. But do keep in mind that although newer therapists may lack experience, they may be more knowledgeable about the latest treatments and therapies.

Grandparents Seeking Professional Help

How often do custodial grandparents seek help with personal problems? A study in 1999 suggested that the children in their care have a lot to do with it. The researchers compared three groups:

- "traditional" (non-parenting) grandparents
- custodial grandparents whose grandchildren were considered "normal" behaviorally
- custodial grandparents with children regarded as "problematic" behaviorally

The children in the last group—those with the problem behaviors—were about twice as likely as the other children to have oppositional defiant disorder or hyperactivity. (Read more on those diagnoses in chapter 9.) They were also at greater risk for such issues as depression, trouble with the law, and learning difficulties.

The grandparents in each group were asked whether they had ever sought help for a personal problem. How did they answer?

- Of the traditional grandparents, 27 percent said yes.
- Of the custodial grandparents dealing with normal behaviors, 50 percent said yes.
- Of the custodial grandparents dealing with problem behaviors, 57 percent said yes.[12]

What's the lesson? Being a parent can be a tough job when you're a grandparent—but more of us are seeking help when we need it and realizing that asking for help when we need it is a positive step.

Caveat: You may see "patient ratings" of physicians and other professionals on the internet, but these can be unreliable. Average doctors may owe their five-star ratings to the fact that they have lots of open appointment times and they are able to quickly see and help people with minor problems. But truly wonderful doctors may have long wait times and long-term patients who tend not to give reviews at all.

Tip: Be a patient patient. If you need help from a mental health professional—or think that you might but you're not sure—take the initiative to seek out someone. Be persistent in getting an appointment. After you see the person, don't expect same-day results. This is not a quick fix. Be patient and listen to what the expert tells you. Does it seem to make sense? If so, use the recommendations and see if your depression, anxiety, or other symptoms slowly ease up.

》

CHAPTER 3

Let's Get Real

Strategies for Dealing with the Middle Generation

"I didn't realize there was a problem until one day I drove a few hours to visit my daughter and grandchildren," said Ruth. "The door was unlocked, and I went in and found my daughter Sophie, who appeared sound asleep. She was still breathing, but I couldn't wake her up. My five-year-old granddaughter was making a mac and cheese lunch in the microwave for her and her three-year-old brother. Nobody else was in the house. I called 911 and they took Sophie away in an ambulance. She had overdosed on drugs—but she lived. And she gave me emergency custody of the children. Within a few months, I realized I needed permanent custody, and I got it. That was a year ago, and Sophie is still addicted and mostly out of the picture. She hardly ever sees the children."

• • •

Ruth's story is all too common. But often the birth parents do stay in the picture. They may see the child and the grandparents, regularly or irregularly. And sometimes their relations may become strained and even adversarial. Adult children may greatly resent their parents for taking over "their" job of parenting (despite their own failings in that department), and birth parents may try to undermine the grandparents or threaten to do so.

On the other hand, some custodial grandparents get along very well with the birth parents: fully 40 percent, by one measure: 2013 data from the US Centers for Disease Control and Prevention. Another 36 percent said they got along "somewhat well," for a total of 76 percent.[1]

In the Adesman Grandfamily Study, those rates of "getting along-ness" were lower, both with birth mothers and birth fathers. Just 35 percent of grandparents said they currently had a good relationship with the birth mother; 32 percent said the same concerning the birth father.[2]

Data-gathering methods may account for the differences in findings. Dr. Adesman's results were submitted anonymously by respondents to an online questionnaire. In contrast, the CDC data were gathered by telephone. Perhaps it is harder to be negative about birth parents on the phone or the children were within earshot, although there could be other reasons for the differences.

When Worlds Collide:
You Clash with the Child's Parents

There are many areas of possible dispute between you and the child's parents, and in this chapter, we'll cover some common clashes. Even when their child is placed with the grandparents by state or county child services authorities, many birth parents still feel like they are—or should be—in charge of the child. Birth parents may resent losing custody and don't want the grandparents to make *any* decisions concerning their child, ranging from haircuts to the choice of preschool. Birth parents may expect their parents to offer financial help to *them*, along with raising the child. Our advice in cases like these: stand your ground. Let's look at these and some other common flash points.

Showing Some (Tough) Love

Anna's daughter Talia, twenty-two, moved back home a few months ago, along with her toddler, Micah. Although she's unemployed, Talia hasn't been helping out around the house or paying rent. She expects her mother to provide a clean home and hot meals, and when Anna comes home from work, Talia hands her the baby, saying she's "done." Whenever Anna suggests she find a part-time job, clean house, or cook, Talia threatens to move out and take Micah with her.

Is Talia serious? Anna doesn't know, but she worries about what might happen if Talia started staying at friends' homes. Would Micah be safe? Would he eat right? Anna stops pushing. Child neglect that *might* happen in the future isn't a reportable problem, but the possibility haunts her. The stress is getting to her, and she knows she has to take a stand.

What should Anna do? In some families, an impasse is broken only when there's a crisis or a blowup. But that's also the worst time to make decisions. People are upset, and words can be said that can't be taken back.

If you're in a time-bomb situation like this, try to act *before* the crisis point. To get to the root of the problem, Anna could try talking calmly with Talia at a time when they won't be interrupted. (Involving a therapist or other third party is an option too.) Anna might first ask nicely if she could help with any obstacles preventing Talia from meeting her home-sharing expectations. And then she should listen closely, giving Talia time to answer. Talia may be depressed but afraid to admit it. The conversation might reveal other underlying issues or new solutions for making home-sharing beneficial for both of them.

continued

If that doesn't work, Anna might choose to take these "tough love" steps:

1. Anna tells Talia verbally and in writing what she expects and needs her to do to continue living in the home, whether it's helping with household chores (itemize them), paying some rent, caring for her own child, or all of the above.

2. Anna gives Talia a deadline for complying, making it clear that noncompliance will mean that Talia must move out by a specific date.

3. If the date passes and the conditions haven't been met, Anna tells Talia she must leave. She might offer to babysit for Micah in her own home or even to let Micah continue to live with her; that's Anna's choice to make.

She can expect Talia to react first with anger to any of these steps and, if Anna offers to care for Micah, to insist that no one else can raise her child. It's difficult, but Anna can only do her best to take any initial verbal abuse in stride.

When the Birth Parents Try to Overrule What Grandparents Tell the Child

If and when the birth parents visit the child—we say "if and when" because some birth parents visit sporadically or not at all—they may try to exert their authority by telling the child to do the opposite of whatever the grandparent set as rules. For example, if the grandparent doesn't allow sweets within an hour before a meal, the parent may knowingly bring a half gallon of ice cream just before dinner. She'll give the child a big dish before you realize what's happening, then say she "forgot" this was not allowed. If this happens to you, you could schedule the next visit at a time further away from a meal.

Or maybe you have told the birth parent that the child goes to bed at 8 p.m. If the birth parent calls at 9 p.m. and wants to speak to the child, he needs to be told that the child is asleep and he should call back tomorrow or later in the week.

If the birth parent repeatedly attempts to thwart your authority while in your home, consider setting up visits away from home, such as at a park where you can limit the timing of the visits.

Stand your ground but try not to lose your temper. Realize the birth parents may have underlying hurt feelings. But as long as you have custody of the child, you are in charge. (A few exceptions may apply: for example, if the child needs major surgery, you may need state or parental permission.)

When the Birth Parent Criticizes the Grandparent to the Child
Some parents badmouth the grandparent in front of the child or others, saying the grandparent is too strict or too lax, the home is too messy or too perfect, or other criticisms. Although birth parents may believe these opinions, they are largely offered (consciously or unconsciously) to prove to themselves, the child, and others that the child would be better off with the birth parents—whom they may believe are really still in charge.

But the birth parent is *not* in charge when you are the custodial grandparent. Simply state that you like your rules and the way your home looks, and do not argue. If more barbed comments are made, ignore them—up to a point. If the tone goes too toxic and dramatic, tell the birth parent this behavior must stop, or the visit will end. If it continues or escalates further, tell the birth parent to leave now. Try your best to not be goaded into a shouting match in front of the child.

When the Birth Parent Makes Last-Minute Changes to Plans or Is a No-Show

It happens a lot: the birth parent promises to be on time for a birthday party or other event that is important to the child and then either shows up too late or backs out at the last minute, often with a lame excuse or no reason at all. If this has happened repeatedly, it's often best to tell the child ahead of time that you're not sure if the birth parent can make it. (You may be quite certain that the birth parent could be there if so desired, but don't say that to the child.)

This policy may also be wise when the birth parent repeatedly fails to show up for scheduled visits. After frequent cancellations, some grandparents don't tell the child at all about upcoming scheduled visits. They don't want the child to be upset if the parent is a no-show yet again.

Be Present and Listen to All Conversations

At least until the child reaches adolescence, maintain some control during the child's phone conversations with the birth parent. Put the birth parent on speakerphone to make sure nothing upsetting is said to the child. With video call apps such as Skype, stay in the same room during the call and make your presence known by asking the child if the system is working okay or briefly greeting the parent. If the birth parent speaks abusively to the child or you, state that the conversation is over now. And end it.

If the child is at least eleven or twelve and the calls have been constructive, you may consider allowing some private calls to see how they go.

When the Birth Parent Disagrees about Medical or Quasi-Medical Issues

With medical decisions, the stakes can be even higher. Imagine that you've taken your energetic, irritable grandson Charlie to several sessions with a pediatrician, who has made a diagnosis of attention-deficit/hyperactivity disorder (ADHD). The doctor prescribes an ADHD medication to help stabilize Charlie's energy levels and improve his focus. Even though these meds often have calming effects, they are technically stimulants. They're controlled substances, available only by prescription. The pediatrician discusses them with you, explaining the benefits and assuring you that research shows that for children with ADHD, these meds don't raise the risk of later developing a substance use disorder.[3]

You agree and go home with the prescription. But when you inform your son Tom, Charlie's dad, about the diagnosis and prescription, he balks. He's a drug user himself, and he's reluctant to see Charlie treated with a controlled substance. You explain the doctor's reasoning and show him the research studies. But what if Tom still disagrees? In such a case, it's important to do what's right for the child: follow the doctor's advice. Your son's objection to a legitimately prescribed drug may strike you as ironic, especially if you've had to confront and overcome your own biases about mental health and medication. But whatever the ironies, place your grandson's medical well-being first.

Or, in a lower-stakes example, maybe your daughter Trish thinks that four-year-old Alisha is ready to get her ears pierced, and you think she's too young. When you are the custodial grandparent, it's your call. Let Trish know: no pierced ears for Alisha. Then stay on alert. You might not want to let Trish take Alisha to the mall with the piercing studio, as she might decide to "surprise" you.

When the Birth Parent Misleads Others about Who Has Custody of the Children

Some grandparents get very annoyed when the child's birth parent posts pictures of the child on social media, sometimes pictures the grandparents have posted on their own site. Here's one solution: If this happens to you on social media and you don't like it, then "unfriend" or "unfollow" the birth parent and post all your pictures privately on a closed site for grandfamilies.

Possible Problems during Visits

When the visits with the child are held in your home, you may experience some clashes with the birth parents. Remember, although they're adults (by age, if not by behavior!), it's your house, so your rules apply. If you don't allow smoking, swearing, or littering, don't relax your rules. Here are some parental behaviors that upset grandparents and grandchildren:

The Birth Parent Breaks Promises

What happens when, for example, the birth parent offers the child a future gift and then fails to deliver? For example, a birth father might say he'll pass along an old PlayStation gaming system or electronic device that's being replaced. The child does not forget this promise, but sometimes the birth parent does and the grandparents must explain it. Rather than vilifying the birth parent, which will cause the child more distress, simply say that some people make promises and don't always keep them. This is still upsetting, but at least the child won't be waiting (sometimes years!) for a forgotten promise to be fulfilled.

The Birth Parent Shows Up Intoxicated or High

If parents are on drugs or drunk during the visit, then it's usually best to end the visit. If they insist they are not on any drugs, you may wish to insist that they provide a urine sample for home testing (a test kit found at many pharmacies), which they will likely refuse. People are not on their best behavior when under the influence of drugs or alcohol, and your grandchild should not have to witness such conduct. If the parent becomes abusive, threaten to call the police. And follow through, if necessary. Keep in mind that people who are high may also have drugs in their possession, and you do not want illegal substances in your home.

When a Child Takes a Stand

Children sometimes handle difficult issues in their own way. Grandparents don't always have to fix everything.

George had no relationship with his birth mother, Carly, who lived in another state. He had no memory of Carly from his babyhood; the only home he knew was his grandparents'. His grandma Lucy showed George pictures of Carly, but she never called or wrote. A few times Carly promised to visit for the holidays, but she always canceled at the last minute.

George was eleven when Carly finally came to visit for a weekend. A few hours into the visit, George suddenly announced, "Mama, you owe me for eleven years of birthday and Christmas presents!" Carly, clearly stunned, didn't say anything, and George walked away satisfied. He'd made his point. Lucy decided to *not* intervene because, what the heck, George was right. Carly had never bought him any gifts or gone to any of his birthday parties—so Lucy let the comment stand and didn't embellish it. Of course, if George had been mean or disrespectful, Lucy would have corrected him. But what he had said—it felt right.

The Birth Parent Ignores the Child

Some birth parents see visits in your home as a chance to eat well, watch TV, play video games, text constantly with their friends, and do everything except pay attention to their children. In fact, they may feel awkward around their children. If you sense this, you could suggest they interact with their child by

---

A Birth Mother Ignores Her Children during Visits

Even when they do show up, some birth parents aren't really consciously present. "My daughter Sherry drives me crazy!" said Ellen. "She comes to my home to visit her beautiful children, but then she ignores them!" Ellen recently took over parenting Sherry's toddler and infant, and the court has ordered visits at least twice a week for at least two hours each time. "She walks in the door, and before she even sits down, Sherry is checking her phone for any new text messages. Meanwhile, the older child is literally begging for attention. It hurts me to see this!"

Ellen says her daughter is lucky she can see the children at all, after she was arrested and incarcerated for possession of hydrocodone (an opioid). Sherry will go to court soon for sentencing. (Yes, Ellen bailed Sherry out of jail, although now she regrets it.)

"What *is* it about this constant texting?" asked Ellen. "I don't get it. God forbid she should miss a text message from just about anyone." When Ellen asked her daughter to turn off the phone during visits, Sherry looked at her as if she'd lost her mind. "It's like shutting off the phone is unimaginable," said Ellen with a sigh. Before the visit starts, it's best to set ground rules, such as shutting off cells during visits with the child.

---

playing a game or other age-appropriate activity. Consider board games or puzzles, card games (Uno is a good simple one), or playing catch outside if the weather is nice.

The Birth Parent Brings a New Boyfriend or Girlfriend Along

Sometimes the birth mother wants to show off her child to a new boyfriend, and she brings the new man along with her to the visit. It's up to you whether to allow this. You might choose to allow it once, and then observe. Does the birth parent pay attention to the child and offer some quality interactions? Or does she pay more attention to the guy she brought along? Either way, if the new person is someone who feels threatening to you, set a boundary by telling the birth parent that future visits should be between her and the grandchild only.

The Birth Parent Makes Threats

Sometimes birth parents threaten the grandparents. They may even threaten to call child protective services and allege that the grandparents have been abusive to the child. And sometimes they *do* call. A CPS worker comes out, sees that all is well, and closes the case. The birth parents may also threaten to take the child away without your permission. In some cases, they may also threaten physical harm to you or your property.

When there is *any* concern that the child's birth parent could harm you or the child, call the police: especially when the birth parent is under the influence of alcohol or other drugs, is severely mentally ill, or is actively threatening you or the child, either with words or actions.

What if a birth parent is actively violent or threatening violence and is already inside your home? Psychiatrist Joel Young, coauthor of *When Your Adult Child Breaks Your Heart*, advises that you should not let the birth parent get between you and an exit door in case you need to leave in a hurry. (Make sure the child is safe too.)

Young has specific advice if birth parents are exhibiting paranoid delusions, believing that you or others are plotting against them:

- Avoid looking the person in the eyes, which is often seen as a direct threat.

- Try to stand next to the person rather than looking them in the face.

- Act as if you and the other person are united against the world, even if that contradicts how you really feel; use pronouns like "they" or "we" rather than "I" or "you"—they sound less confrontational to a person who is paranoid.[4]

The Birth Parents Place Their Own Priorities Ahead of the Child's Needs

Adult children may be used to asking for help in the form of money, a place to live, a car, and so forth. Yet parenting your grandchild takes a great deal of your time and money—even when you receive some financial support from the state or another source. In some cases, there will be a direct conflict between what the birth parent wants and what the grandchild needs. Emma handled the situation this way. She told her son Ian, "If you need something and little Ethan needs something else at the same time, and I have to choose, he will win. Every time."

Emma meant it, and she has followed through when conflicts have arisen. One afternoon Emma was on her way to Ethan's school to watch his performance in the second-grade play. Her cell phone rang, and it was Ian. His car had broken

down and he needed a ride. He said it was urgent because he had
to get home to pick up tickets to tonight's concert of his favorite band, and he'd been looking forward to it for a long time.

Ethan had been talking about this play for weeks and was
really excited this morning. Emma knew he would notice if she
didn't show up. So Emma told Ian she couldn't make it: she'd
made a promise to Ethan for this afternoon. Ian was angry and
tried to argue with her, but she said firmly, "I would come if
I could, but I cannot do it. I have to go now." And she hung
up and pulled into the school parking lot. Did Emma agonize
during the entire play that maybe she *should* have gone to help
Ian? No, Emma did not. Ian was an adult, age thirty, and not her
primary responsibility anymore. Instead, she concentrated on
Ethan. When the play was over and the little boy flung himself
into Emma's arms, she was a very proud grandparent.

The Birth Parent Objects When the Grandchild Calls You Mom or Dad

Some birth parents and some grandparents may be surprised
when their young grandchild (or even an older child) suddenly
starts using the names Mom or Dad rather than Grandma,
Grandpa, or any of the other names grandparents have pre-
selected for themselves. This situation is less likely if the birth
parents are regular visitors and active in the child's life. But for
many birth parents, it could feel like a shock.

The child may have lived with the grandparents since infancy and eventually realizes that most other children call the
people they live with Mom and Dad. In one case, a playmate
at daycare told a child, "Here's your mom!" when her grandmother walked in. The girl was initially startled, then beamed
and adopted the term herself. Because the birth parents hadn't
seen the child in years, this grandmother decided to allow this.

Others might make a different choice—there is no one right answer here.

How do you feel about the child calling you Mom or Dad? Is it okay with you? Maybe the birth parent is largely or completely absent from the child's life and it feels okay. But maybe it doesn't. In that case, gently ask the child to call you Nana

---

A Grandson Becomes a Son

From the age of one, Marc had lived with his grandparents, Sandy and Warren. When Marc was six, they officially adopted him: it was clear that their daughter Julie wouldn't be up to the parenting task. She'd been diagnosed with bipolar disorder and had asked her parents to care for Marc. It had taken some time to bring her symptoms under control with psychiatric medications. Because her mood swings were still unpredictable, Julie decided she still couldn't handle the stress of raising a child. She'd taken a job in another part of the state, and now she visited on holidays. Marc, now an adult, remembered that he had always known Sandy and Warren as Grandma and Grandpa, so when the adoption was official, they asked him if he wanted to change what he called them. He didn't, and they agreed.

But one Saturday afternoon soon after, Marc called to Warren from the kitchen table. "Grandpa, would you help me with my new plane? I want to spend some Grandpa-son time with you." Warren was startled for a second, but then he laughed and said, "Sure, son, I'll be right there." Marc knew where he stood with Warren and Sandy. They were his parents. And Julie knew it too. This grandfamily had become the new normal for everyone involved. Marc and Grandpa fondly remember their Grandpa-son times together.

---

or Grandpa or whatever name you've used for yourself. Some grandparents have the child call them Mom, Dad, or a variation of that, while the birth parents are Mommy and Daddy. Decide what works best for you and the child.

Drawing the Line: When Contact Is Too Difficult

What circumstances might prompt you to end the birth parents' contact with the child? What incidents should you report to child protective services—or to the police? Some situations seem clear; others are murkier.

In general, if the child's case is being monitored by a state or county agency, any highly distressing behavior on a birth parent's part should be reported to the agency monitoring the case. The agency may decide the child needs supervised visits (supervised by a caseworker) or may even end visits altogether. Do not report minor arguments or inconveniences, but do report abuse or other illegal activities. Find a state-by-state list of toll-free numbers to call or websites to access at this site: www.childhelp.org/wp-content/uploads/2014/07/CPS-Phone -Numbers.pdf.

If the case is *not* under the control of an agency and you are the custodial grandparent—one with legal permission to make decisions for the child—then you usually can decide yourself to end the child's contact with the birth parent. Let's look at some circumstances in which you might make such a choice.

The Birth Parent Is Violent or Emotionally Abusive

If you are at risk for imminent harm—or if the child is—contact the police and report the threat right away, and also call child protective services: see appendix 2 for a list of hotlines, state by state. If the child's case is supervised by state or county child social services, you should also report it to the child's caseworker immediately. If you are required to allow the birth parent to visit the child, insist that someone other than you supervise the visits; that way, the person supervising can witness the dysfunction firsthand. If the child is not under the control of state or county child welfare officials, then ask the police if you should call the CPS hotline or if an officer will call.

Some grandparents seek a restraining order in court against an abusive birth parent so they are not allowed to be in the same area as the grandparent. A restraining order means the birth parents cannot come to your home or even come near you out of the home. (You may be able to obtain a restraining order at no cost, although states and counties differ.) If birth parents violate the restraining order, then they are arrested. Restraining orders are granted by the court, and each jurisdiction varies with respect to the process by which they are obtained.

A Case of Sexual Abuse

Ever since her daughter Alicia became addicted to meth, Denise had been caring for her five-year-old granddaughter Carrie, with Alicia's approval. Alicia had recently split from Carrie's father, Tony, who asked to see Carrie once a week for an overnight stay at his apartment. He didn't seem impaired by drugs, so Denise agreed.

Then one week, Tony asked to keep Carrie for two days. When Denise picked Carrie up afterward, the girl was crying, and Tony was acting strange, shouting to Denise that Carrie was only crying because he'd made her brush her teeth. Denise could see it was something more than that: Carrie had never minded brushing her teeth before. Could it be a lack of sleep? Maybe two nights was too long a stay. But Denise also recalled Carrie's nightmares recently after another stay with her dad.

Denise gave Carrie a hug and put her in the car. On the way home, they stopped at the supermarket, and what happened next shocked Denise. Carrie stood up in the grocery cart, pulled her panties down, and screamed, "It hurts! It hurts!" Denise abandoned her cart and rushed Carrie to the restroom to check her. She found a little redness, but Denise thought Tony probably hadn't bathed Carrie or made sure she cleaned herself after toileting. An exhausted Carrie fell asleep on the car trip home.

When Carrie woke up from her nap, Denise bathed her, but the child kept saying, "Daddy put something on me," pointing to her vagina. Denise showed her some baby powder: Is that what Daddy put on you? No. Denise decided to call Alicia and describe the situation. "He must have touched her!" Alicia said on the phone. "Take her to the hospital now! I'll meet you there." At the emergency room, the doctor said to Carrie, "I hear you don't feel good." Carrie said, "My daddy pulled my pants down and then he pulled his pants down and he put his thorn in me!"

A police investigation ensued. When Denise called Tony on a tapped phone, he admitted the sexual abuse. Tony soon fled, but a warrant is still out for him. Denise doesn't know where Alicia is; her phone went dead and she can't find her. Denise concentrates on keeping Carrie safe: she has gained permanent guardianship from the court. Carrie is in play therapy, and her recurrent nightmares have subsided. Tragically, Carrie had to learn, at a very young age, about good touch and bad touch.

The Birth Parent Steals from the Grandparent or the Child

Sometimes grandparents don't want birth parents in their home because they steal things from them: money, jewelry, cell phones, or other valuable items. It's unreasonable for you to continue to allow a thief in your home, even when that thief is your own adult child. Report thefts to the police department, and if birth parent visits with the child are required by the court, insist on supervised visits somewhere outside your home.

The Birth Parent's Visits Distress the Child

If a child is upset by a birth parent's visit, the reasons may be simple or complex. Sometimes a visit prompts the feeling of wanting to return home with the parent—because children usually love their parents, even if they've been abusive or neglectful. It may sound crazy, but it's true. If a child is upset after a visit, it doesn't necessarily mean the birth parent did something wrong. The mere presence of the birth parent can be upsetting, as it prompts mixed feelings for the child.

But sometimes the child clearly does *not* wish to return to the birth parent's home because of worry about being abused again. The child may beg you to end the visits. Who decides whether the visits will continue? It may be your choice, but often it is not. For example, if the child is in foster care and was placed with you, the caseworkers (and maybe the judge) will decide, and they may insist that visits continue. This doesn't mean you ignore the child's distress. You can report the child's concerns and behavior to the caseworkers. Also, if you don't want to view your grandchild's distress and if you want case-workers to see that it is real, you can request supervised visits that don't involve you from now on. If there is no social services involvement while you are raising your grandchild, you could ask the parents to stop visiting, but they are likely to argue with you. If you suspect abuse or neglect during the visits, you can report your concerns to child protective services anonymously—however, your adult child may suspect that you are the person who made the report. When in doubt, consider what is best for your grandchild, rather than what is best for you or your adult child; it is nearly always best to report suspected abuse or neglect.

If the child becomes very upset after a visit, try to find out why by asking questions calmly. Don't assume the birth parent hurt the child, maybe while you were briefly absent. Here are some sample questions you could ask:

- Did someone say something that hurt your feelings or made you sad?
- Are you sad because Mommy/Daddy had to leave?
- Was there a smell or touch or something else that upset you? (A preschooler may resist affectionate gestures, and sensory-sensitive children may dislike the smell of someone with poor hygiene or dirty clothes.)
- Are you hurt anywhere on your body? (If so, ask the child to show you where.)

Asking such questions may provide the information you need. Remember, this is not *Law and Order,* and you are not a police detective investigating a murder. So don't push too hard. You can always revisit the issue later when the situation is calmer.

The Birth Parent Makes Hurtful Statements

Sometimes birth parents make nasty statements while impaired by drugs, alcohol, mental illness, or some other problem. Here are some examples:

"YOU STOLE MY CHILD."

Many custodial grandparents hear that claim at least once: "You stole my child" or "You kidnapped the baby." You need not take this claim seriously, even if the birth parent seems convinced of it. Tell the birth parent that if you had kidnapped the child, you'd be in trouble with the law—so the claim is not valid. Still, it's a common protest, often prompting upset and worry. But remember: you can't control other people's behavior—only your own response to it.

"I HATE YOU BECAUSE YOU STOLE MY CHILD."

Closely related to "You stole my child" is "I hate you because you stole my child." Birth parents may be projecting their own personal failures on you—pinning guilt on you (instead of themselves). Nobody likes to admit that failure as a parent, whether because of drugs, mental illness, criminal behavior, immaturity, or some other problem. It's always easier to blame someone else, and you're a handy target. Unfortunately, it may be true that the birth parent really does hate you now, at this moment. But keep in mind that your focus needs to be on your grandchild. And remember, it's hard to change the mind or the emotions of another person, even when that person is your own child. Yes, you may vividly remember the wonderful day this person was born, but today your adult child may be extremely angry and have a distorted view of life.

"SOMEDAY I'LL GET MY CHILD BACK AND YOU'LL NEVER SEE HER AGAIN."

Some birth parents threaten that they'll regain custody and then withhold the child from you. Unfortunately, this sometimes does happen, and spiteful parents who have regained custody decide to take their revenge. And you may or may not have any legal standing: grandparent visitation rights vary dramatically from state to state when children are living with their parents. If your state allows for grandparent rights, you may be able to pursue visitation. In other cases, the children are sent home with the birth parents, a problem occurs or recurs, and they are sent back to you again. There can be several cycles of this back-and-forth.

"MY PROBLEMS ARE ALL YOUR FAULT."

People who are unable or unwilling to parent their own children often don't like themselves much. And when people are unhappy with their own actions and behaviors, they often lash out at others. Who better to lash out at than their mother and father? Especially when the birth parent suspects that Mom and Dad are fearful that there's some truth in the accusation—that somehow, it really *is* their fault that Cathy is now addicted to heroin or that Casey is in jail for stealing cars. If you hear this blaming statement, and you may hear it more than once, let it roll off your back. It is *not* your fault.

"YOU'RE GOING TO RUIN MY CHILD, JUST LIKE YOU RUINED ME."

Playing the blame game, some birth parents claim that the caretaking grandparent will destroy the grandchild's life too. This is nonsense. And just remind yourself who's spewing the nonsense: a person whose own life is out of control and who cannot handle parenting duties. You did your best in raising this child, and later you stepped up to raising your grandchild out of love and caring. So pat yourself on the back for doing that!

If and When the Birth Parent's Situation Changes

If the situation changes, take time to reevaluate. Circumstances could improve or worsen as new factors come into play. Or the situation may become ambiguous, with many uncertainties. Often you may be unsure of what is going to happen next. For example, the birth parent may recently have been released from jail or prison, and she may assume that the child should immediately be given back to her. Or the birth parent may have completed a drug rehabilitation program and believe that he is ready to be a parent again right away.

One general rule applies in most situations: if the birth parent will be granted legal custody of the child, who will be leaving your home, it is best to slowly transition the child to the birth parent's care, whenever possible. For example, share a meal at your own home with the child and the birth parent; then have a few meals at the birth parent's home with you present. Next, allow the child to have meals and visits with the birth parent *without* you for a while; then have the child stay at the birth parent's home for longer periods and without your presence. Make sure the child is allowed to bring along any important objects, like a favorite blanket or teddy bear. A treasured item can help ease the transition. Also, ask to visit your grandchild at least weekly after the transition is complete.

The Birth Parent Is Incarcerated

If a birth parent enters jail or prison, the family dynamics shift dramatically. It's jarring for everyone. If it happened before you stepped into your new parenting role, you may be trying to figure out how your grandchild is perceiving the situation. Some birth parents haven't told their child they're in prison because they believe the truth is too painful for the child. Instead, the parent might tell the child by phone that they're "away" or on a long trip or offer other vague explanations. And that might continue for months or years. The problem is, eventually children will come up with their own ideas about what's really going on, which may be worse than the reality: they may think the parent is dead or was kidnapped or some other scenario. (Read more on talking to your grandchildren about birth parents' situation in chapter 4.)

Many stressors can make children likely to "act out," and a parent's incarceration is certainly one of them. But one research study suggested that two factors can be a big help for these children: (1) feeling supported by a caregiver—that's you!—and (2) having fewer *other* life stressors at the time of the parent's incarceration, stressors such as a new baby entering the family, moving, changing schools, the hospitalization or death of a family member, or seeing someone beaten or shot.[5] Of course, some of these stressors may be out of your control. And when it comes to decisions such as moving, you might choose to trade a short-term stress for a longer-term benefit for your grandfamily. That is part of your new parenting job, and it takes lots of judgment calls. Another study focused on caregiving grandmothers whose adult daughters were incarcerated and whose crimes were related to substance use. On top of their other stressors, the caregivers often worried that the birth mother would return to alcohol or other drug use after release. Meanwhile, the birth mothers often felt torn: both grateful for and jealous of their own mothers' new role with their children.[6]

The Birth Parent Is Released from Jail or Prison

When the incarcerated birth parent is released, many questions arise: Will the parent want immediate custody of the child upon being released? Will the parent be able to handle what it takes to parent again? Is substance use or addiction likely to be an ongoing issue? Keep in mind that when people are released from prison, they often are on parole and expected to comply with basic requirements such as getting a job, passing drug screenings, and reporting to parole officers. If they fail to meet these obligations, they may be sent back to prison. There's a lot of joy with being released from prison, but there's considerable stress as well.

Some experts say children go through several stages of adaptation when a parent is released from prison. Counseling may help with all these stages. First, there is the honeymoon period, when children may be on their best behavior in front of the birth parent, yet they feel anxious under the surface. Next may come a period of suspicion, when some of the children's concerns and worries begin to emerge. A period of resistance may occur when children act out on purpose in front of the parent, to see if this will drive the parent away. Next, children may begin to express their feelings about the relationship—or may continue to withhold their emotions or try to push them down.[7]

Within the family, there may be vastly different expectations about what life will be like with the birth parent newly out of prison. The birth parent may unrealistically hope to take over parenting five minutes after being released. You may be torn between hoping the birth parent will have a normal life from now on and fearing that this won't happen—that the children will still need you. The children may perceive the birth parent as a sort of an older sibling, an ideal figure, or have some other unrealistic ideas.

In a best-case scenario, everyone should take it slow. It will take time for the birth parent to establish a new life by finding a job and a place to live, perhaps getting a car, and (you can hope) finding new friends to help support a productive lifestyle.

A Clash Leads to New Understandings

Sometimes the differences in expectations can show up in a dramatic clash. When thirty-year-old Nina was released from prison after serving three years for drug dealing, the paternal grandparents said she could live with them for up to six months so she'd have time to organize her life. They'd been caring for Nina's kids during her sentence: Tory, age seven, and Sammy, age four. After Nina moved in, the children couldn't get enough of her. In fact, Jerri, the paternal grandmother, said she felt a little resentful, like Nina was the bright, shiny new object who got all the attention.

But one evening, the tables suddenly turned. The family was gathered in the living room when Jerri told Tory to pick up her toys from the floor. Tory said, "Yeah, old woman, I'll do it later!" Nina rushed over and slapped Tory on the butt, shocking everyone. "Whoa! Stop right there!" said Jerri to Nina. "What?" asked Nina, baffled. She felt like Tory had been sassing Jerri and needed punishing. "In this home, we don't hit," said Jerri. At this, Tory began crying as if she were mortally wounded and she screamed that Nina was a child abuser and should go back to prison. And Sammy ran to his room, crying, apparently afraid he'd get hit next.

The clash was painful, but what can everyone in this family learn from it? Nina needs to learn she overreacted, and she will likely learn this lesson fast. When things calm down, Jerri needs to talk to Nina about what types of discipline she has used successfully, such as time-outs or withholding of privileges. On her part, Tory needs to learn to speak respectfully to her grandmother. And Sammy needs quick reassurance that he's safe. Jerri also needs to realize that Nina was, in her misguided way, trying to defend Jerri.

The Birth Parent Claims to Be Clean and Sober

Maybe the birth parent truly is in recovery from drugs or alcohol. We certainly hope so! But you must do due diligence, because people who use substances often lie and misrepresent themselves. For the short term, some grandparents insist on witnessing a negative drug test before letting the adult child visit the grandchild. Such test kits can be purchased at local pharmacies. Nearly all employers now require a clean drug test before they hire workers at any level—so why should you demand any less?

For the long term, remember that relapse is common. If the birth parent has been clean and sober for a few weeks or months, don't assume that the person has "recovered." In fact, recovery is a lifelong process, requiring daily vigilance and healthy habits. If a slip happens and the person uses again, notice what happens: Does the slide continue into frequent or constant use? Or does the birth parent treat the slip as a wake-up call and then get serious about recovery efforts again? That person's long-term health may hinge on the response to that slip. Of course, you may not be in a position to know. But don't let wishful thinking tempt you into "believing" a person is truly in recovery. Look for actions and evidence in the person's life.

The Birth Parent Becomes a Parent to Other Children

Here's a common scenario: while one or more children are being raised by the grandparents, their biological mother gets pregnant again. Sometimes the newborn baby will be immediately removed from the birth mother, particularly if there are strong indications that she is using substances or that the baby would be harmed or neglected.

But if the birth mother is in the process of recovery from her previous issues, such as alcohol or drug addiciton or criminal behavior, she may be given a chance to raise the newborn child. That's a tough call, though, and if the child is in the foster care system, it is not your call to make, although you should certainly offer your opinion to the caseworker.

There may also be problems during family visits with the older children. Sometimes birth mothers insensitively lavish affection on the new baby in front of their older children, ignoring the older children—who are justifiably upset. Grandparents worry about those hurt feelings. Will the older children wonder why the parent "kept" the younger child—and not them? The reality is that such hurt feelings are common among children who don't live with the birth mother. Understanding such feelings can be very helpful.

In some cases, the birth parent clearly favors one child over another. "She ignores my wonderful grandson and lavishes all her attention on her daughter who lives with her," said a grandmother. You can't change how another person feels, but you can ask the birth parent to come alone to visits with the grandchildren you are caring for. Or you can offer to watch the other grandchild in another room while the birth parent pays attention to the older children. The grandparent can also counsel the birth mother to be more sensitive to this issue. In addition, you can take pains to make the ignored children feel special without slighting the sibling who may be the parent's favorite. For example, point out to the older children that they have a later bedtime (if they do). Other "older sibling" privileges can be conferred on them, ostensibly based on age but really just to help make the slighted children feel more special.

The Birth Parent Enters a Serious Romantic Relationship
If a new relationship develops for either of the birth parents, it may take up much of their time, and they may wish to bring the person to visits with the child. The grandparents, in contrast, may think that the birth parents should devote all their visiting time to the child and leave the new friend at home. The question is, will the birth parents refuse to visit without the new significant other? If so, you'll need to decide if you will allow the other person to visit the child. Your job is to do what is in the best interests of the child, not comply with whatever makes your adult child or the other birth parent happy. If the new love seems problematic to you, then insist that person be left at home. But be reasonable. Ask yourself sincerely if your objections to this new person are valid.

Keep in mind that in raising your grandchild, you have three jobs: to keep the child safe, healthy, and happy. "Safe" trumps healthy and "safe and healthy" both trump "happy." If the birth parent's new love does meet the child in your custody, it is best to supervise the birth parent, the new partner, and the child yourself, or ask social services to supervise them. The new person may be kind and loving, or indifferent, or worse: keep an open mind, but exercise due diligence.

Favorable and Concerning Signs
The problems that caused your adult child to lose custody of the children often are not resolved. Remember that recovering from alcoholism or drug addiction is a lifelong process. That's why many people say they're an alcoholic or addict "in recovery"—not "recovered." Recovery from heroin addiction is very difficult, but it is possible with ongoing vigilance. Overcoming addiction to alcohol or drugs such as meth or cocaine is also challenging,

Recovering or Backsliding? Some Signs to Watch For

Birth Parent's Main Issue	Favorable Signs	Causes for Concern
Opioid or other drug addiction that led to child abuse or neglect	• Multiple negative drug tests • Successfully completing a rehab program • Regular attendance at Narcotics Anonymous or other Twelve Step group • Holding a job for at least a month • Healthier appearance than in the recent past • Use of addiction treatment medications such as naltrexone (Vivitrol) or buprenorphine (Subutex)	• Positive drug screens • Combativeness • Homelessness • Continuing to associate with friends, relatives, or others who abuse alcohol or other drugs • Inability to hold a job • Driving a vehicle under the influence of drugs
Alcohol use or addiction that led to child abuse or neglect	• Abstaining from alcohol • Regular attendance at Alcoholics Anonymous meetings • Holding a regular job for at least a month • Recognizing and admitting that alcohol is a problem • Completing inpatient or outpatient treatment, if appropriate	• Continuing to drink to intoxication • Driving a vehicle under the influence of alcohol • Homelessness • Continuing to associate with friends, relatives, or others who abuse alcohol or other drugs • Denying any problem with alcohol use (despite what others think) • Having no coping skills to deal with stress other than alcohol use

continued

Birth Parent's Main Issue	Favorable Signs	Causes for Concern
Anger problem leading to child abuse or neglect	• Attendance at anger management classes • Attendance at therapy sessions • No angry outbursts • Use of healthy stress-release outlets (exercise, for example) • Holding a job for at least a month • Undergoing treatment for substance use disorder, if appropriate for anger management	• Refusal to take anger management classes • Belief that there is nothing wrong with behavior • No focus: not in school or a training program nor holding a job
Incarceration for crimes committed, unable to care for child	• Completing jail or prison term • Holding a job for at least a month • Successfully completing probation or parole	• Joblessness • Violating terms of probation or parole • Continuing to associate with people involved in past crimes
Mental health disorders, unable to care for child	• Seeing a psychiatrist • Taking psychiatric medication as prescribed • Not hallucinating or delusional • Seeing a therapist, if recommended	• Refusal to admit any mental health problem— now or ever • Refusal to take psychiatric medications • Belief that most people are evil or plotting to cause person harm • Severe mania or suicidal depression

yet it can be done. Mental health disorders can be treated; anger issues can be improved with new skills and habits. Incarcerated parents can rebuild their lives after release. All of these outcomes are possible, but it's wise to be wary. Keep an eye out for signs of progress in your adult child—but also for signs of slipping. See the chart "Recovering or Backsliding?" for an overview of these signs, both favorable and unfavorable. Read on for some general advice.

CONSIDER ACTIONS RATHER THAN WORDS

Instead of relying on what birth parents say, look for active signs of improvement or deterioration, and look at actions. For example, if the birth father says he is ready to be a good parent again, does he have a place for the child to live? Does he have a job that enables him to support the child? Does he now avoid his former drug-using or alcoholic friends, who might tempt him back into using drugs again? Or, if the birth mother is mentally ill, is she now taking her medication consistently and seeing her psychiatrist or therapist on a regular basis?

RECOVERY FROM SUBSTANCE USE DISORDERS

True recovery from addiction—also called a substance use disorder—is a lifetime commitment. Treatment may be the first step on that path, although many people find recovery without a rehab program. Ongoing abstinence is key, but active recovery means more than that. It means adopting healthy routines and social circles. It means identifying one's own "relapse triggers"— the risk factors for reverting to substance use—and having a plan to avoid them and to address relapse if it does occur. It means having a support system such as a Twelve Step program or other mutual support group. And it means recognizing personal problems and starting to resolve them.[8]

How do you know if a person is actively recovering from drug or alcohol addiction? As the saying goes, recovery is an inside job—it's not just behavior change; it's a new attitude. And you may not be in close enough touch to see evidence of a new attitude—or lack of it. Still, a person in active recovery is likely to show signs of better health, both physical and emotional. Of course, one good sign is to repeatedly test negative for drug use in urine screens (blood and hair can also be tested)—although one "clean" test is insufficient for planning a child's return to the parent. It's also encouraging to see healthy daily habits and a new, healthy circle of friends.

Another good sign is consistent activity in Twelve Step groups. In addition to Alcoholics Anonymous and Narcotics Anonymous, there's Crystal Meth Anonymous, Dual Recovery Anonymous (for people with co-occurring substance use and mental health disorders), and others. These groups don't take attendance and you can't verify a person's attendance, but if group members speak authentically about their own experiences in these meetings, that's favorable. Remember, though, that attendees don't reveal details about other attendees; confidentiality is a hallmark of these groups.

RECOVERY FROM A MENTAL HEALTH DISORDER

Mental problems can affect parenting skills to various degrees, ranging from the clouded judgment of a person with major depression, to the intermittent impulsivity of a person with bipolar disorder, to the possible delusions of someone with schizophrenia. In extreme cases, birth parents might lose custody of their children because their dangerous psychotic behavior causes them to be unfit parents. This situation may change after loss of custody; for example, the birth parent may start taking antipsychotic medication, and the symptoms may abate.

In fact, many serious mental health disorders can be improved with prescribed psychiatric medications. If a mentally unstable birth parent is now taking medications as prescribed, that person is likely to be much more grounded in the real world and more competent as a parent. Conversely, if the birth parent stops taking the medication, the problematic symptoms likely will return, and it will be difficult for the person to think logically and care for a child. Unfortunately, people sometimes *do* stop taking their psychiatric medications, for many reasons, including to avoid side effects such as weight gain, lowered mood, and impaired creativity.

In addition, other mental illnesses may be so debilitating that they make it extremely difficult or impossible for the person to be a good parent. For example, severe agoraphobia may prevent a mother from ever leaving her home, or mysophobia (fear of germs) could preclude her from changing diapers. The distractions of severe obsessive-compulsive disorder could also affect a parent's ability to set priorities and follow through with them. Treatment can improve all of these conditions.

If the birth parent starts to consistently put the child's interests first, this is a sign of a true turnaround. Before she was diagnosed with bipolar disorder, Beth didn't see her own impulsive behavior as a problem. She knew she was moody—she'd have long low periods, often followed by days of high energy when she'd feel inspired, creative, up for any adventure. At those times, whatever it was or whatever the consequences, she'd pack up her young daughter Kaylee and just do it.

After some dangerous scrapes and job losses, Beth finally sought help and started taking mood-stabilizing medications. Now, whatever choice she has to make, she first considers the possible effects on Kaylee, age six. For example, an overnight trip during the week would cause Kaylee to miss school, so Beth limits those trips to weekends. Staying up all night will cause Kaylee to be overtired the next day, so Beth makes sure that Kaylee goes to bed at a reasonable hour. By her actions, Beth has shown that she considers possible effects on Kaylee before she acts. This is one indicator of a good parent.

RECOVERY FROM CRIMINAL BEHAVIOR

Often crimes are linked to substance use or mental health disorders. If birth parents who have criminal records sincerely acknowledge their past mistakes and are pursuing treatment for any problems with alcoholism, drug addiction, or a mental illness, then they may be able to parent their child again at some future point. Past crimes may have been committed while the birth parent was under the influence of alcohol or other drugs or to obtain money to pay for those substances. Those who are in recovery, we trust, should have addressed their substance use problems and ceased their criminal behavior.

Whether or not substance use or mental health problems were involved in the birth parent losing custody, positive signs to look for include a healthy circle of friends, job stability, and good management of both time and money.

■

Every grandfamily has a different set of circumstances. And often they're shifting conditions, making it even harder to predict what situations you may face. But the examples we've discussed offer up several important lessons: use common sense whenever possible. Pick your battles with the birth parents—don't argue over trivial points. And always consider what's the right and best decision for the grandchild. If you keep these points in mind, you will usually make wise choices.

>>

PART 2

ADJUSTING TO
THE NEW NORMAL

After you start raising your grandkids, you are truly no longer just Grandma and Grandpa. The spoiling stops, because the children aren't going home at the end of the day—they are home.

—*A grandmother, reflecting on her grandfamily*

CHAPTER 4

"Why Aren't My Birth Parents Raising Me?"

Two weeks after their granddaughter Dana was born, Sam and Brenda brought her to live with them, at their daughter Kate's request. Kate had stayed off drugs during most of her pregnancy but started using again after Dana's birth. Sam and Brenda weren't shocked—they'd suspected they might be raising this child, given Kate's history of drug use. They were now a grandfamily, and they officially adopted Dana when she was two, with Kate's permission. (The father was unknown.) Kate visited the family sporadically, and Dana called Brenda "Mommy" and Sam "Daddy."

That same year, Kate moved across the country with her boyfriend. After a four-year absence—with very little phone contact with Dana—Kate came back for a visit. Now six, Dana called Kate "Miss Kate," the same way she'd referred to her teachers in day care. Kate didn't like it much, but she accepted this designation. Sam and Brenda were wary but hopeful that Kate might be pulling herself together. She seemed fine for a few days, but then her behavior became nervous and erratic, and she left earlier than planned. After Kate's departure, little Dana had many questions for her grandparents. Why did she leave so early? When was she coming back again? But mainly, if Miss Kate was her first mommy, why didn't Dana live with her all the time, like the other kids in her kindergarten class? Usually a cheerful child, Dana was irritable, and she demanded answers. Sam and Brenda provided age-appropriate information, such as that Kate couldn't be a parent because she had some serious problems with drugs.

After this visit, Kate did not return for six more years and called only occasionally. When she did visit again, she received some hostility from the now-adolescent Dana, nearly thirteen, who didn't try to hide her animosity. No longer calling her "Miss Kate," Dana called her "birth parent" to her face and sometimes "the egg donor" behind her back. Although Sam and Brenda understood that some anger is healthy in such a situation, they discouraged the name-calling, as it served no real purpose. Instead, they offered a listening ear to Dana and encouraged her to tell them about what she was feeling.

• • •

Explaining why your grandchildren's birth parents aren't raising them can be challenging. Many grandparents say they don't understand it themselves. How could their son have chosen drugs over his children? Or why did their daughter decide to stay with her abusive boyfriend rather than regain custody of her child? These choices make no sense. Yet grandparents need to develop a narrative for the benefit of the children they are raising. This chapter offers advice on how to do that—how to explain to your grandchildren their life situation in ways that make sense at their level of understanding. We'll also cover common situations that you may encounter, such as needing to explain major substance use or addiction, mental health disorders, and other problems that led you to parent your grandchild.

Back to our story: Why did Kate's behavior change during her first visit? Sam and Brenda were unsure. Maybe she was using drugs again. Or maybe the visit brought up feelings of sadness and guilt about the choices she had made. Sometimes we never know or understand why people act as they do, including our own children. But the initial visit prompted questions in Dana's mind, primarily: Why wasn't she living with Kate? This question and others came up again, along with a lot of negative feelings, when Kate visited her parents and twelve-year-old Dana. Brenda and Sam explained how their grandfamily came to be, and more explanations will be required to help adolescent Dana come to terms with her heritage.

Explaining to a Child's Level of Understanding

The explanation to questions such as "What happened to my first mom and dad? Why am I living with you instead?" needs to be tailored to the child's level of understanding, which differs dramatically depending on whether the child is four years old, ten, or an adolescent. It also needs to be tailored to the particular child's maturity level. Very simple and upbeat explanations are often sufficient for a young child, but the true picture needs further layering and sophistication as the child grows older and has more questions.

At every level of understanding, however, it's important to say that it wasn't the child's fault in any way that the birth parents aren't raising the child. Even young children may wonder if they cried too much or did something else wrong. Maybe you can't imagine how children possibly could blame themselves when they are completely blameless. Yet children seek explanations for their life situations, and if none are forthcoming, they may come to the wrong conclusions, including self-blame. This is human nature. After all, it is very unlikely that parents are to blame for their adult child's poor choices. Yet many parents agonize, especially at first, over how they might have caused their adult child to become addicted to drugs or to commit crimes. Children are even less able to dissociate themselves from the cause of a problem. Children are also more self-centered than adults. Thus, they reason that they must have done something wrong to be rejected by their parents.

Preschool Children, Ages Four to Five

To very young children, we might say that they grew in their birth mother's "tummy" but then moved in with their grandparents, who were so happy to have a wonderful little child to live with them. The birth parents brought them into the world, but then something happened so that the grandparents needed to take charge of the children. Preschoolers cannot understand concepts like substance use, addiction, mental health problems, incarceration, death, abandonment, or adult immaturity. They can, however, understand that some people can't do a job very well. Their birth parents couldn't do a good job as parents, so the grandparents, who were very experienced at raising children, became the preschoolers' caregivers. Many children can also understand that it wasn't their fault that their parents couldn't raise them, nor was it their grandparents' fault. But be sure to tell them this.

What if a birth parent has died? Very young children can't understand the idea of death. They may ask the same questions over and over, such as "When is Daddy coming to see me?" Try to be patient with these questions. You may be digging deep yourself at this challenging time in your life, especially if the deceased birth parent was your adult child. (You'll find more on talking about death later in this chapter.)

Don't ignore the questions, and also try to avoid feeling annoyed or harassed. Instead, say something like, "Remember when I said Daddy had a bad accident and did not get better? It's sad, but Daddy died, which means we won't see him anymore." (Or you could say "He went to heaven" if the concept of "heaven" is okay with you.)

Children, Ages Six through Twelve

School-age children likely know where babies come from, so you might substitute "womb" or "uterus" for the "tummy" where the child grew inside. These children may also learn in school that illegal drugs are harmful, causing sickness or addiction, and they may even sign pledges to never take drugs. They may also learn about mental illness in school. You can explain that some parents need to take a special kind of medicine to think clearly, use their skills, and be good parents. But if they don't take the medicine, they can't be good parents. (Often people who are mentally ill refuse to take their medication because of the side effects, such as tiredness, mood problems, or weight gain. Cost can also be a factor.) This may prompt the question, "Why didn't my dad take the medicine?" You could say that you are not sure, that the birth parent didn't think it was really necessary, or provide another explanation. Many children will then ask, "Why didn't you make my mom take the medicine? You are still her parent." Here you might respond that adults decide whether to take their medicine, and parents can't make grown-up children take medicine, even if they wish they could.

How much to share with the child about the birth parent's mental health disorder is up to you. Important note: Children who are told their birth parents have a mental illness may worry that they will develop the illness too. You can tell them that the illness is very rare, and they are unlikely to develop it.

If the birth parent has died, school-age children can understand the finality of that fact but may worry that they somehow caused or contributed to their parent's death. They may also worry about dying in their sleep or from a minor illness like a cold. Assure them that they are healthy children (if they are);

that they can expect a long, long life; and that death won't come for a long time. And remind them that they were in no way at fault for the death of their parent.

Teens, Ages Thirteen through Eighteen

Teenagers may see themselves as very mature people indeed, but surging hormones and major body changes can make it difficult to think clearly sometimes. Teenagers can also be very critical and judgmental toward both their birth parents and grandparents. For example, they may ask if their birth mother was a drug user, why didn't she go to rehab and get herself straight? Or why didn't the grandparents force her into treatment? If the birth father was in trouble with the law for multiple crimes, why didn't he stop getting into trouble and pull his act together? Also, why didn't the grandparents make the birth father act like a responsible adult? Grandparents need to explain that adults make their own choices and, unfortunately, sometimes they make choices that are not conducive to parenting children. And parents cannot force their adult children to make good choices.

If the state or county child services agency was involved in the children's removal from the birth parents' custody, the grandparents may wish to tell teenagers that they were removed from the home because of abuse or neglect. Often the abuse or neglect was directly linked to the abuse of alcohol or addictive drugs.

If the birth parent has died, death may have occurred as a result of addiction or an accident related to substance abuse—or it could have happened as a result of natural causes. You can share what you know about the death with your teenage grandchildren, trying to be sensitive and not judgmental. For example, try to avoid making statements like, "If she had just given up drugs, she'd be alive today!" Adolescents may come to that conclusion on their own, and if they ask you if their parents would still be alive had they given up drugs, you could say that they probably would, and it's very sad.

Think Again: Avoid Unhelpful Explanations

As children grow up, you'll need to revisit the story of how your grandfamily came to be, helping them understand and accept it more thoroughly. As with many complex topics, such as talking to your children about sex, it's not a simple story that is told a few times and then, whew, the parents are relieved it is over. Instead, the story about why your grandchildren are living with you needs to be explained very simply when children are young, and then later it should be overlaid with more details. Let's look at some of the common mistakes grandparents make when explaining how the grandfamily came to be.

Think Again . . . If You're Avoiding Explanations Unless the Children Ask for Them

Let's not assume that if children don't ask questions about their family situation, it means they don't *have* any questions, ever. Some children might have trouble formulating a question. Others may be afraid to ask because they fear upsetting their grandparents. (They may be trying to protect *your* feelings!) So it's wise to open up the subject once in a while: "Sweetie, we've talked about how you came to live here with us when you were younger. Do you ever wonder more about what happened? Do you have any questions?" You've given the child an opening to ask about it, now or in the future. When children don't have answers to their questions, including the unasked ones, they make up their own answers to fill in the gaps. And their imagined answers may be more disturbing than what really happened.

Think Again . . . If You're Sugarcoating the Story

Many grandparents want to sugarcoat or altogether avoid the adversity that is almost invariably connected with children being raised by their grandparents rather than their birth parents. Yet it's important to keep in mind the way children think when these stories are told. For example, some grandparents may tell children that their birth parents asked the grandparents to raise the children. That might be true, but it's not enough. *Why* did the birth parents ask the grandparents? Even if children don't ask that question, they are certainly thinking it. And if it's not addressed, children may think that it was somehow their own fault. They may believe that in some way they just weren't good enough—and that's the last thing you want them to think. You need to gently explain the birth parents' problems at a level the children can understand.

Think Again . . . before Saying the Children Are
with the Grandparents Because the Birth Parents
Really Loved the Children

If we simply tell Alex that his birth mother loved him so much that she gave him to his grandparents to raise, that's also avoiding the issue. Alex may then wonder if the grandparent might place him with someone else—*because we love each other too, right?*—equating love with loss. Maybe the birth parent did love Alex, but that's not the main reason he's living with you now. Instead, for some reason, the birth parent could not handle the job of parenting Alex, and that's what you need to explain, in simple terms.

Think Again . . . Before Saying the Birth Parents Were "Bad"

The birth parents of your grandchildren may have emotionally harmed you deeply by their behaviors, whatever the reasons they couldn't or didn't choose to raise their children. One of these birth parents was your own adult child, and it often hurts—a lot—that you can't be a "regular" grandparent. Nevertheless, don't paint the birth parents as bad people. If the birth parents had problems that prevented them from parenting their children, it was their *behavior* that was problematic, such as abusing substances or committing crimes. This is what you need to stress.

Here's why: Your grandchildren know they were born to their birth parents. And if their birth parents are frequently depicted as "bad guys," then does that mean the grandchildren are bad too? Avoid this interpretation by staying away from the bad-guy explanation.

This is easy to advise but may be hard to follow sometimes. When your daughter is pregnant yet again, and you know she can't raise child number four, it's hard to refrain from making critical comments about her irresponsibility. But do keep those comments to yourself or strictly among the adults in the family (and remember, children love to eavesdrop). And even if you think—or even say—snide terms for the birth parents such as "sperm donor" or "egg donor," make sure the child never hears them. It's very painful for parents when their own adult children aren't good parents, but it's best to keep at least some of the pain away from your grandchildren.

*Think Again . . . before Describing the Birth Parents
as Too Poor to Raise a Family*

Yes, money may have been a problem for the birth parents. But
rarely are finances or even joblessness the bottom-line reason
that parents give up or otherwise lose custody of their children:
there's usually an underlying issue (substance use or gambling,
for example). And if children think that money was the reason,
what if they later hear you talk about how money is tight this
month? Will that mean that they must go elsewhere? Maybe the
birth parents could not financially support their children, but
most grandchildren will wonder why their grandparents didn't
help them out. The children may know other families who don't
have much money but know they receive help in the form of
government payments or subsidies. "If they have been told that
being poor was why their parents gave them up, they may feel
confused or distrustful of the adults around them."

*Think Again . . . before Describing the Birth Parents
as Too Sick to Raise a Family*

Framing the problem as sickness can also be misleading—unless
the birth parent has a progressively debilitating condition or
a terminal illness. The children may wonder, *Why didn't my
grandparents—or doctors—help my parent get better?* Perhaps in
reality, however, the birth parents were "too sick" because they
were abusing drugs or were mentally ill, and they didn't listen
to guidance from the grandparents—or doctors, for that matter.
If young children are told that their birth parents couldn't be
good parents and keep them safe, that explanation usually is
sufficient. Later, more information can and should be provided.

Explaining can be a way of framing a situation for the children. This chart shows some helpful—and harmful—ways to
help children understand and accept their family background.

Helpful and Harmful Ways to Explain

May be harmful	Probably helpful
Your birth parents loved drugs/alcohol more than they loved you.	Your birth parents couldn't/can't be good parents because of a problem with drugs or alcohol.
Your birth father abused you/neglected you, so the state took you away.	Your birth father couldn't take care of you and be a good enough parent because of a problem with drugs.
Your birth mom was mentally ill and you needed a normal person to raise you.	Your birth mother has an illness that makes it very hard to think clearly and be a good parent.
Your mother was nothing but trouble, and she went to prison for her bad behavior.	Your birth mother made some serious mistakes that were against the law, and she went to jail as a punishment.
Your birth mother loves her idiot boyfriend more than she loves you.	Your birth mother lives with a man who isn't nice to children.
Your birth parents were stupid teenagers who didn't know how to raise a child.	Your birth parents were very young and didn't know how to be good parents. They decided later for you to stay with us permanently.
Your birth mother can't hold a job or a man because she's immature and irresponsible.	Some people have trouble with everyday life, and your birth mother is one of them. She couldn't be a good parent.

More on the Underlying Issues

At an age-appropriate level, children need to learn the underlying reasons their birth parents could not be good parents to them, whether the problem was a substance use disorder, child abuse or neglect, incarceration, a mental health disorder, immaturity, or the birth parent's death. Let's look at each of these issues.

When the Problem Was Substance Use or Addiction

Many children are raised by their grandparents because their birth parents are in thrall to drugs or alcohol. The birth parents refuse to seek treatment, or they go to rehab and check themselves out after a few days. People who are dependent on substances cannot be good parents, which is what children should be told at a level they can understand. Alcohol and other addictive drugs affect the brain, and they control the person's behavior in harmful ways. People who abuse substances often are too distracted by their using to pay attention to the needs of their children—including feeding them regular meals, taking them to the doctor when they are sick, or making sure they have clean clothes and get to school on time. Children need safety, food, clothing, health care, and a loving home—and grandparents can often provide that.

Preschoolers can be told that medicine helps sick people, and medicine is okay if it's taken for certain reasons—so they don't fear that taking "drugs" will cause them to become sick with addiction like their birth parents. School-age children will learn that some drugs are abused, and you may wish to tell them that substance addiction is the birth parent's main problem. When children become adolescents, talk to them about their feelings—when they are open to such talk—and you may wish to recommend they avoid alcohol or other addictive drugs, particularly as stress relievers. Suggest other stress-busters, such as playing sports, dancing, meditating, or walking outside. And let them know they should be careful with alcohol and drugs because some people are more susceptible to the influence of those substances than other people are. They may have an inherited risk for this susceptibility. But make it clear they're not doomed to be alcohol or drug addicts. Instead, they should be cautious and aware of their behavior choices and find the lifestyle and habits that lead to real happiness.

When the Problem Was Abuse or Neglect

Abuse or neglect is often linked to substance use or mental health disorders, although this is not always the case. In explaining these issues, authors Betsy Keefer Smalley and Jayne Schooler recommend the subject be addressed at the child's level of understanding.[1] For example, preschoolers who were physically abused may be told that their birth parents did not keep them safe, which is an important part of being a parent.

Children who have been beaten or hit may be skittish and fearful, especially in any situation where others express anger. Tell children of any age that everyone gets angry sometimes, and talk about ways to deal with anger, such as counting to ten or taking deep breaths. Ask the children, "What are some good ways to handle feelings of anger, and what are some not-good ways?" If the children do not answer, you can say, for example, "Hitting another person is a bad way to deal with anger. The other person will become angry or be hurt, it gets you into trouble, and it resolves nothing. A better way would be to tell the person why you are angry or to walk away until you can control your emotions. It may be better to talk about it a bit later."

School-age children may be told that they weren't hit because they were bad, even if that is what they were told at the time. (Children may have memories of being told they were bad by one or both parents.) Instead, the birth parents hit the children because they were not in control of their own behavior, maybe due to using drugs or alcohol or because of other problems in their lives. Teenagers may be told that their birth parents had problems with anger and didn't know how to control their anger, so they took it out on their children.[2]

Your grandchildren may also ask why their birth parents didn't take anger management classes so they could learn to control their anger. You could say that you don't know or that the birth parents didn't take the classes because they didn't think they needed them. (Whichever explanation is true.)

When the Parent Was Incarcerated

Sometimes birth parents can't raise their children because they're in jail or prison for months or years. Rather than telling your grandchildren of any age that their birth parent is incarcerated for being "bad," you can say that the parent broke the law and that the punishment was to stay in jail or prison for a while.

Should you bring the children to visit their birth parent in jail or prison? That question is beyond the scope of this book, but keep in mind that correctional facilities can be very forbidding places. Make a visit by yourself or with a friend first to gauge whether it would be appropriate for your grandchildren to visit. If you decide to bring the children next time, help them prepare for what they might see—high fences, concertina wire, armed guards—and let them know that although it may seem a little scary, they'll be safe with you during the visit.

When the Problem Was Mental Illness

When parents have a serious mental health disorder, such as clinical depression, severe anxiety, bipolar disorder, or schizophrenia, sometimes they stop taking medication that helps them function well and may begin to exhibit bizarre behavior. The parents may have lost custody of their children because they were not providing good care or were neglectful or abusive. You can tell your grandchildren that their mommy is sick in her mind and that doesn't happen much, but it happens sometimes. If Mommy gets the help she needs, she may be able to be a parent again, but you are not sure if that is going to happen.

Older children may worry that when they reach a certain age, such as the age when their birth parent began to suffer from major depression, bipolar disorder, or another mental disorder, that they, too, will become afflicted with the same condition. Reassure your grandchildren that it is extremely unlikely that they will develop any of the psychiatric problems of their parent. However, if they are worried that they may be having some symptoms of mental illness, it is okay to share this information with you and you will talk about it with them. If they need help, then of course you will help them find it.

The Parent Was Immature

The concept of a parent's immaturity is difficult for a child of any age to understand. However, some birth parents cannot be good parents to their children because they are too self-interested and not able or willing to learn how to be effective in a parenting role. You might explain it this way: "Your birth father didn't understand that being a dad is a big job and that he would need to set a good example all the time." Or, "He didn't get how

Medication Compliance: The Stakes Can Be High

Luisa's daughter Elena was in college when she started acting distant during her visits home. Her speech was confused at times, and she seemed to be hearing voices. On a day when she seemed particularly disturbed, she told Luisa that the students in her classes were planning to kill her. Luisa asked questions and satisfied herself that there really was no plot against Elena's life—the problem was literally in her head. But Elena wouldn't be comforted; she *knew* that she was in danger. Luisa found a psychiatrist who saw Elena that week. He subsequently diagnosed her with schizophrenia and prescribed an antipsychotic medication.

For several years, Elena took the medication under the psychiatrist's care. She functioned well, graduated from college, and found a job. But a year later, she told Luisa she didn't need the medication anymore—she'd thrown it away. She was cured, so why did she need it? Luisa was aghast. Both she and Elena's psychiatrist insisted she still needed the medication but to no avail. Elena's boyfriend too wanted her to continue taking it but said there was nothing he could do. Within a month, Elena refused to see her mother: the voices told her that Luisa had turned against her and didn't love her anymore. Nothing Luisa said made a difference. She and her daughter became estranged.

One day the following summer, Luisa saw Elena across the supermarket parking lot. She looked pregnant, about four months along. Luisa gently approached Elena, not looking at her and not touching her—as the psychiatrist had recommended, if they should meet. Such restraint took every ounce of Luisa's strength, but she knew a strong show of emotion could alarm her daughter. Elena said she was okay. Then she added that for some reason she hadn't gotten her period for several months.

When Luisa gently suggested that missing several periods could mean she was pregnant, Elena was stunned. That idea had never occurred to her. She looked down at her belly. "What do I do?" she moaned. With great trepidation, Luisa suggested maybe a doctor could help her with prenatal care—and someone might want to adopt the baby. (*And it might be me,* Luisa thought to herself.)

Luisa soon made that suggestion out loud, but Elena wanted to consider other options too. Elena had trouble deciding, but after Kyra was born five months later, Elena chose adoption for her baby, and Luisa adopted the child with the help of an adoption attorney.

Why couldn't Elena parent her own child? The key problem was that she refused to take her medications, and Elena's intermittent delusions made her behavior unreliable: she said voices were sending her secret messages through her television, telling her to harm others. They were hard to ignore, and Elena was worried what she might do if the voices told her to harm her child. It might be very hard to resist them.

Luisa keeps in touch with her daughter as much as she can, and she reminds Elena that she needs to take her psychiatric medication. She hopes someday Elena will agree. But a key problem with untreated schizophrenia is a lack of insight—Elena doesn't think anything is wrong with her.

Could baby Kyra develop schizophrenia when she is an adult? It's possible; this illness has a genetic component. About 1 percent of all adults in the United States have schizophrenia, and their children's risk of developing it are about 12 percent.[3]

Turning the percentage around, this also means that Kyra has about an 88 percent chance of *not* developing schizophrenia. Luisa is hoping for the best and prepared for the worst.

important it is to be a good parent every day." The next obvious question is, "Will he ever learn how to be a good parent?" It's okay to say that you don't know.

The Parent Has Died

If the birth parent has died, whether from a drug overdose, an accident, a crime, or some other reason, children do need to know that their parent is never coming back. (It's up to you whether you talk about your own religious or personal beliefs concerning death. Some might wish to say that the birth parent is in heaven; others might talk about how to honor the person's memory by remembering the good about them. Or you might ask your grandchildren what they think.) If there is a gravesite to visit, the children may wish to see where their birth parent is laid to rest.

When children are young, under age three, when their parent dies, experts recommend that grandparents—or other foster parents—keep the routine for newly placed infants and toddlers as normal as possible, sticking to the previous mealtimes and bedtimes. (The same is true for older children, but infants and toddlers depend even more on these consistent patterns.) Young children may be shown photos of their parent and told simply that the parent died. As noted earlier, preschoolers cannot understand death and may ask repeatedly when the parent is coming back.[4] Children in elementary school can grasp that death is final but it may terrify them, and they may be afraid of dying themselves. They may also fear that something they did or said caused their parent to die; they need to be reassured that it was not their fault.

If the birth parent recently died, you can decide whether the children attend the parent's funeral or memorial service—but don't force a child to go. If children do go, prepare them ahead of time. You might say that many people will be there; they will be sad, and some may cry. People will speak about the person's life and remember the good things, there might be singing, and so on. Prepare them gently for any graveside service or other rituals.

In all cases, remember this: look for the positive. You may feel very critical about the child's parents for a variety of reasons. But usually there is something positive to say, even if it's a minor point, such as that the birth mother has (or had) a great sense of humor, or the birth father was a good dancer. Or he loved animals as a child and quickly found a family for every stray dog in the neighborhood. Avoid the tendency to wipe out the positive with more negative, such as by saying, "Your biological mother was very bright—just not bright enough to give up drugs, I guess."

Why try to say something positive? Because children know that that they are genetically related to their birth parents. If all they ever hear about them is negative, then they have no sense of the gifts they may have inherited from them, such as a great mechanical ability or an artistic or athletic talent. As for the parent who was not your adult child, find something positive to say about that person too. Yes, you can!

Other Issues That May Need Discussion

Beyond the story of how your grandfamily came to be, you'll certainly encounter other issues that need discussion and explanation—maybe on an ongoing basis over the years. For example:

- Racial and ethnic differences within your grandfamily: How do you frame them?
- Birth parents who pull themselves together and then start a new family: Where does your grandchild fit in?

- Birth parent visits that cause problems: How can we prevent some problems and respond wisely to the ones we don't anticipate?

Entire books could be written on these subjects, but let's look at some of the most common issues.

Differences in Racial or Ethnic Backgrounds— Visible or Invisible

When you're a grandparent whose skin color is noticeably different from your grandchildren's, eventually they will notice and wonder why. Young children can be told that everyone is the same on the inside and skin color does not matter; older children will benefit from a more nuanced discussion. However, other people may not be so kind, and if your grandchildren notice this, tell them that you don't agree with saying mean things about another person because of skin color, because people are born with their skin color and it's just a part of who they are. In fact, if you are raising a child of a different skin color, then you are a mixed-race family now. People who adopt "transracially" make this choice voluntarily, but as a grandparent, it is the way it is, and you need to accept your mixed-race or biracial grandchildren fully and completely—or let someone else raise them.

When you are raising a child of another race, the whole family is affected, and this needs to be a reality that you can accept. For example, if your grandchild has a white mother and a black father, then many people in society would consider the child to be black. President Barack Obama had a white mother and a black father, but he clearly identified with the black community and called himself a black man. At the same time, President Obama seemed to move comfortably in all circles, perhaps because of his mixed heritage and wide travels, even as a child.

And from about age ten, Obama was raised largely by his white grandparents in Hawaii.

If you and your grandchildren have different skin colors, are you willing to associate and befriend individuals in your grandchildren's racial group? Would you have a problem going to a barber or hairdresser of another race than yours? Don't deny your grandchildren's skin color. It's part of their identity.

Native Grandmothers Step In and Stand Up

In most Native American cultures, grandparents have an honored role. Traditionally, grandmothers are true matriarchs, caring for children while parents work, passing along values and knowledge to children through daily interactions. But on many reservations today, women are taking in their grandchildren full time at record rates. Some sources say that Native American grandparents are about five times as likely to be raising grandchildren as their white counterparts,[5] although they represent only 1.4 percent of all parenting grandparents.[6]

As in the wider population, the birth parents' alcohol or other drug addiction is often the main reason. And in these Native American grandfamilies, some grandmothers are banding together to raise awareness of the problem and begin to heal the damage. On Montana's Northern Cheyenne Indian Reservation, grandmothers have marched, gathered to pray, held ceremonies, and talked to reporters. One grandmother spoke of the need to show tough love and use tribal courts to mandate treatment programs for their adult children. Another, Margaret Behan, said that "On the reservation . . . the norm is grandmothers are raising grandchildren. They should not be."[7]

And now that your grandchildren are in your family, it is part of your familial identity as well. You will be perceived differently by others when you are raising children of another race. You may be seen as a "saint" for raising mixed-race children, or you may be perceived as an oddity. For you, however, it's just your family and it's normal.

"I'm Everything!"

Veronica, a multiracial child, age eight, had been bullied in school by some of her classmates at the start of third grade. "What *are* you?" they asked her, over and over. Her dark-olive skin, thick hair, and slightly Asian facial features made the other kids wonder, *Is she white, or black, or what?* It didn't help when Veronica visited the school nurse for a scraped arm and came back to class with a peach-pink Band-Aid on her dark skin. Veronica knew about her mixed racial heritage, but that was the day she came home from school and asked her grandma if she was "white enough."

One day, during a world geography lesson that involved looking at a globe, Veronica spontaneously cried out in front of the teacher and all the students, "My family is from all of these places. I'm Asian, I'm black, I'm white. I'm *everything.* I'm everyone. And I love everyone."

It's been three years since Veronica shared her revelation of self-acceptance, and she hasn't said another word to her grandmother about her skin color. No one in school has teased her about racial issues either.

The bottom-line lesson is that grandparents can and should provide positive information about racial differences while also sharing that some people don't like others, merely because of the color of their skin, as crazy as that sounds.

What if your grandchildren are part Hispanic, Asian, or Native American, for example, and you are not? It could open some new doors for your grandfamily. Some grandparents, whether they share their grandchildren's racial heritage or not (as with biracial or multiracial children) participate in activities oriented to the race or ethnicity of the children, such as arts and other cultural activities, language use, and holidays, street festivals, or powwows. You may wish to consider these ideas at various times and discuss them with your grandchildren as they grow up.

What about how the children themselves perceive race? Children generally do not notice much about skin color until

---

"People Do a Double Take"

"My two grandsons have different mothers, and their skin color reflects that fact," said Shantelle. "Lamar is eight, and he's pretty much the same color as I am, but James, the little one, looks like a white boy." His skin is lighter, and his hair is smoother than hers too. Shantelle is raising both boys and has legal custody of them: her son, the boys' father, is out of their lives now. She says sometimes people hear five-year-old James call her Grandma, and they do a double take, like she and James don't belong together. Some ask if James is her foster child, assuming he couldn't be related to her, and it aggravates her. "They are both blood relatives, and they are both my grandsons," said Shantelle. She worries that when they get older, kids may tease James about looking white and may make comments to Lamar about his "white" brother or to James about his "black" brother. But she's decided she'll handle whatever comes up. "I love them both with all my heart, and we'll work through any problems," she said.

---

they are school-age and others make comments to them, although they likely *do* notice if their skin color is different from a grandparent's. Sometimes a spontaneous comment a grandparent makes can help. Carole says her biracial grandson Eric, born to a white father and a black mother, first mentioned skin color when he was about three: "Grandma, I wish your skin was the same color as mine," he said. Grandma responded, "So do I! Your skin is beautiful!" earning herself a brilliant smile from her grandson. This answer suffices for a young child, but of course older children and teens need more of an exchange of views on the subject.

The Birth Mother's New Family

Imagine this scenario: Seven years ago, you gained custody of your infant grandson Jamal when it became clear that your daughter Marian's alcohol problem made her an unreliable parent. A county social service agency had removed him from her home, and you took him immediately, officially adopting him a year later. Now Jamal is in second grade, a happy child. All along, you've let Marian visit him once a week—as long as she was sober at the time. Jamal calls her "Auntie Mari." (He calls you Mommy.)

Now Marian seems to finally have found a solid recovery from her alcoholism. She's been sober for two years and goes to Alcoholics Anonymous (AA) meetings twice a week. She has a new job and a fiancé. And guess what: she's already pregnant and thrilled about it. She hopes to have at least one more child too. You hear this news, and although you're still wary—alcoholism is a relapsing disease—you believe that yes, Marian would probably now be judged fit to be a mother.

Your question is this: How will Jamal feel about this new family in the future? Any child in this situation could take it very personally: *Something must be wrong with me, because Auntie Mari didn't want to raise me, but now she'll have a family with the children she really does want.*

Will Jamal's birth mother, Marian, bring her new baby with her when she visits Jamal? That's for you as the grandparent to decide, weighing all the factors when the time comes. Will Jamal spend time with this new family as he grows up? Again, when you are Grandma, you may need to play it by ear. But Jamal is your child now, and you can call the shots. He might enjoy playing the "big brother" role from time to time as Marian's child grows. (And by the way, to a child, there is no such thing as a half-brother or half-sister. There are only brothers and sisters.) There could be a real upside to this development.

But there could be downsides too. Keep an eye out to make sure Jamal feels he's being treated fairly. And, over time, you might want to notice what rules Marian sets in her own home for her new children and use that as a factor in gauging Jamal's involvement there. In any case, her rules should not undermine your own. Your house, your rules.

"Is Something Wrong with Me?"

It's also important for children to know—and for you to remind them, if need be—that they came to your grandfamily not because of any fault or flaw that they had. It was their birth parent's problem. Even if the child is disabled and the birth parents could not handle the disability, that is *their* problem and not the child's fault.

For example, Delia had bacterial meningitis when she was a baby, and her birth parents delayed in bringing her to the pediatrician for evaluation of her fever and irritability. As a result, two-year-old Delia became deaf. Her grandparents were shocked to learn of her deafness a year later, when a state social worker discovered extensive neglect in the home. Not only that, but the birth parents hadn't sought any resources for raising a deaf child: learning sign language, giving visual cues instead of auditory ones, and so on. Delia's grandparents resolved to immediately learn sign language and do everything they could for their beautiful grandchild. They are a happy grandfamily today.

Problems with Parental Visits: Explaining Them to the Child
Unannounced visits. Forgotten birthdays and no-shows. Power plays. They're all potential problems that may occur with parental visits. Many grandparents complain about the effects of parental visits on the child, saying that the child acts up a great deal after each visit, and they wish the visits could be suspended altogether. Children may have mixed feelings of loyalty to both you and their birth parents. They may worry that a visit means

---

Understand the Question before Answering

Sometimes adults provide too much information—or information that's off the mark. You might be anticipating questions that the child isn't ready to ask. For example, if your children ask you where they are from, they may be wondering how babies get born, why they are with you rather than their birth parents, or whether their home city is Boston or Chicago.[8] How do you figure that out? By asking questions in response, such as, "When you ask where you come from, do you mean what town do we live in? Do you mean how do babies get made, or do you mean something else?" These questions will help children clarify what they want to know.

---

they will be leaving your home soon—but at the same time, they might long to live with one or both birth parents again. Emotions run high all around. So you need to establish some basic ground rules with the birth parents about visits and then do your best to enforce them. If the birth parents cannot or will not follow these rules and visits are required by the state or county or a court (as sometimes happen), then you should ask that the visits be supervised by someone else, such as a caseworker from social services.

Parental visits can raise some complex problems, perhaps upsetting the child or the birth parent (and you). To resolve them, you may need to talk with both the child and the birth parent to understand the feelings and set appropriate boundaries. So let's look at some of the most common issues.

THE BIRTH PARENT SHOWS UP UNANNOUNCED

Some birth parents seem to think they can drop in and out of their child's life anytime they feel like it. Perhaps they feel privileged because it's family—not strangers—who are serving as foster caregivers or adoptive parents, but the birth parents lost or gave up custody of the child. It is best to schedule visits—no drop-ins—to avoid hurt feelings on all sides.

An example: Pam, age twenty-five, was in the neighborhood (or so she said) and dropped in to see her nine-year-old son, Daniel. But Grandma and Grandpa were taking Daniel out to dinner, an event they had planned since last week, when Daniel's report card showed how much he'd improved lately. It was a celebration dinner, and they didn't really want to invite Pam along, because they never knew whether she would be on drugs and cause embarrassment in public. But neither did the grandparents want to cancel a scheduled event. They reluctantly invited Pam to join them on this occasion, and fortunately, she was on her best behavior. But later that evening, the grandparents asked Pam to please call first before she came and not to drop in unannounced anymore. They told Pam this was very important for Daniel. Pam didn't like it much, but she agreed.

What if Pam did not agree and continued dropping by unannounced? Then the grandparents would need to tell Pam politely that now was not a good time, ask her to leave, and suggest that she call later to find out when would be a better time for a visit.

THE BIRTH PARENT IS A NO-SHOW FOR A SCHEDULED VISIT

It can upset children terribly when they are looking forward to a visit and the parent never shows up at all. Children may blame themselves or worry that something happened to their parent. If this is a pattern with your grandchildren's birth parents, try this: *don't* tell the children about scheduled visits in advance. If the parent shows up, then fine. If not, then the children are spared the disappointment: They have no reason to become upset, self-blaming, angry, and so forth, because they never expected the visit to happen in the first place.

Note: If the birth parent is a chronic no-show, consider documenting this information for later use in court, particularly if you think you may wish to become a permanent legal guardian or adopt the child. Keep a log of scheduled visits and record times of arrival and departure as well as no-shows. (See chapter 7 for more details and a sample visit log.) Be sure to have the parent initial the visit log for verification purposes. You may need to show this log to the judge later.

One judge was all set to give custody of little Zachary back to his birth mother, Sherry, until the caseworker asked the judge to look at the schedule of visits. The log showed that over the course of three months, Sherry had visited her son only three times. The judge rethought his plan. He asked Sherry if the log was accurate, and she confirmed it was. The judge decided that Zachary would stay with his grandparents and the case would be revisited in six months.

THE BIRTH PARENT TELLS THE CHILD THEY WILL BE REUNITED "SOON"

Sometimes birth parents are convinced that they've recovered from whatever problem resulted in their loss of child custody. Sometimes they are right. But on many occasions, they are not. So it's cruel for the birth parent to tell the child that they will be reunited—especially if they say it will be soon (to many children, "soon" means tomorrow, next week, or at the latest, next month). This message is deeply confusing to the child. If it happens, insist that the birth parent not say so again. The child needs to feel safe and stable in the grandfamily, and often the birth parent's judgment is not reliable on this score.

If there's a real likelihood of the birth parents regaining custody, you might tell your grandchildren that someday they may go live with their birth parents again, but it's not going to happen today, tomorrow, or even next month. Tell the children that you'll let them know if you think they may be going to live with their birth parents again. Meanwhile, they've got their own family right here with you.

THE BIRTH PARENT FORGETS AN IMPORTANT EVENT

It happens often: the birth parent forgets a child's birthday or fails to be in touch on a major holiday. The birth parent may forget because of an alcohol or drug addiction, a mental health disorder, or for another reason—but it still can be deeply disappointing to a child. Consider reminding the birth parent in advance about the upcoming birthday. If the birth parent still forgets to bring a gift or to call, you could tell the children how very important they are and that it would be good if their birth parent did remember, but she sometimes forgets things like birthdays and holidays.

Don't buy your grandchildren a gift yourself and say it is from their birth parent. This is dishonest, and the children may feel deceived if they find out later that all those nice presents they thought were from the birth parent were really purchased by you. (Santa Claus strategies notwithstanding.) Even if the children enjoy these false presents, they may build a false impression of the birth parent in the mind—one that might be more painful to let go of later.

THE BIRTH PARENT TRIES TO ACT LIKE THE ONE IN CHARGE: YOUR HOUSE, YOUR RULES

Keep your eyes open for power plays. When you have custody but the birth parent shows up and starts acting like the parent in charge of the child, it's time to assert your authority. Your rules may be very different from the parent's rules, but your rules should take precedence. Explain to the birth parent (privately, whenever possible) that the children need to follow the rules that you have set. And no, it's not okay for the children to stay up for hours past their bedtime so that they can watch a movie with the birth parent, nor is it okay to load them up on cookies and ice cream just before bed, if that is not usually allowed in your home.

THE BIRTH PARENT IS VERBALLY OR PHYSICALLY ABUSIVE

Sometimes tempers flare and words are said that should not have been spoken. If what is said rises to the level of a threat, showing an intent to harm you or the child, the visit needs to end. Tell the birth parent to leave now, and then call 911 if you must. If the birth parent is physically abusive (which is often more likely when substances are involved), *get help*. Leave with the child as soon as you can, and call 911 for help. You may later wish to obtain a restraining order in court. Your physical safety, and that of the child, should not be endangered.

■

These are challenging problems, but as your grandchild grows, the situation is likely to stabilize, and problems are resolved. What's more, your bonds with the child often deepen over time. That's what one research study showed in a study of forty-one adolescents ages eleven to eighteen who were raised in a grandfamily.[9] The researchers asked the adolescents questions about their relationships with their birth parents (if they had any such relationship) as well as about their relationships with their grandparents. Here are some of their findings:

- Eighty-three percent of the grandchildren said they had a close, enjoyable, and loving relationship with their grandparents.
- Eighty percent said their lives were better because their grandparent was raising them (and the longer they'd lived in the grandfamily, the more likely they felt this way).
- Sixty-one percent were grateful to their grandparents. And that figure probably rises once they're past their teens, looking back!

Another noteworthy fact: it was the grandchildren who had been with their grandparents since infancy who made statements such as, "She's been like the only mom I've ever had."[10]

〉〉

CHAPTER 5

Responding to
Problem Behaviors

When Billy first arrived at his grandparents' home, he was a highly fearful and hyperactive four-year-old. He seemed anxious and afraid of everything, and what scared him the most was sleeping by himself in the bedroom his grandparents had prepared for him. Turning on a night-light didn't help, nor did leaving on the overhead light. Grandma tried sitting with Billy until he finally fell asleep out of sheer exhaustion, reassuring him and patting him gently, and leaving him, sometimes hours later, for her own bed. But nearly every night Billy woke up screaming. Later his grandparents discovered that Billy had previously experienced real-life nightmarish problems—he had been physically abused by his mother's boyfriend, mostly in the evenings when the man was intoxicated and raging.

Grandma knew that it's best to leave a child alone to fall asleep. But in those early days, common sense told her to make an exception for a while. She suspected he'd had some trauma, and she learned she was right.

• • •

This chapter discusses some problematic behaviors common for grandchildren who are feeling stressed or who may have experienced neglect, abuse, or abandonment before they came to live with you. These are serious issues, but don't skip this chapter if the child has no history of abuse or neglect. We'll address other issues that can occur in any child. Even if you have parented your grandchildren since they were newborns, difficulties may occur with sleeping, eating, toileting, regressive behaviors, temper tantrums, or aggressive behaviors. The problems may stem from the drug use of the birth parents, genetic issues, premature birth, or other problems. Sometimes you may never find out what causes the behaviors, and you must cope with them as best you can. The guidance in this chapter gives you a place to start.

Sleep Problems

Children from infancy through adolescence may have problems with sleeping: trouble falling sleep, frequent wake-ups at night, recurrent nightmares, night terrors, sleepwalking, and bedwetting. We'll discuss all of these, but one piece of advice first. Experts report that as many as 50 percent of all children experience some form of sleep problems. The good news, however, is that often they "outgrow" these problems with time. For example, only about 4 percent of children continue to experience night terrors and sleepwalking by adolescence.[1] We strongly recommend establishing a nightly bedtime ritual: children often thrive with predictable schedules. They like knowing what is going to happen next. Make sure you have a winding-down period of at least a half hour beforehand, so the child is not overexcited from an active game or boisterous playtime. At least thirty minutes before bedtime, turn off the television, the computer tablet, the cell phone, and any other electronic devices the child uses.

How much sleep does your grandchild need? It depends on the child's age. The chart here shows the average amount of sleep recommended for children from ages four months old to eighteen years old. Getting enough sleep is linked to better behavior, improved emotional regulation, and both physical and mental health.[2] Sometimes more sleep is needed, as during an illness.

Sleep Guidelines for Children Ages 4 Months to 18 Years[3]

Age of Child	Hours of Sleep Needed Each 24
Infants 4–12 months old	12–16 hours (including naps)
1–2 years	11–14 hours (including naps)
3–5 years	10–13 hours (including naps)
6–12 years	9–12 hours
13–18 years	8–10 hours

The Nightly Ritual: Helping Your Child Fall Asleep
Many children have trouble getting to sleep at night, especially those who have been traumatized in the past. But even healthy children who have not experienced trauma may not want to go to bed in the evening. They may not want the fun to end and may also feel like sleep is a waste of time. A nightly ritual helps the child ease into sleep. For example, a regular ritual might include a bath or shower, teeth brushing, and then for a young child, a drink of water and a book or two at bedtime. Dimming the light in the room is also helpful, either by using a dimmer switch in the ceiling or table lamp fixture or simply using a lamp with a lower-wattage bulb. Some children also may wish to have their favorite blanket or stuffed animal sleep with them every night.

When children are new to your grandfamily, try repeating the various steps to the nightly ritual each night until they start reciting the steps to you themselves. For example, you could say, "Remember, first you have your bath and then you put on your pajamas. Then you brush your teeth. Then you have a drink of water and then you lie down with Harold the Cat and then we read the next story in your book." (All of these "thens" help accentuate the separate steps of the nightly ritual.) This repetitious dialogue can be comforting to a child who has had a tumultuous past. A nighttime ritual can also be reassuring to a child who has *not* had a difficult past life.

CHILDREN'S DELAYING BEHAVIORS

Consciously or not, many children try to delay their bedtime because they don't want to go to sleep for a variety of reasons. Children may insist they're not tired, even as you observe them yawning widely, staggering with exhaustion, and struggling to keep their eyes open. Reassure your children that sleep is normal and important, and it helps their body recharge—like when you plug in a phone to recharge it. Except human bodies recharge through sleep.

Delaying tactics may include asking for multiple cups of water, just one more story—and then one more after that. Remind your grandchild that too much water means too many trips to the bathroom (and may cause "accidents" if the child tends to wet the bed). Two books or stories should be enough for most children to relax at bedtime. If the child is afraid of the dark, try using one or more night-lights.

Some children do well listening to soothing music at bedtime, such as relaxing classical music specifically meant for children, available for download or on CD. One grandchild listened to the same CD every night for a year. He found the sameness of the music to be comforting after a very unstable past life. Then after a year, the child suddenly didn't need or want the music anymore, so his grandparents stopped playing it. Nor did he want any substitute music. This grandchild announced that he wanted a quiet room, and that is what he received. So be adaptable. What works today may not work well tomorrow because children's needs and wishes change over time.

If you start to leave the room and your children beg you to stay, reassure them that you will be nearby, and they are safe. Avoid insulting the children by calling them a "baby" for being fearful. The fear, if it is present, is real. It may be completely irrational, and often fears *are* irrational—yet they are nonetheless real to the person who has them. Children need to learn that they can separate from your sight and still be safe. If children ask you to check under the bed or in the closet for monsters, go ahead and do it. A fear of monsters is very common.

Or the fear might be based on past feelings of insecurity. Some children insist on checking that all the outside doors are locked, and this can be added to the nightly pre-bedtime ritual if it helps them feel safer.

If children three or older scream and cry when you leave the room, try delaying your return for several minutes. If the crying continues, go back and reassure them that they are safe, and everything is fine. Use a gentle and calm voice. Then leave. The crying may still continue, in which case you should increase the time between your returns until the children finally do fall asleep. Yes, it may be time-consuming and frustrating for you, but eventually they will learn that they are able to fall asleep on their own.

To help children sleep the whole night through, a baby monitor is a good investment—especially if your late-night bedroom checkups tend to wake the children inadvertently. With kids of all ages, the monitor lets you hear your grandchildren's regular breathing and know that they are asleep and all right.

Melatonin as a Sleep Aid: Dr. Adesman's Views

If your grandchild still has trouble falling asleep, should you try giving melatonin? Widely available as an over-the-counter supplement, the hormone melatonin has an off-label use as a sleep aid. An off-label use means that a drug is not specifically recommended for that purpose by the US Food and Drug Administration.

I have no objection to the *occasional* use of melatonin to help your child fall asleep at night, if the child is three or older and your pediatrician has recommended a safe dosage in advance. It should, however, be an option of last resort if the child is having trouble getting to sleep.[4]

Melatonin is usually given in the evening before bedtime, and it may take thirty minutes to an hour to take effect. It is available from pharmacies, supermarkets, and many online sites. If possible, choose a formulation with the United States Pharmacopeia (USP) designation, which means it is manufactured according to pharmaceutical standards. For younger children, consider the chewable type of melatonin. They come in flavors such as strawberry and cherry. But keep these medications and all others well out of reach of young children! They are not candy, even though they may taste like it. Avoid giving melatonin to a child with an immune disorder or who is taking immunosuppressants, because melatonin could affect the immune system in people with an impaired system.

If insomnia is a pattern with your grandchild, you're not alone. One study showed that up to 25 percent of healthy children may have insomnia, and the rate rises up to 75 percent for children with psychiatric or neurodevelopmental problems.[5]

Problems during the Night

For some grandparents, helping the child fall asleep at bedtime is only part of the challenge. Especially for children who have experienced trauma, or who had irregular sleep patterns due to chaos in their home of origin, sleep problems can surface during the night. Let's discuss some of the most common ones and how to address them.

FREQUENT WAKING UP AT NIGHT

If you are successful at getting your grandchildren to sleep but they keep waking up every few hours, this isn't healthy for them or for you. (Babies and toddlers may wake up frequently, but they should grow out of that tendency.) Children two or older should be able to sleep through the night unless they are ill or have another problem.

As children progress through the various stages of sleep, as described in the sidebar, during a period of semi-wakefulness, they may wake up, notice that you are not there, and call for you or get up and look for you. Reassure them that they are fine and need to get back into bed and lie down. What if a child crawls into bed with you? It's okay to allow this occasionally, for example, when a child is ill or extremely upset about a problem or because of anxiety due to life changes. But if it becomes frequent, you will have allowed a pattern to occur. It's up to you to decide whether this is a pattern you can accept.

To help prepare children for sleep, consider singing to them (you *don't* need a great singing voice) and patting them gently on the back. However, it is very important that these soothing behaviors are used only until the children are quiet in bed and not until they fall asleep. If children depend on your presence to fall asleep, this will create a continuing problem. (In the opening anecdote to our chapter, the grandparent did stay with the child until asleep; however, this was an exception to the rule because of the extreme trauma the child had experienced.) In any case, do not share your bed with an infant—it's not safe.

RECURRENT NIGHTMARES

Some children suffer from recurrent nightmares, possibly indicating some unresolved issues in their life. If this happens with your grandchildren, reassure them that sometimes children

---

Understanding Sleep Cycles

During sleep, all humans—children and adults—alternate between two main types of consciousness. To better understand the kind of rest your child is getting, it's good to know about these sleep stages.

REM sleep. Rapid eye movement (REM) sleep is the stage when most dreams happen. In an extended sleep, we all have intermittent periods of REM sleep, which is when most of us dream. During this stage, our eyes move under our closed eyelids, as if we're watching a movie. During REM sleep, breathing and heart rates are usually just a bit slower than they are during wakeful rest.

Non-REM stages of sleep. To reach the first REM stage, the sleeper needs to drop through three stages of non-REM sleep. Stage one is a light sleep: it is the period of moving from being awake to being asleep. The brain waves change from the wakefulness pattern, and breathing and heart rate slow down. Stage two of non-REM sleep is a slightly deeper sleep state, with body temperature dropping slightly. Stage three is a deep sleep, when the heart rate may drop further and the muscles relax. It is difficult to awaken a person in this stage of sleep.[6]

---

have bad dreams and that they are not real. They are fine and nothing bad has happened or will happen tonight. Talk to your pediatrician about this issue and see if, between the two of you, you can find the cause of these frequent nightmares so that you can help the children resolve them. A child psychologist or psychiatrist might help too.

NIGHT TERRORS

For toddlers and preschoolers, night terrors (also called sleep terrors) are more common than actual nightmares. The child with night terrors is experiencing a heightened state of fear, may have an elevated heart rate, and may perspire. According to some experts, age eighteen months is the most common age for night terrors, and about a third of all children this age may experience them.[7] The good news is that most children outgrow night terrors. Your job is to keep children safe during the episode. Don't try to talk them out of it while they are in the middle of it—they can't hear you. Simply wake the children up to end the

---

How Do Sleep Cycles Change Over Time?

Infants spend about half of their sleep time in the REM stage. That fraction gradually shrinks over time; adults typically spend only about one-fifth of their sleep in the REM stage. In an eight-hour period, adults generally go through the whole cycle four to five times. For both children and adults, the first dream is usually a short one, occurring about ninety minutes after falling asleep. With each REM cycle, the dreams get longer, and most dreaming occurs at the end of the last cycle. Whether a person is in REM or non-REM sleep can be determined by an electroencephalogram (EEG), a machine that measures brain waves.[8]

episode; they will then fall asleep and be fine. In the morning, they will have no memory of it.[9] Up to 6.5 percent of children may have night terrors, but the prevalence drops to about 4 percent among individuals ages fourteen years and older. The incidence may increase when children feel under stress or after seeing a frightening TV show or movie.

SLEEPWALKING ("SOMNAMBULISM")

Your grandchildren may never sleepwalk, or they could be frequent sleepwalkers. It's much more common in children than in adults: about 5 percent of children sleepwalk, compared to only about 1.5 percent of adults.[10] And it's worth noting that preschoolers who had night terrors are more likely to sleepwalk when they're school-age. If your grandchildren are sleepwalkers, your pediatrician may recommend waking them up at night so that their sleep cycle will be reset. This is also referred to as "anticipatory awakening" and is done before sleepwalking occurs. The pediatrician can provide advice on how to handle anticipatory awakening.

Usually sleepwalking occurs when children are deeply asleep, although it can occur in a light sleep. When children sleepwalk, their eyes may be open but they are not awake, and this behavior could pose a danger—for example, if they leave the home. Children who sleepwalk may dress themselves or take items out of the refrigerator. It's not true that you should never wake a sleepwalking child. As mentioned with night terrors, some doctors recommend that you *do* wake up children who are sleepwalking so that they come out of their deep sleep. Then put them back to bed, and they will be unlikely to sleepwalk for the rest of the night. (Although you may have trouble sleeping yourself, Grandma and Grandpa!)

BEDWETTING

Also known as "nocturnal enuresis" (pronounced en-yoo-REE-sis), bedwetting is a frustrating problem. When your grandchild wakes you up and tells you the bed is wet, yet again, your heart may sink. *But this child is toilet trained! What is going on?* Don't blame the child. It's not bad behavior and should never be punished. Research has revealed that the bedwetting tendency is affected by genetic heritage. For example, if one of the child's parents wet the bed during childhood, then the child is 44 percent more likely to have a bedwetting problem. If *both* parents did, then the risk is as high as 77 percent.[11]

There are five key reasons for bedwetting in children, including a reduced bladder capacity, increased nighttime urine production, an arousal disorder, constipation, and psychological factors. A reduced bladder capacity simply means the children have a smaller bladder than others their age. As a result, when they are asleep, their bladder cannot retain all the urine in their body until they wake up in the morning, so these children have an "accident." Another cause of bedwetting is an increase in the nighttime production of urine. The cause is an insufficient amount of vasopressin, a hormone that releases at night and controls the amount of urine that the kidneys make. Next, with an arousal disorder, another cause of bedwetting, some children don't respond to their body's signals that it is time to use the toilet, like having a feeling that they have to "go" right now. Another common cause of bedwetting, believe it or not, is constipation, and a colon that is full of stools may press down against the bladder, causing the bladder to "think" it is fuller than it is. In this case, the good news is that simply by treating constipation, bedwetting dramatically improves. Last, with regard to psychological problems, some children develop secondary bedwetting after experiencing a period of severe emotional stress.[12]

Very few people in high school or college still wet the bed. (And if they do, a doctor should check them out.) Up to one-fifth of five-year-old children regularly wet the bed, and this percentage plummets to about 1–2 percent by age seventeen.[13]

Keep in mind that bedwetting, when present since infancy, is not considered a problem by doctors unless the child is older than five and has been wetting the bed for at least three months.[14] If a child who previously had no accidents begins to have occasional accidents during the day, this should be discussed with the pediatrician. It might indicate an infection or other problem. It is also concerning if a child who has been completely accident free for an extended period suddenly starts wetting the bed at night. This fact should also be reported to the pediatrician.

Analyzing the problem. When regular bedwetting persists past the age of five, consult your pediatrician. The doctor will check the child's urine for a possible bacterial infection and for signs of diabetes. There may be no abnormal findings, because many children with bedwetting problems are otherwise completely normal. It may also be a genetic issue, or the child may have a maturational delay and the problem will resolve with time.[15] The doctor will also want to determine if the child is having any accidents during the daytime. The doctor may suggest that you limit the amount of liquids a child drinks before bedtime.

Treating bedwetting. To decrease episodes of bedwetting in a toilet-trained child, as mentioned, limit fluids at bedtime, especially those that contain caffeine. Make sure the child uses the toilet before going to bed, and ensure a clear path to the bathroom during the night. Some doctors recommend waking the child up at night to use the bathroom. Others recommend moisture-sensing alarms that wake the child up with a sound or a motion of the device if the child wets the bed. If the child does not wake up despite the alarm, then the grandparents should wake the child.

Behavior charts can be very effective. The child may be rewarded with stickers or other motivators for each dry night. If the bed does get wet, involve the child in the morning cleanup, calmly and not punitively.[16]

For a child who is seven or older, you might consider asking your pediatrician about having the child take desmopressin (DDAVP), a prescribed medication, but only for special occasions such as sleepovers with friends or summer camps, to avoid embarrassment for the child. The medication is not recommended for long-term use, because children may relapse when it is stopped. Sometimes low dosages of older prescribed antidepressants such as imipramine are used to treat bedwetting: a side effect of the drug may be to increase urinary retention at night.[17]

Food Problems

As with sleep troubles, children from unstable, problematic homes may have a higher rate of food-related issues. Some are picky eaters, although that is a common childhood issue everywhere. Others may show signs of past food deprivation: eating too quickly or hoarding food, for example. Let's address some of these issues and how to approach them.

Picky Eaters

Many grandparents insist that their grandchildren are very picky eaters and eat "practically nothing." However, if your grandchildren fall into a normal weight range and are healthy according to your pediatrician, then by definition, they are eating enough. The children may not like the same foods you do; they may like bland while you like spicy, for example. Adapt. Introduce new foods slowly and don't pressure the child to try them. And remember that even a child who's getting enough calories may not be getting enough vitamins and minerals. Check with the child's doctor about whether a vitamin or mineral supplement is needed.

Many people, up to 50 percent of parents, believe their children are picky eaters.[18] However, the rate of truly problematic pickiness is likely much lower. Kathryn Walton and colleagues point out that preschool children are learning to make their own choices and exercising their free will, and refusing some foods is one way to achieve that goal (even though it can be very frustrating for you). The researchers also note that using food as a reward, pressuring a child to eat, and restricting some foods are all means of controlling the child and should be avoided. Why? These tactics can lead to poor habits, such as using external cues to eat (eating as a reward or a self-comforting mechanism or to please others), rather than eating as a response to internal cues like hunger or the tastes of foods. Walton and her colleagues also advise against tactics such as urging children to "eat three more bites" because this could discourage them from heeding their own feelings of fullness. Instead, they recommend asking children such questions as, "Does your tummy have more room?" or "Does this food taste all right to you?"[19]

Food neophobia—a resistance to trying new foods—is common among young children, who may reject the taste or even the texture or appearance of a food that is new to them. (Let's face it: guacamole really does look yucky.) Most children eventually grow out of this, although some children may become adults who loathe spinach or other foods.

If picky eating has been identified in the child (by the doctor and not by you), one recommended tactic may be to discourage the child from drinking too many fluids between meals. In addition, food grazing should be discouraged.[20] "Food grazing" refers to putting out food and leaving it for long periods so the child might eat some food and then come back later and eat more.

Experts recommend more frequent and smaller meals to help picky eaters. Another tip is to offer previously rejected foods on at least ten separate occasions.[21] This means that if your grandchildren turn up their noses at green beans once, try again later at least nine more times—on time number nine, they may eat them. And do *not* remind children that they have always hated green beans in the past. Just offer the food and see what happens. If your grandchild tries the food and likes it, be happy silently in your mind. Chalk up another victory for the grandparent!

Signs of Past Food Deprivation

It's disturbing to think that some children go to bed hungry at night, but it happens, and it may have happened with your grandchildren. In 2016, 17 percent of US households with children under eighteen were "food insecure," that is, the household's food supply was uncertain. In some cases, the children were well fed while the adults were not. But in about three million US households, both children and adults were food insecure.[22] It's safe to say that millions of children suffer from hunger each year.

Children who are insecure about food may behave in these ways:

- hiding, hoarding, or stealing food
- gobbling food very quickly when it is available
- eating to the point of vomiting
- eating faster if told to slow down eating

If you know or suspect that your grandchild has been food insecure in the past, you may wish to overstock the child's favorite foods for a while, suggested Katja Rowell, MD, an expert on this subject. She cited a case of one child who gorged on breakfast cereal when the box was running low because he believed there would never be any more cereal. When the boy could see that more boxes were available to him, however, he ended this survivalist-type behavior.[23]

It's also important to tell, and show, your grandchildren that you will always have enough food. Eventually they will realize that you have a kitchen full of food and that they will never go hungry again. In the meantime, you may wish to provide a place in the kitchen for the children to have individual stashes of food. Tell them that they can take food from this place anytime they want, and include at least a few foods that you know they like. Some grandparents fill a mini-fridge and keep it in the children's room until it is no longer needed. Eventually the children will realize that food is plentiful, and they will not suffer from hunger in your home.

Childhood Obesity: Helping Correct It and Prevent It

Sometimes children who are overweight or obese will hoard food, particularly if their caregivers are trying to control the food intake to help correct the overeating problem. They will also eat when they are not hungry. This seems to be a greater problem when parents or caregivers are very controlling regarding what the children can eat. The solution may be to help your grandchildren learn more about foods and nutrition, but at the same time, to avoid labeling any foods as "bad" or "good." There's a natural human tendency to want foods that you cannot or should not have—this elevates these foods in the person's mind to a high desirability.

Some new research suggests that prebiotics (supplements that are high in bulk and that include a substance known as "inulin," *not* to be confused with insulin) may help reduce weight in obese children, probably because prebiotic supplements increase satiety, or the feeling of fullness.[24] Ask your pediatrician for an opinion on this. (For further information, check the *ScienceDaily* article cited here: the link appears in the endnotes at the back of this book.)

Whether the child is overweight or not, strike the right balance between healthy foods and treat foods. It's important to instill good nutrition habits in children when they are young. These patterns will serve them well throughout their lives. But it's also a matter of balance. It's a bad idea to provide a constant array of cakes, chips, cookies, pies, and other carb- and sugar-filled concoctions, but, on the other hand, forbidding them altogether can make them seem overly important or too special to a child. Moderation is the key.

Water is the best fluid for children, both at meals and between meals. The amount of water a child needs depends on age, weight, and gender. For example, boys and girls ages four to eight years old need five cups of water a day. For children ages nine to thirteen years old, girls need seven cups of water a day while boys need eight cups. And for adolescents ages fourteen to eighteen years, girls need eight cups of water a day, and boys need eleven cups daily.[25]

Skim milk is okay too, but avoid flavored milks, which are often full of sugar. Avoid sodas, both diet and regular. Although young children are often given lots of fruit juices or fruit-flavored drinks, think twice before offering any juices, because these calorie-laden beverages contribute to the risk for childhood obesity. In fact, the American Academy of Pediatrics recommends *no* juice be given to children under age one. Give fresh fruit instead. For children ages one to three, limit juice to four ounces a day. Children four to six may drink up to six ounces; children seven to eighteen, up to eight ounces.[26]

It probably will not shock you to learn that children who frequent fast-food restaurants will likely have a higher body mass index (BMI) than children who don't.[27] This does not mean you should never take your grandchildren out for fast food or ice cream. It may mean, however, that you should not take them to such places every week. If you have concerns that your grandchild may be overweight, speak with your pediatrician.

Regressive Behaviors

Under stress, children sometimes revert to the behaviors of a younger child. For example, a small child who is toilet trained may regress to needing diapers. Regressive behaviors may also lead to interrupted sleep routines, eating problems, and other behavioral issues. So try to discover, whenever possible, what may be underlying the regression. Sometimes fear and anxiety may be caused by frequent moves, abuse and neglect, or other factors. For children of any age, regressive behavior may also occur after a visit with birth parents, even when the visit appears to have gone well. Children may become confused about why they are no longer living with their birth parents. No matter how well and often you explain what has happened, it's still hard for a child to understand. You can likely relate. Most grandparents have trouble understanding how or why their adult children, if they are living, have ended up in their current situation. When children are confused by a situation, then they may act out, consciously or unconsciously—and one way to act out is to revert to earlier behaviors.

When Regressive Behaviors Occur

In general, regressive behaviors such as "forgetting" their toilet training or using baby talk may occur when children are feeling insecure or distressed about a new situation, like starting a new grade in school or seeing their birth parents for the first time in many months or longer. In addition, if you are particularly stressed by a new illness or other serious problem in your life, your grandchild may pick up on your anxiety and start behaving in a more childish manner. Some situations may also induce regressive behaviors, such as a move to a new home, the addition of a new family member, the divorce of a family member, or a death in the family.

What to Do When Children Regress

First, don't panic. Try to identify the event or problem that has caused the child to regress to an earlier stage of behavior. If a child has been talking about using diapers again, ask why the child feels like diapers are necessary now. Could it be that the birth mother has had a new baby and the child feels sad to be living with the grandparents while that baby is with the birth mother? Or maybe the child is feeling lonely and needs more attention, and one or both grandparents have been very busy lately with other issues.

Temper Tantrums

We've all seen them, and maybe we've had to handle them. A temper tantrum is an out-of-control meltdown: children may scream, throw their body about on the floor, flail their arms and legs, cry hysterically, say mean things ("I hate you!"), and upset you and anyone else in the area.

What prompts a tantrum? Most likely, an adult has set a limit. The child is told "no," and the tantrum is a protest that, if it were rewarded, would lead to future tantrums, as a form of learned behavior. Children are more likely to have temper tantrums if they are overtired, overstimulated, or overwhelmed. They might also be coming down with a virus or other infection; they don't feel well, and consequently, they're acting out. Children usually don't throw tantrums just because they want extra attention or a toy—although occasionally this can happen.

If your grandchild throws a tantrum in public, make sure he is safe and can't hurt himself if he is thrashing on the floor. Physically remove him if necessary, although it can be tough to relocate a writhing forty-pound child using all his surprising strength. Hold him from behind, gently putting both your arms around him so that his arms are pinned close to his body, and watch out for him jerking his head backward into your head or chest. Reassure the child that everything will be okay. If you're in the supermarket, abandon your cart and leave with your grandchild. If you're in line at the post office, get out of line and mail your package later. If the child is demanding some item, *never* buy it for her. This only teaches her that tantrums work.

Take the child home. If she is hungry, feed her. If she is tired, put her to bed. How will you know what she needs? Offer a snack or a drink, and eventually she will accept it if she is hungry or thirsty. If she is tired, she may fall asleep in the car on the way home, even if you live just two miles away. If she is sick, she will probably develop a fever or other symptoms within a day or so.

The one thing you should *not* do is to blame yourself for somehow causing the temper tantrum. And don't worry about what bystanders may say you should do, such as walk away from the child or other unsolicited advice. Yes, a child's temper tantrum can be very embarrassing, but it's not the end of the world. Eventually, tantrums stop as children grow older and gain more control over their behavior. Maybe your adult children never had tantrums when they were little. But that was then, and this is now. Learn to deal with it. If tantrums occur several times daily, ask your pediatrician for help.

Aggressive Behaviors

Are your grandchildren behaving aggressively toward others—or themselves? Most such behavior arises out of frustration and anxiety. Hitting, throwing or breaking things, throwing tantrums, or self-harming: these are distressing to see, but they may not indicate a serious problem. Simple discipline or other behavioral interventions can probably bring such behavior under control. On the other hand, if the aggression is more frequent, purposeful, or severe, or if behavioral interventions prove inadequate (as may occur with children with conduct disorder or sometimes autism spectrum disorder, ASD), this behavior requires a stronger intervention (covered in chapter 9). Aggression may also be verbal, as when a child threatens harm to property or to others, such as threatening to break a window or harm another person. For now, let's look at some more common aggressive behaviors, remembering that they may be modeled on parental behavior or the behavior of others who formerly lived with the child. For example, if the birth parents constantly cursed and threw items at the child or others, then this behavior may have been learned as acceptable—even though it is not. It will take time to reverse aggressive behaviors.

Hitting Others and Throwing Items

When a child who is normally well behaved starts hitting others or throwing items in an aggressive manner, this may indicate that the child is overtired or feels frightened or upset about something. Take away the thrown objects and gently ask the child to calm down. If it happens frequently and seems willful— say, hitting others purposefully and throwing objects that are directly aimed at others—then discuss your concerns with the child's doctor; the child may need extra help, such as from a child psychologist, behavioral pediatrician, child neurologist, or child psychiatrist.

Cursing and Verbal Abuse

Most children are fascinated by the power of certain words to upset their grandparents or other adults and children. It can be exciting to see the shock on people's faces when a child uses these forbidden words. But at the same time, the child knows (or quickly learns) that it's not a nice way to talk. Tell the child that those words are unacceptable and that you don't want to hear them again.

Of course, you probably *will* hear them again—children constantly test adults. In that case, you can frown at the child or shake your head but don't give a lot of attention. (As you know, sometimes children seek attention, even negative attention.)

However, if the cursing continues to be a problem, you can have the school-age child write down, "I will not curse" fifty times on some lined paper. This is not a fun task. Taking away a privilege such as TV, video games, or computer time is another option you may choose to make your point that those words are unacceptable and that you don't want to hear them again.

Avoid using these words yourself as much as possible, lest the child copy your behavior. If you accidentally step on a toy and a choice word issues from your mouth, it's okay—any adult does that from time to time. Just don't use such words routinely if you don't want to hear them issuing from your grandchildren's mouths. And remember, do *not* wash the child's mouth out with soap. Many soaps have ingredients that could be dangerous for a child.

Breaking Things on Purpose
In most cases, when a child breaks an object, it was an accident. But sometimes it was clearly not an accident, and in such a case, it was an aggressive act. Help the child clean up the debris or clean it up yourself if there are dangerous shards. If the broken item was a child's toy, don't rush out to buy a new one. Let the lesson sink in: broken things can't be immediately replaced all the time. In addition, if the broken object belonged to you, such as a lamp or dish or other object, have the child do some chores to help cover the cost of the replacement item. Even if you decide to not replace the item, the child should still do some chores as a penalty for breaking an item on purpose.

Self-Harming Behaviors
Children who injure themselves in some way—such as banging their heads against the wall or otherwise hurting themselves—may behave in this manner because they are seeking attention

or feel extremely frustrated. These can also be signs of autism spectrum disorder, a subject that is covered in chapter 9. In the case of head-banging, children may also have a specific problem with their head, such as the itching caused by an infestation of lice (see chapter 10), a severe headache, or another medical problem.

But take action when you see such behavior: your grandchild must be protected from self-harm. Head-banging or other self-harm such as cutting oneself can be very dangerous. If you see these happening, consult with the child's pediatrician right away.

Myths and Realities about Child Discipline

In the Adesman Grandfamily Study, the majority of grandparents—56 percent—agreed with the statement, "Disciplining my grandchild has been more difficult than I expected." Discipline can be tough for any parent, and it's hard for grandparents too. Nobody enjoys punishing their grandchildren, but sometimes discipline is necessary because all children test boundaries: What is allowed and not allowed? They are not always purposely aggravating you—they are learning the boundaries of what is okay or not okay.

Consider some of the examples in the chart "Dos and Don'ts of Discipline." Many parents—and parenting grandparents—have found these to be effective rules of thumb. But remember, there are exceptions to every rule. Yelling for a child's attention may not be advisable most of the time. But if your grandchild runs out into the street, holler your head off!

Dos and Don'ts of Discipline

Do This	Don't Do This
Do explain briefly to the child what behavior was a problem.	Don't give the child a speech about the behavior.
Do correct the child with a time-out or a warning.	Don't spank or hit the child.
Do move closer to the child when misbehavior occurs, and speak in a soft and kind voice. If you're very angry, calm down until you can speak in a normal voice and decide on a fair punishment.	Don't yell and scream because you're so angry.
Do use "time-outs" or "time-ins" if rules are broken, and use a timer to make sure you and the child know when the time is up. Be consistent. Children notice inconsistencies and are confused by them. Another option is to use consequences, such as "no tablet time today."	Don't be inconsistent with respect to punishments; for example, imposing a time-out for hitting on one day, then changing the punishment for hitting the next day. (The child does notice.)

Let's remember, too, that discipline doesn't just mean punishment: it can mean giving children a chance to practice self-discipline. How do we motivate them? Many people believe that "bribing" a child with a promise of a few candies or a toy is always a bad idea. We disagree. In a pinch, bribery works very well. (It's also a form of positive reinforcement, which sounds much nicer.) For example, standing in a long checkout line at the supermarket may be boring for you, but it can be excruciating for your grandchildren. In such a circumstance, you may prolong good behavior by telling them that if they are "good," then they can have a cookie as soon as you pay the cashier. (You'd better define what good means: keeping their hands to themselves, not whining, and so on.) Even the most impatient child usually can maintain calm for a brief period when the reward is a desirable one. And the ability to stay calm improves with practice.

Why is it so hard to discipline grandchildren? One reason may be that the "traditional" role of the grandparent is to indulge the child. But now you are parenting the child, so you must take on the discipline part of the parenting job as well. Another reason discipline may be difficult is that the child may have been abused or neglected before arriving at your home. In some cases, the child may have never received any form of discipline before.

Grandparents may feel sorry for their grandchildren and want to make everything better. A little extra tender loving care may well be indicated in the early stages when the children first arrive. But eventually, children will need to learn the meaning of the word "no," and they'll need to learn it from you.

No Spanking, Please

Your parents may have spanked you when you were a child, and you turned out okay, right? It doesn't matter. Extensive years of research have indicated that corporal punishment—physical discipline, such as spanking or other forms of striking—is both cruel and unwise. It scares the child and it's not an effective form of discipline. Some grandchildren have been physically abused by their parents or others, and the last thing they need is to be hit by their grandparents.

Another reason for avoiding spanking is that it is ineffective in changing behavior, according to experts. Sociologist Murray Straus says spanking causes stress and fear in children rather than insight. In addition, young children often do not correlate the spanking with the "bad" behavior. This means they often don't connect the punishment with the infraction (the problem behavior)—so you're likely to see the "bad" behavior again if you spank. Instead, Straus recommends explaining to the child why you are displeased and imposing other consequences.[28] If you swat your grandchild's behind once in anger—and we're not talking about physical abuse—apologize to the child and make it a point to avoid spanking in the future.

Some grandparents still believe in spanking and other forms of physical punishment. For example, in the Adesman Grand-family Study, 20 percent of the respondents strongly or somewhat agreed that corporal punishment is acceptable. Still, most of the grandparents agreed with our no-spanking rule, and that proportion is likely to increase further in the future.

If You Make a Mistake with the Child, Apologize

If you lose your temper with your grandchildren and yell at them, calm down and then apologize. Doing so doesn't mean that you're ignoring the misbehavior, and it doesn't mean that you are demeaning yourself or undermining your authority. Just say you're sorry that you yelled, and end the apology right there. No "buts," such as "I'm sorry but you drive me crazy sometimes." That is not a real apology. When you say you're sorry, you're teaching children that it's good, even for adults, to apologize when they make a mistake. It's a great example. Of course, the children still will receive a consequence for the misbehavior, if they deserve one.

Use Your (Brief) Words

When correcting your grandchildren, use words, but be brief! Too many grandparents (and parents) give a mini-lecture about why that glass got knocked over and the milk spilled everywhere, while the children's eyes and brain glaze over. Instead, simply say that spills happen. Then give them a paper towel and tell them to clean it up, unless it's a dangerous spill involving broken glass. In that case, clean it up yourself, saying that it's important to be careful. Avoid long-winded lectures. Children realize when they made a mistake and are already unhappy about it.

Tone of voice matters too. Children misbehave quite a bit sometimes, and you could yell yourself hoarse trying to make corrections. Save the shouting for emergencies and try speaking in your "indoor voice," so the child pays more attention. Move closer to your grandchildren so they can hear you. Speak in a kind voice.

A Helpful Book on Discipline

Want to learn more? We recommend Thomas Phelan's helpful book *1-2-3 Magic: Effective Discipline for Children Ages 2–12,* published by Sourcebooks in 2016.

Reward Charts: The "Carrots" Approach to Discipline

Carrots or sticks? We've already talked about speaking softly—and we know that sticks (or paddles, or swatting hands) are no longer acceptable. Let's try carrots: rewards, that is. Many preschool and grade-school children respond to a chart with visible symbols for good behavior. With this system, adults define the desired behavior—brushing teeth or making the bed in the morning, say—and each time the children deliver the behavior, they get a gold star or happy face or another symbol on a chart you've created. (It works great for potty training.) You can use a gold pen or purchase stickers. When the children receive a certain number of symbols on their chart, say seven of them, then they receive a reward such as a trip to an ice-cream shop or a favored park. Over time, you might up the ante: ten stars wins the reward. As the behavior becomes more ingrained, you won't need the chart anymore.

Considering "Time-Outs" and "Time-Ins"

The "time-out" refers to the disciplinary practice of sending children to stand in a corner or elsewhere by themselves after an instance of bad behavior. It's an isolation form of punishment generally used for children ages two to eight. In general, the rule is to give one minute for each year of age. Thus, a four-year-old who misbehaves will receive a four-minute time-out. However, before using time-outs, it's important to consider whether the child has attention-deficit/hyperactivity disorder, autism spectrum disorder, or an intellectual disability. In such cases, this may mean that a significantly shorter time-out is needed, because children with such developmental disabilities may have difficulty handling a more typical time-out.

The time-out works best for repeated misbehavior, such as annoying the cat or pulling another child's hair. Give one warning first and if it persists, give a time-out: send the child to a corner of the room or to face a wall (not to another room; time-outs should always be monitored). Don't interact with the child during the time-out. When the time-out is over, briefly discuss the misbehavior so the child is clear on what mistakes were made.[29] If the time-out is effective at changing the child's behavior, then use it as needed.

If your grandchild has been recently abused or traumatized, you may wish to make the time-out shorter. Of course, if a mental health professional advises against using time-out, heed this advice but ask how you should correct behavior. Another time-out tip: use a simple timer that rings when the time is up. It's easy to get distracted, and you don't want a three-minute time-out to extend to ten. (This timer can be used in other settings too; for example, to limit TV time—the child will just look at the timer and know.)

With the "time-in," children sit close by their grandparent (or even in their lap, for a young child), and when they are ready, the two discuss what was done and how the behavior should have been different. The time-in involves interacting with the child for five to ten minutes. Sometimes it may be a better choice than the time-out. The time-in is best used when you notice the child starting to misbehave. Some experts see the time-in as preventive action before full-blown misbehavior happens.[30] However, if you're angry with the child, it may be better for both of you to choose the time-out to avoid saying something you may regret. The time-out gives both the grandparent and the child an opportunity to recover from intense emotions.[31]

Be Consistent

Say what you mean, and mean what you say, consistently. Another crucial point, and one that several of Dr. Adesman's survey respondents emphasized, is the need to be consistent with your method of discipline. Set realistic expectations and communicate them clearly to your grandchildren. And then let your actions reflect your words. For example, if you tell the children there will be no candy today unless they come inside the house within the next five minutes, then don't change your mind and give them candy when they show up a half hour later. If you do, you're practicing "intermittent reinforcement"—and that's a very risky thing to do. If you promised the answer would be "no," but if one time you say "yes," then your grandchildren will always wonder if this will be the time when the reward will be forthcoming, despite what you said. This is why adults gamble on slot machines—because they know that eventually, it will pay off. However, if someone who worked at the casino said that a machine was broken and would never pay off, then no one would play it. So stay consistent: don't let your grandchildren start playing you like a slot machine!

▦

Keep in mind that many of the concerns discussed in this chapter will resolve themselves in time and don't signify a true problem, while others, such as continued aggression or childhood obesity, may indicate a more difficult problem. Do your best to identify potentially serious problems early on and to use the expertise of your child's pediatrician.

〉〉

CHAPTER 6

Challenges at School—
and Where to Find Help

"Kids' social lives are so fast and complicated these days," said Frank, furrowing his brow. "When I was growing up, bullies were the tough guys who taunted us when the teacher wasn't looking or ganged up on us on the way home. In my case, they also made fun of me because I was dyslexic and a slow reader for a while. But once I got home, I felt safe. I got a break from that social pressure.

"But these days, a bully might be someone who mocks a kid relentlessly on social media or posts pictures that make them look foolish. And there's no break! Kids are 'always on.' They need to be online to do a lot of their homework, which means they're checking those sites constantly. And it can be really agonizing. Our thirteen-year-old grandson came to us practically in tears last night. For weeks, some classmates had been saying embarrassing things about him online. After he explained what happened, my wife and I looked at each other, wondering, What can we do?"

• • •

Many grandparents feel like they need a new education themselves as they guide a child through school, twenty or thirty years after their first family was school-age. Online bullying, the ever-changing uses of classroom technology, new ways of approaching learning disabilities: those are just a few of the topics we'll discuss in this chapter.

Getting Started at School

Meet your grandchildren's teachers at the earliest opportunity. Sometimes teachers are available at school on registration day for the new school year, and even a brief meeting in their classroom may be very helpful. Let teachers know that you're the person raising your grandchildren—but don't overshare about why you have custody. Teachers don't need to know the personal details. But you do want them to know if your grandchildren may have some difficulties because they missed a lot of school in the past, have been diagnosed with learning disabilities, or have other issues that are directly relevant to schoolwork and school performance.

See the "Don't Overshare" later in this chapter for ideas on how to frame issues to your grandchildren's teachers. Let them know about any general problems—the children missed a lot of school in the past, for example—but keep your focus on the future: let's help them catch up. Resist the urge to explain why so much school was missed and assign blame for that fact. Respect the children's privacy and focus on resolving problems from where you are now.

As the year gets underway, many schools have an "open school night" or a "meet my teacher" night, often in the first few weeks. If this is an option, attend if you can. See what you can learn about the classroom and ask questions too. How frequent are homework assignments, tests, and quizzes? What regular weekly routines are there? (For example, you may learn that younger children may be provided with spelling words on Monday and then be given spelling tests every Friday.) You may also discover whether the teacher assigns longer-term projects or reports. Older children may be given projects to work on over a period of weeks or even longer, often with

Can You Enroll Your Grandchild?
State Educational Consent Laws

Imagine this: You took six-year-old Ben into your home last month, in July, with the permission of your daughter Kim, his birth mother. No social service agency was involved. You intend to be his long-term caregiver, but you don't have legal custody—at least not yet. If Kim agrees to it, can you enroll Ben in your local public school?

It depends on where you live. In situations like this, twenty-eight states now allow grandparents to register their grandchildren for school (as of late 2017): Alabama, California, Connecticut, Delaware, Georgia, Hawaii, Indiana, Iowa, Louisiana, Maryland, Massachusetts, Michigan, Montana, New Jersey, New York, North Carolina, Ohio, Oklahoma, Oregon, Rhode Island, South Carolina, South Dakota, Tennessee, Texas, Utah, Virginia, Washington state, and Wyoming.[1]

To check the laws in your state, use the resources at the Grandfamilies.org website, including the "State Fact Sheets": www.grandfamilies.org/State-Fact-Sheets/. For more details, visit the "Search Laws" page (www.grandfamilies.org/Search-Laws) and enter the search term "educational consent."

You may also wish to call the local school and ask what type of consent is required to register a child. School staff probably won't find your question unusual; many grandparents and other relatives are raising children today.

Don't Overshare:
What to Tell (and Not Tell) Your Grandchild's New Teacher

Say This	Not This	Why
Colton has missed some school and needs to catch up. I'd like to work with you to help him get up to where his classmates are.	Colton has missed a lot of school because his parents were too drunk or doped up to send him to school most of the time.	Creating a plan to work together with the teacher is better than inducing sympathy for Colton.
Shayla has ADHD, and we think she may also have a learning disability in reading.	Shayla's mom didn't get any prenatal care and this probably messed Shayla up.	Defining known and possible problems is more proactive than blaming the birth mother.
Dwayne lost both his parents last year. He's working with a counselor but is still sad sometimes as he processes his grief.	Dwayne's parents overdosed on heroin and he found them both dead.	Explaining the sadness is good but overexplaining is not. Also, the teacher will be reassured to know that you have a counselor for Dwayne.
Mara has some issues with trust, but once she knows you, she accepts you.	Mara was abused by her brother and that's why it's hard for her to trust people.	Talking about abuse and neglect in general conjures up all sorts of negative images and may make the teacher overly protective.
Thomas can be impatient when he doesn't understand something quickly.	Thomas will have a fit if he doesn't grasp something in five seconds.	Giving Thomas a chance in the new school but also informing the teacher of his impatience is helpful. Exaggerating the problem is not helpful.

interim dates when some aspect of the project is due, such as an outline or other milestone. (If so, you might want to find out those dates and give periodic reminders to your grandchild.) Ask teachers how they prefer to be contacted—by notes sent through the child, by emails, or phone calls to the school? The open school night is also an opportunity to briefly meet with the parents of your grandchild's classmates.

School Conferences

Upon review of your grandchildren's report cards—or the "interim reports" that some schools send midway through the marking period—be sure to ask for a teacher conference if you think they are performing below their potential. Many schools set specific evenings aside for parent conferences, often after report cards are handed out, and you can make an appointment with teachers on those dates. However, if you really need an appointment with your grandchildren's teachers at another time, they should be willing to meet with you at an agreed-upon time convenient for you both, such as right after school.

Don't bring the children with you (unless you must), because teachers may feel like they cannot speak candidly in front of the children. If you can't find someone to watch the children while you attend a teacher conference, then ask the teacher if you can have a telephone conference at some time during the school day, when there will be no risk of them overhearing the conversation. Additionally, some teachers are open to email communication, so you can ask if this is an option. Remember, however, that your email may be shared with others, such as the principal, so be kind and be aware.

When the time comes for the in-person conference, arrive on time. Bring notes with you about any ideas or questions you may have. For example, maybe you are wondering if flash cards would be helpful with your grandchild's math problem, and you wish to ask the teacher if this strategy is recommended. If the child's distractibility is a problem, maybe the child could be seated away from the window or closer to the teacher. Feel free to take notes during the conference too.

Your Relationship with Your Grandchild's Teacher

Here are some suggestions for working well with teachers, especially during school conferences but also at other times.

Listen to the Teacher

Listening is more than just hearing—it's an act of open-mindedness. At school conferences, on the phone, or whenever you are communicating with teachers, listen carefully (and take notes). You're listening for new information: teachers may have real insights about your grandchildren. It's helpful to get a sense of the children's progress not only relative to their grade level but also relative to their own recent past. Are your grandchildren's grades and behavior better or worse now than at an earlier time? If so, what has changed? If you don't know, ask their teachers.

Whether teachers are offering praise, criticism, or both, are they offering evidence, such as test scores, grades, or other quantifiable data? Listen for that type of information too. If they don't supply it, ask if it is available. (Many schools do extensive testing, so testing data is likely available.)

Do you see any patterns in the information? Maybe your grandchild is doing well in math but not well at all in spelling or reading, which may indicate a learning disability. Has the teacher requested any testing for a disability?

What is the main point the teacher is trying to convey? Make a statement about it and ask if it reflects what the teacher is saying, such as "I think the main point here is that you are concerned because Carrie has not completed a lot of homework assignments. Is that right?"

Does the teacher have recommendations for what you and the child should do? If you are not sure, then ask.

Most teachers today realize that more and more grandparents are raising their grandchildren. But what if the teacher seems reluctant to talk to you, rather than a parent, at a parent-teacher conference? Explain that you are parenting your grandchild now and that this situation is likely to continue for the long term (if you think that is true). Tell the teacher you are willing and available to help your grandchild, you want to work with the teacher, and you will share any major changes or issues that come up in the child's life. Most teachers will appreciate the opportunity to work with family members. At the same time, respect the child's privacy, and do not overshare.

Remember, the teacher doesn't need to know that Isabella's father is in prison for assaulting her mother, who is now in rehab. But if Isabella has been anxious or sad, you may wish to share that general observation. If she has post-traumatic stress disorder because of past crises or reactive attachment disorder (RAD) because of a lack of early bonding, you might say she has "extra emotional issues we are working on." This can help the teacher to be more sensitive and understanding. You'll learn more about these disorders in chapter 9.

Consider the Teacher's General Attitude

If you're hearing about troubles at school, listen carefully and try to evaluate the teacher's attitude toward your grandchild. Does the teacher seem to be supportive rather than judgmental? Does the teacher seem to know and like your grandchild despite any struggles? And to what extent is the teacher making helpful suggestions, rather than just elaborating on your grandchild's weaknesses and deficiencies?

If you feel yourself getting angry because of possibly unkind or erroneous remarks, keep your temper. Make your points calmly. If you feel that the teacher is behaving in a condescending manner to you, take a deep breath. Maybe you're right, but this teacher is important to your grandchild, so it's not about you—it's about the child. Behaving with dignity yourself will help earn the teacher's respect. At the same time, don't talk down to the teacher because your own adult children are older than the teacher or because when you went to school, things were different and better. This is not relevant or helpful information to the teacher. Stick to the here and now.

The School and the Classroom: How Good a Fit?

In some cases, the fit between your grandchild and the classroom is not a good one. Maybe the child needs a smaller class, one with a teacher's aide, or a teacher more skilled in behavior management strategies. Talk to the teacher about these concerns. You may also need to talk to the principal or another administrator, such as the guidance counselor. These individuals are not only aware of the programs that their school offers but are often knowledgeable about programs available in other schools that might benefit your grandchild.

Moving Your Grandchild to Another School

If you ask the principal to place your grandchild in a new classroom with a different teacher but the principal refuses, you may feel strongly that the child needs to move to another school. (*Note:* If you are thinking about moving your grandchild to another school because of bullying or other social issues—covered in the next section—think carefully before you take that step and talk to school guidance counselors, psychologists, or social workers. They may be able to mediate and resolve challenges that your grandchild is having with other students.)

If you feel you must move your child and another public school is not an option, you might consider a charter school or private school. (Also note that if a public school cannot meet a child's needs for a free appropriate public education, or FAPE, under some quite rare circumstances, it may be obligated to pay for a private school for that child. But because it's a significant out-of-pocket expense for school districts, it does not happen easily.)

A charter school, an option in some states, is a school that is funded by the state or county, while a private school is funded by a nonpublic entity. Charter schools do not charge tuition, but private schools do. For information on states with charter schools, visit the National Alliance for Public Charter Schools (see the resources in appendix 1).

In the same way that public and charter schools come in all shapes, sizes, and areas of focus, many private schools also cater to particular needs and backgrounds. If you're considering a move for your grandchild, you may believe that something is preventing her from flourishing at school—whether it's social or academic or both. Exploring private options (and the scholarships many schools offer) could be worthwhile because there are so many types of private institutions: religiously oriented schools, military schools, schools that concentrate on academic achievement or preparation for college, schools that focus on the socio-emotional or special needs of students, and even schools for highly creative students.

As with any life change, talk to other parents and grandparents before you make the move. Find out what they like and don't like about the school you are considering. If possible, talk to them by phone or email. On social media, people may be reluctant to openly share negative opinions, because they don't want to be chided by others. And consider the pros and cons of various schools for your particular grandchild.

Possible pros of private or charter schools:

- Some private or charter schools have small classes.
- They may offer instruction in specialized subjects.
- They may offer religious instruction, which you might favor.
- The private or charter school may be a good fit for your grandchild's academic needs.

Possible cons:

- Private or charter schools may not offer the help that is needed, such as for children with learning disabilities.
- You may have to provide transportation to and from school every day or join a carpool.
- The school may not offer instruction in art, music, or other subjects.
- Private schools can be very expensive.

Another factor is the child's response to a possible move—but remember that children usually adjust fine, even if they object at first. Most children resist major changes, and they'll want to stay with their friends at the old school rather than risk a new school with "unknown angels." During the transition, your grandchildren will not necessarily thank you, and they may also blame themselves for a while. But regardless of those reactions, do the right thing for your grandchildren.

Social Problems at School

Sometimes children have few or no friends in school. For a child with a difficult early life, involving neglect, abuse, or other troubles, a poor self-image may be hindering friendships. If children don't think they are worthy of having friends, they may shy away from others and may also shun their friendly overtures. After a while, other children give up and move on to the children who do want to engage with them. Sports activities may help shy children make friends, so consider having your grandchildren join a soccer or baseball team, for example. Scouting is another good option, as are clubs for older kids. Some schools may offer social skills training, as may some therapists. If you are a religious person, activities for children and adolescents at your place of worship may help to draw the child out. Keep in mind that not all children are social butterflies, and many children are happy with just one or two friends.

You may also try some role-playing with your grandchild, pretending you are another child having a conversation. Learning basic social skills may be challenging for some children, but practice can help.

Children with autism spectrum disorder may benefit from a social skills group offered by a local counseling organization for children and teenagers with autism. Make some calls to see if such groups are available in your community. There may be a small fee to participate. You'll learn more about ASD in chapter 9.

Bullying

Whether it's in person or online, expecting children to just handle bullying on their own is unreasonable. For this reason, many schools now have anti-bullying rules and programs for their students in place. Ask your child's school if it has an anti-bullying policy, and if so, ask to see it.

What forms does bullying take? Sometimes it's physical violence or threats of violence. Sometimes children band together to taunt and torment their latest victim. Or it may be psychological: a child is taunted about looking or acting in any way that is different from the other children. Words do matter. The adage "Stick and stones may break my bones, but words can never hurt me" is wrong. Words can hurt enormously, and the internet can magnify that pain.

In her book *The Bully, the Bullied, and the Bystander*, author Barbara Coloroso explains that bullying is a lose-lose-lose proposition. The bullied child is the obvious victim because that child may become depressed and angry. But the bully is also affected: this power-grabbing behavior can be habit forming, and it's not a recipe for satisfying relationships. The bystander is also affected, whether the child joins in with the bullying behavior or chooses to ignore it.[2] Sometimes, a bystander reports bullying to others—and this is to be applauded, but the person making the report may also feel at risk. Bullying is very common; according to the Centers for Disease Control and Prevention in 2015, 20 percent of schoolchildren in the United States said they had been bullied on school property in the last twelve months.[3]

Since the advent of social media in the early 2000s, young people have started using this form of communication at earlier and earlier ages. And unfortunately, online bullying, also known as "cyberbullying," has become more common: in 2015, 16 percent of students were electronically bullied in emails, in chat rooms, by instant messages, or by texting. Females were more than twice as likely to be electronically bullied (22 percent) as males (10 percent).[4]

Authors at the Nobullying.com site say that preteens especially need guidance on social media because of their innocence and vulnerability. So they advise that you know all the passwords for your child's email and social media accounts and that you periodically check into them to make sure there are no serious problems or bullying issues. They also recommend that you know the names of all your child's friends, and if a new

---

Online Bullying: An Old Problem with a New Face

Ava's grandparents were shocked when they learned that Ava, fifteen, was being bullied over social media by several girls in her class. The other girls said Ava's clothes were old-fashioned and she had no style, probably because she lived with a couple of old people. Over the last two months, they had posted candid unflattering photos of Ava with mocking captions. A sobbing Ava finally told her grandparents about the problem. *Whom should we contact?* they wondered. Because Ava had no homeroom teacher in tenth grade, they decided to call the principal.

The principal was deeply concerned and acknowledged that the girls' behavior was a problem. Even if Ava wasn't in physical danger, this kind of mocking really does amount to bullying. Like many other schools, the principal said, Ava's school was developing its own "no bullying" policy and program. Next fall, every grade would discuss the problem at the beginning of the year and agree to the school's reporting procedures for all kinds of bullying.

Unfortunately, at this age it's harder to make contact with the bullies' parents, the principal said, as you might do with younger kids. For now, the principal recommended that Ava talk to the school counselor.

---

name pops up in discussion, find out if this is a local child or a "virtual" friend (on the internet only).[5] These virtual friends sometimes are adults pretending to be kids so they can gain the confidence of children or teens through flattery and attention, only to prey on them later. The authors also recommend connecting your computer or device to your grandchildren's devices so you can perform this task. Yes, you're spying on them, but you are also protecting them.

When Teachers Are Bullies

It doesn't happen often, but sometimes teachers are bullies—and often the bullying teachers were bullied as children. That was one finding of a study of 116 elementary school teachers from seven schools, surveyed anonymously with results published in 2006.[6]

The teachers were between twenty-two and sixty-four years old and most (88 percent) were female. In addition, most (81 percent) were either satisfied or highly satisfied with their job—this was not primarily a group of disgruntled teachers. Some of the ways in which they reportedly bullied their students included frequently punishing the same child, humiliating students to halt classroom disruptions, purposefully hurting students' feelings, making fun of students in special ed programs, and setting up students to be bullied by others.

The bottom line is this: some teachers *are* bullies, and if you think your grandchild may have a bullying teacher, you need to investigate further and likely will need to get the child out of that classroom. Your first step should be to speak to the school principal about your concerns.

Children and teens often don't realize how their online words or photographs may affect others, and they likely don't realize that on most social media, what is posted will stay there unless the site manager deletes it or the site itself is removed. Tell your grandchildren that before posting a comment about someone else online, think about how they would feel if someone said the same thing about them. And how might they feel reading their comments ten years from now? It's hard for adolescents to think beyond tomorrow, but you can help bend their minds in that direction.

Grandparents, keep that in mind yourself—whatever you say on social media may likely be there a long time. We advise this caveat: don't say anything anywhere on the Internet that you wouldn't mind reading on the front page of the *New York Times* or hearing on CNN.

Achievement in School:
How to Help Your Grandchild

If your grandchild has trouble grasping new material, consider what the reason might be. Many children have learning disabilities, which are discussed later in this chapter. Others may struggle with an unfamiliar teaching technique. For example, a child learning to read may have been learning to sound out words a few months ago. But now she's in a new school where the teachers are using an entirely different method to teach reading. This can be difficult for the child to adapt to, and it can be quite frustrating—especially if all the other students in her class are used to this method. It helps to let her know that you understand her feelings about this. Also, in a case like this, tell the teacher about the former way the child was learning to read—or to divide numbers or learn any other skill—and ask the teacher for recommendations on ways to help bring your grandchild up to speed.

Ask the teacher and the principal if there are after-school programs or tutors who can help with reading (or math) issues. Many schools pull children out of class for special reading help—although children may resist being singled out and having to leave their classmates. Children with special education needs may be placed in a more supportive classroom (more on that option in a moment). Some children do well with team teaching, which involves two or more instructors teaching the same subject, such as reading or math. Be sure that your grandchild knows that many smart people have struggled with math, reading, or other school subjects.

In recent years, teachers have started paying more attention to different learning styles too. Some people learn best by seeing information (visual learners)—for example, by reading, viewing pictures, or interpreting charts or graphs. Auditory learners learn best by hearing information: a simple example is the ABC song that helps children memorize the alphabet. Kinesthetic learners learn best by engaging in activities, such as building a model or making a map. Think about how you learn most effectively: Would you rather learn a task or lesson visually, watching a video or reading a book? Would you rather hear the material explained or listen to an audiobook? Or would you rather learn through a hands-on activity? Then think about how your grandchildren seem to learn best. You may not know right away which type of learning your grandchildren find most natural, but observe their behavior, read reports about them from teachers and others, and talk to their teachers about what they think.

Eventually, the school (and you) will figure out how to help your grandchildren learn in the best way possible.

Homework Hints

- Some children do best when they do their homework as soon as they get home from school, while others do best with a break and a snack after school before starting homework. See which way works best for your grandchild.

- Provide a clean and clear place for children to do homework, whether it's the kitchen table, their own desks, or another location.

- Remove as many distractions as possible, such as the television, cell phone, and radio.

- You can help with homework by showing the child how to do one or two examples provided in homework. But don't do all the work for the child. The goal is to have your grandchild be able to do the work independently.

- If you don't understand an assignment yourself (and it happens because teaching techniques change!), ask the teacher for some pointers. Don't be shy or hesitant about "asking the internet" either. The terms "Common Core State Standards" or "Common Core Curriculum" might not mean anything to you now, but you might soon need to know all about it. Whether you're trying to navigate the current jargon used by schools and teachers or just realizing you're rusty in algebra, ask members of your support group or other parents you know (or go online). It's a natural area of common ground, even with parents much younger than you are.

- If your grandchild needs tutoring, ask the teacher if there are any in-school resources available, or ask other parents for recommendations.

Technology in the Classroom—and at Home

These days, younger grandparents are probably very computer literate, while older ones may be less comfortable with technology. If you do have some basic computer ability, you may find there are some advantages to connecting electronically with your grandchildren's school. For example, report cards may be posted online. You may be able to email your grandchildren's teachers, if they are willing to provide an email address. Some schools offer their own email system as a channel for general information and sometimes for teacher-parent communications (often, you receive an email alert to check the system for a new message). If you don't have computer experience, consider developing some basic skills in this area. Your own grandchild might be able to teach you some basics. A friend or neighbor might be willing to give you some lessons, or you could offer to barter skills with a parent of your grandchild's classmate. Some public libraries and community education programs offer free or low-cost sessions for computer literacy.

Your grandchildren may tell you that they absolutely need a computer (or at least a device with internet access) for schoolwork—and they may be right, although this is much less likely in the very early grades. But children are increasingly using electronic devices in school and for homework, to gather information for reports, for example. Depending on the grade level and the school system, most students might be using a desktop computer at home, perhaps shared with others in the family. Or they might be issued a laptop or tablet that travels between school and home. Talk with your child's teacher about expectations and practices.

For school purposes, you don't need a computer with all the latest bells and whistles, even if your grandchild thinks you do.

If you can afford a computer, buy one that is within your budget. A printer is handy too, especially for older children. You may choose to buy a used or reconditioned computer from a reputable dealer. If you cannot afford a computer, not a problem. Go to the public library, a fount of knowledge, information, and computers available for free use (sometimes with a sign-up sheet and a time limit).

Periodically monitor your grandchild's internet use. There are software programs that filter out inappropriate websites, such as Net Nanny (www.netnanny.com). Many internet browsers offer parental controls to limit the places that children can visit online, including Google Chrome, Internet Explorer, and Mozilla Firefox.[7] If you do none of these things and don't monitor your grandchild's online use, it's relatively easy for a child to access graphic pornography sites, the last thing a child needs to see. Although these sites say that a person must be at least eighteen years old to enter, children can simply lie and click to affirm that they are old enough.

Tell your grandchildren to not befriend anyone online that they don't know in real life: another reason that you should periodically monitor what your grandchildren are doing on their devices.

If you're short on tech savvy, know that you've got company. In the Adesman Grandfamily Study, respondents were all over the map with computer literacy (although because the survey was online, they may have been a group that was savvier than average). They were asked to rate their ability to help their grandchild with computers and other school-related technology, compared to current first-time parents:

- 27 percent said they were "somewhat less" or "much less" capable.

- 37 percent said they were "about the same" in terms of capability.
- 18 percent said they were "much *more* capable" than other parents.

So learn what you can, even if you'll never be as technologically adept as your grandchild. And that's okay. You can be a wonderful grandparent even if you're not a technological genius.

Does My Grandchild Have a Disability or Need Special Education (or Both)?

If your grandchild is struggling to learn, a learning disability may be the cause. Some learning disabilities make it difficult for a child to read (dyslexia), while others impede math calculations (dyscalculia), writing (dysgraphia), or motor skills (dyspraxia). Many children with learning disabilities also have ADHD.

Sometimes children with a learning disability need specialized instruction. They may receive most of their instruction in a general classroom and then be pulled out to go to a "resource room" for a specialized small-group session. Other children may need to be taught in a self-contained classroom with other children who also have one or more conditions that interfere with learning.

Also, please note that "special education" does not refer solely to helping children with Down syndrome or other forms of intellectual delays. Instead, in today's world, special education encompasses all the many different types of school assistance and accommodations that children with learning disabilities, developmental disorders, or psychiatric problems may need so that they can learn. You may also hear the term "exceptional education," as a term synonymous with "special education."

Types of Disabilities Schools Acknowledge
Having a specific learning disability is just one way a child may qualify for special education services. Children who fall into one of the following categories may also qualify for services:

- speech or language impairment
- autism spectrum disorder
- intellectual disability
- hearing impairment
- deafness
- visual impairment, including blindness
- deaf-blindness
- orthopedic impairment
- emotional disturbance
- traumatic brain injury
- multiple disabilities

As for learning disabilities, unfortunately, children who have them may be told by unaware teachers, parents, grandparents, and others that they are not "trying hard enough," and the children may mistakenly believe that they're not smart. Imagine yourself as your grandchild, trying out a skill that you struggle with or can't do at all. It could be any skill, from swimming to writing a story. Now imagine other children in your grade mastering this skill with no problem, but you struggle. Further imagine that teachers and other people tell you're not trying hard enough to succeed, even though you know you are doing your best. This is what it feels like to be a child with an undiagnosed learning disability.

For more information, use these resources:

- learning disabilities:
  Learning Disabilities Association of America at https://
  ldaamerica.org/and National Center for Learning Disabilities
  at www.ncld.org/

- special education:
  US Department of Education at www2.ed.gov/parents/needs
  /speced/edpicks.jhtml and Individuals with Disabilities
  Education Act site at https://sites.ed.gov/idea/

Asking the School to Evaluate Your Grandchild

If you think your grandchild may have a learning disability (that hasn't yet been diagnosed by a doctor, you may wish to ask the school to test the child for such a problem. (The same goes for emotional, behavioral, or developmental disorders, discussed in chapter 9.) It's best to ask in writing, either by email or in a letter. Explain why you think the child needs testing, and give concrete reasons rather than feelings. For example, you might say that Maria is still reading at the second-grade level even though she's beginning fifth grade, and she doesn't seem to be improving (instead of saying Maria is upset and hates reading). You can expect at least some resistance from the school. Testing costs money and takes time, and often schools don't want to do such testing because they feel they already have plenty of students in various programs. But be persistent if you think your child may need extra help.

Many schools provide some remedial education services to try to help a child without invoking the process known as the Individualized Education Program, or IEP (which we'll discuss in a moment). The term for this remedial solution is "response to intervention," and it may include special help for children who have trouble with reading, math, or other academic areas. This may be an option for your grandchild.

What if you're ignored at the local school level after multiple requests for help? Sometimes, parents and grandparents in this position benefit from writing letters or emails requesting help to the superintendent of schools for their county or school district. If you decide to email the superintendent, whose email address should be available on the internet, be brief, be to the point, and don't be accusatory. An email can be shared or forwarded to other people, and it creates a digital trail.

Don't worry that your local principal will become annoyed or even angry about your letter to the superintendent. Even if this is the case, if you have repeatedly attempted to get the principal's help with your grandchild over months or even years and you feel like you have gotten nowhere, then this person is very unlikely to call you up and yell at you. Keep your eyes on the goal: helping your grandchild acquire a good education. Be your grandchild's advocate.

Learning about Individualized Plans That May Help

If your grandchildren have consistent trouble with schoolwork, whether they have been identified with a learning disability or not, they may be eligible for special adjustments or "accommodations" to help them learn most effectively:

- an Individualized Education Program: a plan for a child who qualifies for accommodations under the IDEA law
- a Section 504 Plan, or also called an Individualized Accommodation Plan (IAP): a plan for a child who qualifies for accommodations under ADA AA

Yes, it's an alphabet soup. (Refer to the "Federal Laws on Education and Disabilities" sidebar to keep things straight.) Complicating issues further, sometimes people may use the term "IEP" when "IAP" would be the right terminology. But

Federal Laws on Education and Disabilities: Which One Might Apply to My Grandchild?

Several key federal laws focus on meeting the needs of children with a variety of disabilities, including learning disabilities. For example:

- The Individuals with Disabilities Education Act (IDEA) of 2004 pertains to the educational benefits children may be entitled to. For example, it provides for Individualized Education Programs (IEPs) tailored to meet students' particular needs.

- Section 504 of the Rehabilitation Act and the Americans with Disabilities Act Amendments Act (ADA AA) of 2008 pertains to children's civil rights to education, for example, allowing wheelchair access in school settings. Further, Section 504 may offer a comparable kind of individualized plan to children who don't qualify for an IEP under the IDEA law.

There are also state educational laws, but federal laws supersede state laws: if there is a conflict, the federal law usually "wins." It is also true that the federal government gives the states money to implement these federal laws, and if states fail to implement the laws, then they may risk losing considerable cash.

Some new-sounding laws may be revisions to old ones. For example, the Every Student Succeeds Act (ESSA), signed into law by President Obama in 2015, was really an update of the 2001 No Child Left Behind Act. (Its history actually dates back to 1965 when Lyndon Johnson signed the Elementary and Secondary Education Act.)[8] Congress often cobbles new legislation onto old laws, adding new sections and deleting others, and renaming it.

for now, as we discuss how one of these plans might help your grandchild, we'll use the term IEP to refer to the IAP as well. For many students, these tailored plans help them overcome specific obstacles to learning. They're created by a team that includes the parent or guardian (or you), the teacher, and other school professionals, such as the guidance counselor and the school psychologist, and they consist of strategies to address a child's particular issues: for example, distractibility, poor hearing, or learning style obstacles. The team may decide that testing is needed—a hearing test by an audiologist or further tests of the child's reading or mathematical abilities are among the many types of tests that may be recommended.

Before the child may receive an IEP, an evaluation of the child's needs is made by a guidance counselor, a school psychologist, teachers, and perhaps others, depending on the issues. Grandparents with legal custody must first agree to such an evaluation (see chapter 7 regarding the difficulties of *not* having legal custody). Working together with these staff members, you will come up with a plan to help your child. For example, if your grandchild struggles to pay attention (whether or not the child has ADHD), it may be best to seat the child close to the teacher. In some cases, the child may be given accommodations to help address the disability or other challenge, such as a reminder sent home every day regarding schoolwork the child needs to complete or tests that are coming up in a few days.

Here are some examples of accommodations that may be requested for children with ADHD:[9]

- The child should be seated away from major distractions ("preferential seating").
- The teacher refocuses and redirects the child as needed.

- Homework modifications; if the child seems to know the material, then allow abbreviated assignments.

- The child may be allowed extra time to complete assignments and tests.

- The child is allowed to take tests in a quiet place.

- Large assignments and projects may be broken down into smaller parts and given deadlines.

- The child may be given both verbal and written instructions.

- The child may be assigned a peer to help with note-taking.

- Private signals can be developed that the teacher uses to help the child get back on task, such as a touch on the shoulder.

- A communication notebook may be used in which a daily report is given to the grandparents on the child's progress and behavior, and the grandparent can respond to these comments.

- The teacher should discuss behavior problems with the child in private, rather than in front of the class.

Many children have IEPs. In the Adesman Grandfamily Study, respondents reported that nearly a third (30 percent) of the grandchildren had an IEP, and 20 percent were in special education classes in school.

By law, public schools in the United States have to place a student in the "least restrictive" environment; for example, a school district cannot place a child in a small special education class if it is believed that a mainstream class would also be appropriate. An IEP can sometimes help make that possible.

Developing an Individualized Plan for Your Grandchild:
The IEP Meeting

If your grandchildren are being considered for an individualized plan, then you may need to attend a scheduled meeting with the children's teacher, the guidance counselor, and possibly others, such as the school psychologist. At this meeting, you'll discuss whether the children need a plan and why, perhaps referring to test results and other evidence. If you agree an IEP is needed, you'll discuss what it should consist of: What special accommodations will help your grandchildren learn to their full potential? At this meeting (or a later one), you will be asked to sign off on a recommended plan. *Note:* You do not need to sign off until you agree with the plan. The initial IEP is planned for one year, at which point it will be reviewed and possibly revised if needed. (Only in drastic situations is it revisited before that one-year point.)

PREPARING FOR THE IEP MEETING

Think carefully about what questions you want to ask your grandchild's teacher (and others) and think about what relevant information you can provide. Bring notes, and plan to take notes at the meeting. Ideally, the meeting will have a collaborative tone, but be prepared to advocate for your grandchild if you feel that school staff members aren't seeing the whole picture. If possible, ask to see the child's testing results *before* the meeting, so you won't be confused or blindsided by test results or other data that is suddenly presented to you. This also may provide you with an opportunity to discuss the test results with a physician or outside educational consultant or advocate.

Bringing more voices into the meeting. You can bring along anyone you want with you to the meeting, whether it is a friend, your child's psychologist or psychiatrist, or others, such as a special education attorney or advocate. (However, it is best to notify the school district ahead of time if you plan to bring an attorney, because then the school may want to send its own attorney to such a meeting. If you do not notify the school in advance, it might reschedule the meeting.)

Realistically, you probably won't be able to get your child's psychiatrist or developmental pediatrician to an IEP meeting. But it could happen, especially if there is a pointed need for it. One mother felt her high school daughter's needs weren't being appreciated by school staff. The girl's psychiatrist was a new physician who hadn't built up a large caseload yet, and this doctor was willing to attend a follow-up IEP meeting with the mother. In this meeting, as the mother had feared, the staff announced that they were removing the girl from the special program that she was now in and planned to send her back to special education classes located in another public school. It was apparently all decided, and the mother said later that she felt like she was being ganged up on and it was helpless and a hopeless situation to protest. Then the child's psychiatrist said, "No. We are *not* going to do that. That is not in the girl's best interest and could cause great harm to her." The result: the girl stayed in her current placement, and other accommodations were put into place.

Here's another idea if you feel you need backup in a tricky situation: if your grandchild has a psychiatrist, psychologist, therapist, or pediatrician who agrees with you but cannot attend the IEP meeting, ask this mental health expert or doctor to participate by phone. If this is not possible, then ask that expert to write a letter in advance about what should be done, addressed to "To whom it may concern." Read the letter, and if you like it, make copies of the letter and bring both the original letter and the copies to the meeting. It's not as exciting as having the mental health expert or doctor being present in the room or on the phone, but it can be a daunting testimony and backup for you nonetheless. Indicate that you want this letter inserted into the official record of the IEP, and provide copies to everyone who attends the meeting. This tactic may increase your probability of obtaining what you believe your grandchild needs.

Getting help from others. There are books written about IEPs and Section 504 Plans, and there are also individuals willing to coach you before the IEP meeting occurs and even go with you, usually for a fee. Legal website Wrightslaw offers "Yellow Pages for Kids with Disabilities," which includes lists of educational consultants, tutors, advocates, and many other experts. For more information, go to www.yellowpagesforkids.com and click on your state on the map.

Talk to any of your friends who have had experience with IEPs, and gain information from their perspectives, whether they are grandparents or younger parents. Their situations may be very different from yours, but there's usually one little fact or helpful insight that you can glean from talking with others.

DURING THE IEP MEETING

The purpose of an initial IEP meeting is to determine if your grandchild needs additional services, and if so, to identify what they are and create a plan for the child. If there is agreement, then everyone signs the IEP and the plan will be carried forward for a year. During the meeting, which should include the teacher and may also include the guidance counselor, school psychologist, principal, and other individuals, ask questions politely, engage collaboratively with the school staff as much as possible, and avoid taking an adversarial tone. Take notes about what is said, because it's easy to forget important comments, and you may need to refer to your old notes at the next IEP meeting. If the teachers or other staff members show you test results and you don't understand them, ask for an explanation. Also, ask if these tests show that your grandchild is doing better or worse than last year (if the child was tested last year). How does your grandchild stand on these tests in comparison to other same-age children? In addition, are these other children from the school or are they drawn from the county, state, or another population? It helps to know if the child is being compared to others within the child's second-grade class or all second graders in the county, a much bigger population.

If staff members make a comment that you don't understand during the meeting, ask for clarification. For example, if they say that they can't tell if Johnny is really trying or if he just doesn't understand the material, ask why they think that. Find out if Johnny's behavior seems to be impeding his progress. An undiagnosed case of ADHD may be causing the child to underperform, and if ADHD is diagnosed, treatment may help Johnny do better in school.

If you do *not* agree with the plan the school has created, remember that you are not obligated to sign the plan. Another reason you may not wish to sign the plan is that further input may be needed from the primary care pediatrician, a developmental pediatrician, an educational consultant, a psychologist, or other expert.

Sample Dialogue at an IEP Meeting

In this sample dialogue, Grandma is advocating for her second-grader, Johnny, and she's thinking on her feet. Ideally, she would have asked to see Johnny's test results before the meeting, but she didn't. So she asks questions on the spot to help her interpret those results. Three people are in this meeting: Johnny's teacher, the school guidance counselor, and Grandma.

Teacher *(showing test results to Grandma):* We're here to see if Johnny needs some extra help in school. As you can see from these reports, Johnny is performing in the bottom 10 percent of second graders in reading.

Grandma *(looking at reports):* Do you mean he's in the bottom 10 percent of the children in his class?

Teacher: No, this is the bottom 10 percent of the second graders in the whole county.

Grandma: Was Johnny evaluated last year? And if he was, how did he do then?

Guidance counselor: Johnny was evaluated in first grade, and he did worse then. He was in the bottom 5 percent last year.

Grandma: So Johnny is still not doing great, but he's doing better than last year?

Guidance counselor: Yes, but we think Johnny still needs extra help, and he may need further testing. We are recommending an IQ test, an intelligence test, to see what his capabilities are.

Grandma: So, the intelligence test may show that Johnny is doing the best he can or it might show that he's smart enough to do better?

continued

Guidance counselor: Yes, that is what it will show.

Grandma: What do you think the result is likely to be? That Johnny is underperforming or doing about as well as he can?

Teacher: We don't know, but we think Johnny is smarter than he shows in reading. He has a pretty big vocabulary for a little guy, and he is very curious and asks a lot of questions.

Grandma: How is Johnny's behavior in school? Could he have something like ADHD?

Teacher: Yes, he could, and we would like your permission to test him for ADHD as well. I have to fill out a behavior form for that, and you also have to fill out a form. Shall we do that?

Grandma: Yes, let's do that. If Johnny has ADHD, does he need medicine?

Teacher: He might need medicine. Let's see if he might have it first, and we'll also need to get his pediatrician involved in the process.

Grandma: That's fine. What kind of help can you give Johnny in the meantime?

Teacher: We have been pulling Johnny out of class to get extra help with reading with two different teachers. Also, we strongly encourage you to have Johnny read at home every day and for you to read to him too.

Grandma: I can do that!

Possible accommodations to request during the IEP meeting. There are many different types of accommodations you may request during the IEP meeting to help your grandchild learn better. David Flink, author of *Thinking Differently: An Inspiring Guide for Parents of Children with Learning Disabilities,* says that it's important to tailor the accommodation to the child, because this is not a one-size-fits-all issue. He notes that giving extra time on tests is a very common accommodation. Others may include providing more frequent teacher feedback to the child, modified assignments, and the use of audiobooks or computers. But some common accommodations may not fit a particular child very well; for example, extra time on tests may translate into more time to be distracted rather than more time to concentrate on the test. Instead, extra breaks from the test or letting the child take a test in a room away from other students may be better for a child.[10]

Other examples of accommodations for learning disabilities provided by the National Center for Learning Disabilities include using large-print books, reducing the number of items on a line or on a page, giving the student directions orally rather than in writing, allowing the student to respond orally rather than in writing, and allowing responses to be conveyed through a computer.[11]

Working with the teachers and other school staff and offering your own input on how the child learns will help you come up with the best interventions and accommodations for your grandchild. Also, keep in mind that a child's needs may change over time and an accommodation that works well one year may need to be adapted or changed in a later school year.

Beyond Counseling: Other Therapists May Be Able to Help Your Grandchild

Who can help with learning disabilities? It depends on the type of disability, but often speech therapists can help with speaking problems, while occupational therapists can provide help if the problem is a motor skill, such as difficulty with handwriting. But before they can help, therapists have a series of tests that they perform with the child to try to determine the key problem and its extent. For example, a child may struggle with tying his shoes not because of a lack of fine motor skills but instead because no one has ever patiently taught him how. (The days when everyone knew how to tie their shoes by age five are long gone—possibly because of the popularity of shoes with Velcro fasteners.) For a school-age child to receive occupational therapy, the evaluation would have to reveal that the child has significant fine motor issues. It should also be noted that often children with learning disabilities have one or more other problems that can be addressed by therapists.

Dyslexia? You're in Good Company

Many bright and accomplished people have learned to overcome dyslexia, for example: [12]

- filmmaker Steven Spielberg
- actors Orlando Bloom, Tom Cruise, Whoopi Goldberg, Keira Knightley, and Keanu Reeves
- news anchor Anderson Cooper
- entrepreneurs Steve Jobs, co-founder of Apple, and Richard Branson of Virgin Galactic
- athlete Tim Tebow
- clothing designer Tommy Hilfiger

What Else Might Be Holding
My Grandchild Back?

Sometimes the problem may not be a learning disability. Something else may be going on with your grandchild instead, or in addition, making it tricky to figure out. So consider the full picture. For example, if a child is having trouble reading, she might have dyslexia. Or she's not getting enough sleep, making it hard for her to concentrate. Or it might be something else, like maybe she simply needs glasses. If your grandchild is squinting at her books or seems to struggle with seeing the words on a page, a visit to the optometrist or the ophthalmologist is warranted to rule out a correctable vision problem. (Of course, in addition, make sure that the child has annual physical examinations with her pediatrician to check for any readily identifiable problems that she may have and to keep up on needed immunizations.)

So it's not necessarily an either-or problem. Often children with one or more learning disabilities have additional problems. In fact, a learning disability often carries an increased risk for coordination disorders, ADHD, and other issues that need to be addressed.

There may also be other issues going on in the child's life, such as a developmental disorder or a psychiatric issue, which are subjects covered in chapter 9.

〉〉

PART 3

LEGAL AND FINANCIAL RESOURCES

USING THEM TO YOUR GRANDFAMILY'S ADVANTAGE

Do everything you can to keep the household stable. And never regard yourself as a second-class parent. You are more than good enough!

—*A parenting grandparent*

CHAPTER 7

Child Custody Issues

"I raised my two grandsons by myself for more than eight years, until they were ten and eleven years old, when the court made me send them to their father in another state," said Idaho grandmother Janice Ausburn. "Their parents were divorced, and I had only a power of attorney [document] signed by my daughter and me and notarized at the bank—that let me put the boys in school and take them to the doctor.

"But if I had known back then what I know now, I would have immediately gone for full court custody of the children after I first got them and when they were little. If you are in this situation yourself, you should seek an attorney and get custody immediately— don't lollygag! You don't know what might happen, and stability for a child is the most important thing there is." [1]

• • •

Janice Ausburn's story is true, and it's a cautionary tale for any grandfamily. You may think you have everything under control now and that you don't need any new legal status. You may be relying on a power of attorney document between you and the birth parent of your grandchild. But situations change, and sometimes people, including your own adult children, may behave in a manner you would never have predicted. This chapter is about your options for legal custody of grandchildren, ranging from power of attorney to guardianship and adoption.

Remember, every grandfamily is different, and knowledge is power! That's what this chapter is all about—empowering you.

See the sidebar on the next page that illustrates the some-times-thorny issues of child custody. This chapter will help you untangle those issues, plan for legal help, and take early action to promote the best options for your grandchildren's well-being. Don't wait! Educate yourself now.

Child Custody: Key Ideas, Terms, and Factors to Consider

Let's begin with an overview of some important ideas and legal terms by applying them to your own situation. Ask yourself these questions.

First, who has physical custody of your grandchildren—that is, who lives with them and cares for their daily needs? Let's assume they live with you, the grandparents. But who chose to place them there? If it was you, or the birth parents themselves, it's likely considered informal placement. But if it was a social service agency, an emergency court order, or a later court ruling, it's likely considered a kinship care or relative foster care arrangement. Either way, the parties involved may have differing opinions about the situation. Is it clearly temporary, clearly permanent, or uncertain? Those questions will play a role as you look ahead at your options.

Who has legal custody of the children now, and should it change? A legal custodian has the right to enroll the children at school, approve their medical care, declare them as dependents on tax returns, get their ears pierced, and so on. Birth parents generally have the legal right to make those choices, regardless of where the children live—even if they've been living else-where for years—unless legal custody has been granted to the

"Don't Lollygag!" A Grandmother Urges Early Action

Back in 2000, when Janice Ausburn's daughter and son-in-law got divorced, her daughter was awarded custody of their two young sons, with visitation rights granted to the father. Janice's daughter and the boys moved into Janice's home, while their father moved out of state. But in March 2001, her daughter moved out and the boys were left with Janice, who became their primary caregiver. For years, Janice raised her grandsons with very little involvement from their mother. Janice fully expected to raise the boys to adulthood. The father didn't visit the children at all for six of those years, although there were some phone calls between him and the boys.

In 2008, Janice was shocked to learn that the birth parents were surreptitiously planning to transfer the children to their father, who now wanted to raise them at his home in a distant state. In fact, the birth parents had gone to court to finalize the arrangement—without revealing to the court that the boys' grandmother was their primary caregiver and had been for years.

When Janice discovered what the parents had done, she immediately filed for custody, but, especially at this late date, her legal standing was limited. The district court awarded sole legal custody to the father and joint physical custody to the father and to Janice: he would keep parental rights and make decisions for the boys and the boys would live with him, but they would also spend six weeks with Janice every summer. The father appealed this decision, and the case ultimately ended up in the Idaho Supreme Court, which upheld the lower court decision in 2011. This custody case has been described in legal documents and articles for attorneys and is an important one regarding grandparent rights.[2]

grandparents. (But certain documents, such as power of attorney, can grant permission for others to make decisions in these areas—for a limited period of time or indefinitely.)

If there's been a termination of parental rights (TPR), who now legally holds those rights, either temporarily or permanently? It might be you, the grandparents; a state or county agency; or a court-appointed third-party guardian.

As you look ahead, what might serve the children best: a legal guardianship arrangement with you (with or without a time limit), adoption, or other options?

Although gaining physical custody can help resolve a crisis, it's often only the first step. Much as you may wish that the birth parents can someday care for their own children again, failing to pursue some form of legal custody can be a very dear mistake. Before we explore more about obtaining legal custody of your grandchildren, starting with understanding the various options, let's review the main ways in which grandchildren originally come to join their grandparents. Maybe your grandfamily has evolved and changed a lot since then, but that early history will often help determine the steps you'll need to take.

How Did the Child Come to Live with the Grandparents?

Custody options are partly shaped by the circumstances under which the child first came into the grandparents' care, which likely occurred in one of three ways: The child might have been placed with grandparents by a state or county agency. Or the grandparents sought emergency custody from the court. Or perhaps the birth parents voluntarily left the child with the grandparents. These circumstances shape the caregivers' legal options going forward, so let's look more closely at each scenario.

Do You Have a Voice in a Custody Dispute?
Check Your State's Laws

In child custody disputes, twenty states and the District of Columbia, listed here, give some degree of legal standing to grandparents who are informal primary caregivers to their grandchildren (as of early 2018).

Arkansas	Mississippi
California	New Hampshire
Delaware	New Jersey
District of Columbia	New York
Georgia	Oregon
Idaho	South Carolina
Indiana	Texas
Kentucky	Virginia
Maine	Washington
Massachusetts	West Virginia
Minnesota	

If your state is on the list, that's a plus. But even with that advantage, grandparents seeking custody may be stymied by problems such as birth parents who can't be found or who are unwilling or too impaired to give the state-required consent. If your state isn't on the list, you probably have no legal standing at all as a grandparent—unless you've taken legal action such as seeking temporary custody, guardianship, or adoption.[3] Either way, think soon about formalizing a new legal relationship with your grandchildren, if called for.

THE CHILD WAS PLACED WITH THE GRANDPARENT
BY A STATE OR COUNTY AGENCY.

In cases of neglect or abuse (physical or sexual), if the child has been made a ward of the court, then state or county caseworkers have thirty days by federal law to find family members—preferably in the same state—who are suitable and willing to raise the child. (A "ward of the court" is a person who is dependent on the court for judgments about issues such as where the child will live, what medical care may be received, and other decisions, depending on state law.) When the child is placed with relatives, the resulting arrangement is a form of foster care sometimes known as kinship care.

THE GRANDPARENT SOUGHT TEMPORARY EMERGENCY
CUSTODY BY COURT ORDER.

In another type of case, if the birth parents clearly cannot care for their child, a grandparent may seek temporary emergency custody from the court. This arrangement will usually have an expiration date of weeks, months, or some other period,

---

New Hampshire Law Paves the Way for Grandfamilies

If you live in New Hampshire, your position may be even stronger. In 2017, the state became the first to pass a law establishing legal preference for grandparents to become guardians of their grandchildren when the birth parents have substance use disorders. In addition, if the birth parents later wish to terminate an existing guardianship, they will have the burden of proof: they must offer compelling evidence to justify it. By signing a related bill, Governor Chris Sununu authorized a study to gather data on grandfamilies and identify the problems they face.[4]

---

depending on the state and on the court. To expedite the process, grandparents can hire an attorney to file for emergency legal custody—or they can do so on their own, unless state laws require representation by an attorney.

THE BIRTH PARENTS VOLUNTARILY PLACED THE CHILD
WITH THE GRANDPARENT.

You may have physical custody of your grandchild yet have no legal rights to custody whatsoever—like Janice Ausburn, the Idaho grandmother. At the very least, in such a situation, it's wise to ask the birth parents for a legal document with the effect of power of attorney, granting you consent to obtain medical care for the child, if needed, or to handle school-related issues.

In fact, power of attorney can play a crucial role in custody issues, so let's look at that option next.

Power of Attorney: How Can It Help, and What Are Its Limitations?

Power of attorney is a type of legal consent document that grants certain decision-making rights to another person. For a grandparent, having a birth parent sign a power of attorney document can be a huge help. Some states have specific forms that they recommend, and there may be different forms for medical or educational consent. These forms must be signed and dated by the custodial birth parent, and often they need to be notarized as well. (Most banks offer notary services at no cost to their customers.)

Colorado attorney Bonnie Saltzman recommends that, at a minimum, birth parents sign a power of attorney with any informal custody arrangement. Without one, she says, "Inevitably, the situation explodes and human services ends up getting involved. I advise [birth] parents to give the caretaker a formal

Limited Power of Attorney or give them temporary guardianship. Colorado actually has a Power of Attorney form on its judicial website that I recommend parents modify for their use."[5]

An important caution: power of attorney may be rescinded at any time and for any reason by the person granting it—in this case, the birth parent. Therefore, power of attorney does not provide a grandparent any protection against a parent who wants to regain custody of the child.

In some cases, grandparents *want* the birth parent to reassume parental responsibility when they're ready. But in others, the grandparents don't trust the birth parents' judgment of their own readiness, or they fear the birth parents may act out of spite. And unfortunately, in that case, a power of attorney offers no protection. If grandparents want to be sure the child will not be removed from their care by an unfit parent, they should obtain formal legal custody—not just rely on informal custody strengthened by a power of attorney document. It is best to consult with an experienced family law attorney to fully understand your options and how the process works in your state.

You Need a Will

Having a will does a huge favor to your family in the event of your death. And if you have legal custody of a child, particularly if you've adopted, it's a good idea to create a will that describes not only your desired financial arrangements but also your recommended plan for who should care for the child.

Your grandchild has a stake in both those areas: the financial as well as the caretaking. And that's true regardless of adoption status. If you haven't adopted your grandchild and you die "intestate"—without a will—then your assets likely will go to your adult children, and your grandchild will inherit nothing. If you *have* adopted and you die intestate, then your grandchild would share a portion of your assets with your (adult) children. But if those children object to that sharing, it could be a testy situation for your grandchild to face.

Whom would you like your grandchild to live with if you should die before the child reaches age eighteen? Discuss this possibility first with the people involved, and include that plan in your will. If that should come to pass, the judge may or may not accede to your wishes, but your wishes won't even be known unless your will names specific individuals to take over your job as parent. Without that direction, the courts will decide on their own. And the judge may not make the choice you would have made yourself.

How do you go about writing a will? You may be able to create your own by learning about the laws in your state and carefully complying with them. Some states have their statutes available on the internet. Nolo Press, which publishes books on legal topics for general readers, also offers WillMaker software and an Online Will service, as do many other trusted organizations (of course, do due diligence in researching these options). A better but more costly option is to hire a family law attorney to produce your will. Explore all these alternatives, and then choose one and proceed. Grandfamily dynamics can be complex when it comes to custody and more, so take this important step to protect the family you've worked so hard to bring together.

Understanding the Options:
Several Types of Legal Custody

We've already discussed the limitations of informal physical custody: the child lives with you, but you have no court-given rights or protections. So, as soon as possible, consider your options for a new legal role. These include temporary custody, fostering your grandchild in a kinship care arrangement, legal guardianship, and adoption. (See the chart "Options for Custody: Pros and Cons" for an overview.) Although adoption is the most comprehensive solution, it requires a high level of certainty and is usually the most time-consuming to achieve. So let's look at the other three first.

Temporary Legal Custody

To fill a short-term need, or when the duration of the need is uncertain, it may be wise to seek temporary legal custody, either from the birth parent or from the court, depending on the situation. The birth parent might be incapacitated for medical reasons. Or the parents might be arrested for a crime and held in jail indefinitely. Someone needs to take over the parenting of the child until the parents become available, and that person may well be you, the grandparent.

One option for a short-term, simple situation: your adult child simply gives you power of attorney to care for your grandchild. But many circumstances are more complex, and you might wish to make an emergency request to the court to grant you temporary legal custody, preferably with the help of a family law attorney. (If your adult child is hospitalized, a hospital social worker may be able to help you make that custody request.)

Note: If you take this action on your own, it's sometimes referred to as a "pro se custody" action, because custody is sought

Options for Custody: Pros and Cons

	Pros	Cons
Informal Physical Custody	• The child is safe with you. • If the parents' problems can be readily resolved, the child can easily be returned to them.	• You have no legal rights over the child. • The parents can take the child at any time and without notice. • It may be difficult to register the child for school or obtain routine medical treatment when needed.
Temporary Legal Custody	• The child is with you, not in foster care with strangers. • You know the child is safe.	• The child can be removed from your custody by a parent or the court, depending on who granted the temporary legal custody. • You will need permission to obtain medical care for the child, and it may be difficult to register the child for school, depending on state law.
Pro Se Custody (Custody obtained without legal assistance)	• You will not incur any legal fees. • In straightforward situations, filing for custody and/or representing yourself may be relatively easy.	• Family law is complicated, and it's easy to make mistakes without the help of an experienced attorney. • Errors made through pro se filing and self-representation could lead to the child's removal from your custody by the parent or the court at any time.

continued

	Pros	Cons
Legal Guardianship	• You don't need permission to take the child to the doctor or register the child for school. • You may make all decisions that a parent would make about the child.	• The parental rights are not terminated. • The guardianship can be overturned at a later point if the birth parents convince the court to do so. • You cannot change the child's name.
Adoption	• Your grandchild becomes your legal child and cannot be taken away from you. • You have all the rights and obligations of the birth parents. • You can change the child's name, if you wish.	• Requires termination of parental rights, which may be difficult to obtain. • Court-ordered child support from the parents will end, although arrears (past due payments) will still be owed (however, many parents fail to pay child support anyway).

without an attorney's help. Pro se custody comes with some potential drawbacks: see the "Options for Custody: Pros and Cons" chart.

Remember, temporary custody is best for a short-term situation. If the need to care for your grandchild continues, use the court system to seek a more permanent legal relationship, such as permanent guardianship or adoption.

What are the limitations of temporary custody? It can be rescinded, depending on the laws of your state and the type of agreement you have with the courts or the birth parents. For example, even if you have a notarized statement from the birth parent granting you temporary custody, the birth parent can cancel that agreement at any time. And even if the temporary

Keep a Log of Birth Parent Visits

How often does the birth parent visit the child at your home, and for how long? Keeping a log can help you provide evidence of a birth parent's positive efforts—or lack of them. If you have temporary or permanent custody of your grandchild (but have not adopted the child), start recording the date of each visit and the time the birth parent arrived and left. Record any scheduled visits ahead of time, and if the birth parent is a no-show, record that fact too. You may also request that the birth parent initial the log at each visit. If the parent refuses, initial it yourself. Ask again the next time and at every visit.

Why keep a log? As a document with relevant data—frequency of visits—it could be very helpful in court. If the birth parents visit very rarely and the caseworker or attorney shows the log to the judge, it may factor into the custody ruling. In contrast, if the birth parents have turned their lives around and are visiting frequently, the log could help support their case.

The log could look like the sample provided here, with just a few days shown. Ideally, each page has a line for each day of the month. If there are few visits, that will stand out. If there are many visits, that will also stand out.

Sample Visit Log for
[birth parent name] [month and year]

Date	Time Visit Started	Time Visit Ended	Birth parent's initials (on dates of visit)
September 15, 2018	6 p.m.	7:30 p.m.	XYZ
September 22, 2018	6:30 p.m.: scheduled, but no-show		
September 29, 2018	7 p.m.	7:15 p.m.	XYZ

custody is court-ordered, the birth parents can still request to have their children returned at any time—as long as that court order hasn't specified a duration for the temporary custody, six months, for example.

So temporary custody comes with some uncertainties. If you don't trust the birth parents' judgment, it may not be optimal. Some grandparents with temporary custody say they would have more peace of mind if the child had been placed with

When the Birth Parent Dies

If the birth parent dies and the other parent is unknown or unavailable, then the grandparents may initially seek temporary custody of the child because they need to act immediately, and then they may seek legal guardianship or adoption later. Unfortunately, this situation has grown more common because of overdose deaths, particularly from opioids and methamphetamine. And, when the pregnant birth mother has abused drugs or alcohol, or both, the child was likely exposed to those substances in utero. Grandparents who are considering providing long-term care for such a child—or, especially, considering adopting the child—should consult with medical professionals first. It's helpful not only to understand the risks of parenting children who were exposed to substances in utero but also to learn what resources and interventions could help the children reach their full potential.

Whatever the reason for a birth parent's death, the grieving parents of the adult child are left to pick up the pieces of their own lives as well as the lives of their grandchildren. Reach out for support and accept all help offered to you. See appendix 1 for resources.

them by an agency. Why? Because in that case, the caseworker and the judge (not the birth parents) would decide if and when the child should return to the birth parents. That, too, has its dangers. Caseworkers and judges have been known to return grandchildren to birth parents who are still unfit. But that is still one step safer than unstable birth parents making the decision themselves, possibly on a whim.

The bottom line is that if you think your grandchild needs to stay with you long term, then you should seek a more permanent option, such as a permanent guardianship or even adoption. But first let's discuss the fostering or kinship care role.

Fostering Your Grandchild

Generally, a grandparent is asked to assume the fostering role by a state or county agency such as child protective services. If a child is removed from a home because of abuse or neglect, social services staff often first seek a nearby relative to care for the child until the situation with the parent is resolved. If no such relatives are found, the agency may place the child with nonrelative adults who are unknown to the child.

But in nearly all cases, the goal of state and county social services is reunification—for the child to be returned to the birth parents. If you, as a grandparent, foster your grandchild, you are not in a parental relationship, technically speaking, but in a kinship relationship to the child. In this case, the state or county is the temporary "parent" and can overrule your decisions if caseworkers wish to do so. The state or county can also decide to remove the child from your custody.

Relatives should be considered first as foster caregivers

If a child is placed in foster care, relatives of the child who may be willing to care for the child must be sought within thirty days of placement, according to the federal Fostering Connections to Success and Increasing Adoptions Act of 2008. Relatives of the child include adults who are grandparents, aunts, uncles, cousins, and so forth, the kinship care discussed in chapter 1. Sometimes the child is placed with relatives in another state, abiding by the Interstate Compact on the Placement of Children, or ICPC. Gaining custody of a child from another state can be very complicated—but grandparents seeking safety for their grandchild can be very persistent people.

Considering the Children in Foster Care

Let's take a look at the numbers of children in foster care in the United States as of 2016. That year, 273,539 children entered foster care, up from 251,352 in 2012.[6]

- Placement: About a third (32 percent) were placed with their relatives, 45 percent with nonrelatives, and the rest in pre-adoptive homes, group homes, institutions, and other living situations.

- Goal: The planned goal in more than half the cases (55 percent) was to reunite the child with the birth parent or main caregivers, and the goal was adoption in 26 percent of the cases. Other goals included guardianship, long-term foster care, and living with other relatives.

- Racial background: Most of the foster children (44 percent) were white, followed by children who were black (23 percent) and Hispanic (21 percent).

- Reason for placement: The largest portion (61 percent) were removed from the home because of neglect, followed by 34 percent who were removed because of parental drug addiction, a stand-alone category now.[7]

A relative who agrees to care for the child may be required to complete foster parent classes, or these classes may be waived for relatives, depending on state law. For example, in 2016 the State of Virginia allowed local social services boards to waive some foster home approval standards.[8] The "kinship" relatives must have a safety check of their home, and they may also undergo fingerprinting and background checks for criminal activity. If you received a minor traffic ticket ten years ago, no problem. But if you have any record of violence, alcohol or other drug issues, this is likely to be a problem for you in receiving approval to become a foster parent.

Researching Your State's Laws

State laws for relatives who want to serve as foster parents vary widely. Here are some resources:

- The FindLaw website offers links to various child custody forms in each state:
    http://files.findlaw.com/pdf/family/family.findlaw.com_child-custody_child-custody-forms-by-state.pdf

- Search for information about state laws at this site:
    www.grandfamilies.org/State-Fact-Sheets

- Many states have their own resources.
    For example, the TexasLawHelp.org site offers information on grandparents' rights at http://texaslawhelp.org/resource/grandparents-rights, and a toll-free number also offers free advice to Texans over age sixty and to anyone receiving Medicare at (800) 622-2520.

- For state-specific information, visit the "Foster Care Licensing" section of the website Grandfamilies.org:
    http://grandfamilies.org/Topics/Foster-Care-Licensing/Foster-Care-Licensing-Summary-Analysis

---

If safety issues arise during the home check, solutions can often be found. In one court case, a grandmother's home had been deemed unacceptable for her two young grandchildren because her stairways had no railings. Installing railings would take time, and the situation was urgent. The caseworker said the children were not safe around their birth mother. The judge asked the worker if the birth mother's *home* was safe. The caseworker said it was, whereupon the judge asked the mother and her daughter if they would be willing to swap homes until the stair railings were fixed. They *were* willing, the agency agreed, and the children were placed with the grandmother after the home swap. This was a case of a very creative judge.

Legal Guardianship

When you are the legal guardian to your grandchildren, you have the right to register them for school, take them to the doctor's office, and act as a parent in virtually every way. But there's a catch: the court can overturn your guardianship if it should wish to do so. For example, if the birth parent petitions the court to regain custody of the children, and the court looks into the request and decides to comply, then you, the grandparent, will lose custody.

Remember this: when you, the grandparent, are granted legal guardianship of your grandchild by the court, the birth parents' rights are simply being suspended, not terminated. Their rights can be reactivated by the court in the future. Even in the distant future.[9]

The state may recognize several types of guardianships, such as a temporary or "standby" guardianship in the event the child needs a grandparent (or other relative) to step up and stand in for the parent. A temporary guardianship may be time limited

From Grandparent to Guardian

"It broke our hearts when our son got a twenty-year sentence," said Kevin. "And on top of that, our grandson's mother, Jandy, could not separate herself from drugs. That was last winter, and my wife and I were taking care of our baby grandson Calvin at our home: informal physical custody. One weekend, Jandy called to tell us to return him immediately because her social worker was insisting on it. We took Cal to her home, met the social worker, and requested a meeting with agency staff, which was granted the next day.

"To our surprise, we walked into a full-scale meeting at the agency office that included several supervisors and other staff. We were told Jandy had tested positive for drugs too many times, and they were going to remove Cal from her home. My wife and I immediately said we would like to take him. After a meeting among the staff, they agreed, and now we have legal guardianship. This was of course after lots of paperwork, jumping through bureaucratic hoops, and taking some legal steps. It's been a year, and Jandy is still on drugs, living who knows where. But as guardians, we can make all the choices Calvin will need, for health care, school, you name it.

"Here's what's uncertain, though. What if our son gets early release? He'll still have parental rights. If he gets out of prison when Calvin's a teenager and he can convince the court, our guardianship could be rescinded. But that's a lot of 'ifs.' Doesn't it seem unlikely—especially since we're the only family Cal has ever known?"

in some states. In contrast, a permanent guardianship stays in effect unless or until it is terminated by the court. Notwithstanding its limitations, a court-ordered guardianship protects the guardians and children from irrational and impulsive behavior by the child's parents. It can be set aside only by the court, usually only after the court has held a hearing and considered the child's best interests.

Note that if you pursue legal guardianship while the child is already in your care as a foster child, you may be eligible for monthly payments when the guardianship is granted. See appendix 3 for information on the states that offer these subsidized guardianships.

Adoption

To keep your grandchild as a member of your immediate family, the most enduring move is, of course, to adopt. Adoption is the lawful transfer of parental rights and responsibilities for another person—usually under eighteen[10]—from the birth parents (or from one birth parent, if the other one is deceased or unknown) to the new parent or parents. When you adopt your grandchild, you become the adoptive parent, whether your grandchild still calls you "Grandma" or "Grandpa" or not.

But before you can adopt your grandchild, if the parents are still living, they must either willingly consent to the adoption or have their parental rights terminated by a judge in court, depending on the laws of your state. Some states have a two-step process that involves first terminating parental rights and then granting the adoption. In other states, a final decree of adoption automatically terminates parental rights, with no need for a separate step.

Laying the Groundwork to Adopt Your Grandchild

You've decided you want to adopt. How you lay the groundwork depends on your current situation: Are you caring for the child in a fostering or kinship care role? Or have you been caring for the child informally, with no legal or social service intervention? Or are you already a legal guardian? Let's look at each of those scenarios.

FROM FOSTER CARE TO ADOPTION

When a child is in foster care—even in grandparental foster care—the federal Adoption and Safe Families Act applies. This law requires that children who have been in foster care for at least fifteen of the last twenty-two months must either be returned to their parents or the parental rights must be terminated—unless the court has a specific reason for upholding them. Parental rights are usually not terminated unless someone else (like you!) wishes to adopt the child. In general, courts consider parents as the best custody option for children, including abused or neglected children, which is why it is difficult to terminate parental rights.

Despite the law, some cases drag on for years before a permanent plan is made for the child.

FROM INFORMAL CARE TO ADOPTION

Imagine you've been caring for your grandson at home, with no involvement from child service agencies at all. If you're ready to adopt, your first choice may be to ask the parents if they are willing to let you adopt him. If they are both willing to voluntarily relinquish their parental rights, the adoption process may be fairly straightforward and affordable. Still, you will need to hire an attorney to help you accomplish this goal. You may (or may not) be required to have a home study, depending on state law.

What is a home study? Contrary to popular belief, it's more than just a safety check of your living quarters. It also includes a review of all household members, including a check with the local, state, and federal authorities for any criminal behavior. You may be required to hire an agency that has experience performing home studies, such as an adoption agency.

FROM LEGAL GUARDIANSHIP TO ADOPTION

If you are the child's legal guardian and now want to adopt the child, then a court case will need to be initiated. Depending on the state where you live, you may need a full home study or, at least, a criminal background check, performed by a state agency or an adoption agency. A full home study involves a caseworker checking your home, your health, and other aspects of your life to ensure the child would be safe and happy if adopted by you. If the birth parents willingly give up their parental rights, the path is much simpler than if the birth parents wish to fight. When the birth parents wish to retain their parental rights, the legal rights of the birth parents must be involuntarily terminated by a court for you to adopt. Basically, you must prove to a judge that the birth parents are unfit parents or have abandoned the child. The grounds to dispense with a parent's consent to adoption varies from state to state. You need to consult an experienced adoption attorney in your state to understand what must be proven and your chances of success. If the child is in the foster care system, the state may prove this for you, at no cost to you. If the child is *not* in the foster care system, legal proceedings, which you are financing, can be prohibitively expensive. Getting a reliable assessment of the likelihood of success and the total cost to litigate should be considered before deciding to pursue an adoption in which a birth parent or parents will not consent or whose parental rights have not been terminated.

Agreements with the Birth Parents before Adoption

When you adopt a child, you become the legal parent, with all of a parent's rights and obligations. In most situations—we'll look at the exception in a moment—the birth parent or parents and the adoptive parents must all "consent" to the adoption unconditionally, with no strings attached. The birth parents can't tell you, for example, "We'll let you adopt Nina as long as we can see her every weekend." Nor can you tell the birth parents, "If you let us adopt Wally, we'll bring him to visit you during school vacations." Whether you continue to let the birth parents see the child will be entirely up to you. You can make any arrangements you wish to, *after* the adoption. If you have already promised some visits to the birth parents, that's fine. But under that scenario, the adoption consent would not become unconditional until all promised visitation had taken place. The court will not grant an adoption that is conditioned upon future events (such as visits). Courts have usually ruled in those situations that the adoption consent is not valid because it was not unconditionally given.

Here's the exception: some states have statutes governing postadoption contact agreements (PACAs). In these states, the birth parents and adoptive parents may, before the adoption is official, make an agreement regarding birth parent contact with the child. But even in those states that allow for PACAs, courts tend to favor the adoptive parents. For example, a court will not overturn an adoption if the adoptive parents fail to abide by the terms of the PACA, although it might hold the adoptive parents in contempt of court. Even if your state law permits a PACA, don't agree to anything you are uneasy about. For example, a request for daily phone calls or visits is an unreasonable request that you should not agree to. However, if you are open to weekly or monthly visits, that may be worth considering.

WHAT IS "TERMINATION OF PARENTAL RIGHTS"?

Whether voluntary or involuntary, the termination of parental rights means that the birth parents essentially stop being the child's parents in the eyes of the law. In a voluntary termination, they willingly agree to give up their rights as parents of a child in court and in front of a judge. (That's what Avery's parents did in the story that follows.) If a court appearance is required, the judge may ask the birth parents if they are sure that they really

---

An "Open Adoption" That Works

Avery was adopted by her grandparents when she was five years old. She had been living with them since she was an infant because her birth parents had issues with emotional immaturity. They have grown up a lot in these five years, and both now have jobs and support themselves. But they also agreed that Avery should stay with her grandparents, and they voluntarily gave up their parental rights in court so Avery could be adopted.

Avery frequently sees her birth parents (who are no longer a couple), and she also sees their other children on many weekends and all major holidays. "It's sort of like an open adoption," said Avery's grandmother Annette. "Avery understands that her birth parents couldn't handle raising a child when she was a baby, but we're always open to questions." Annette says that many people adopt children who may wonder where their birth parents are, what they look like, and if they have brothers and sisters. Avery doesn't have that issue.

---

want to give up their parental rights, giving them one more chance to change their minds before signing the termination document. In other cases, the birth parents' attorneys may arrange for the consent to TPR.

In an involuntary termination, the birth parents do *not* agree to give up their parental rights, and a court takes away those rights against their wishes. A TPR hearing will be held in court and the judge may decide, based on extensive evidence, that the birth parents have failed to fulfill their parental responsibilities or are otherwise unfit to parent, to involuntarily terminate the rights of the parents. Note that an involuntary TPR process may take years to finalize. The birth parents may file multiple appeals, appeals that child services officials often take seriously because reunification of the birth family is usually given a very high priority. Some grandparents say it took three or four years—or longer—before they were finally able to adopt their grandchildren. TPR is generally irrevocable, sometimes after a waiting period.

Who can seek an involuntary TPR? In general, it is the state that does so, under these conditions: the child is in foster care, the state agency has decided that adoption is in the child's best interests, and someone is waiting in the wings, ready to adopt. But it's also possible for a private attorney to seek an involuntary TPR in front of a judge on behalf of the grandparents, though this can be quite costly. The lawyer must prove to the judge not only that it is in the child's best interests to be adopted but also that there are grounds to terminate parental rights because of the birth parents' unfitness to be parents.

The court will not terminate the birth parents' parental rights simply because you would be a "better" parent. If that were the standard, nearly all parents would be in jeopardy because, arguably, there is always someone who would be better parents: more experienced, skilled, and so on.

Whether the termination is voluntary or involuntary, grandparents can have strong mixed emotions on the day of the TPR hearing. On the one hand, they are thrilled that the way has been cleared for them to adopt their grandchildren and keep them safe. On the other hand, they are sad that this action had to be taken. Emotions can run so strong that many grandparents delay taking TPR action for as long as possible, even years, hoping the birth parents will somehow and someday recover from their issues of substance use, mental health disorder, criminal behavior, or whatever problems led to their failures as parents.

The Adoption Process
State adoption laws and procedures vary. But in general, adoption entails a home study with several visits and requirements, consideration of a name change for the child, and finally, on adoption day, a court hearing.

THE HOME STUDY
Some people who plan to adopt are terrified of the first home study visit. What are "they" looking for? What can you do to make sure your home passes inspection? Relax. The caseworkers simply want to see if your home is safe and comfortable for a child. A little clutter won't matter—but nobody believes that. So go ahead and make your home sparkling clean and try not to agonize too much.

In fact, the caseworkers are more interested in talking with you about your commitment to the children and the children's relationship to you and other family members. The caseworker will observe what you say as well as your actions. Don't worry if the children come into the house muddy and puddle-splattered from outdoor play. The caseworker will observe the children and whether they seem generally happy and healthy.

You may be asked to respond to essay questions in writing about your family and why you want to adopt. Answer honestly but positively. For example, one grandmother was asked what she'd like to change about her husband, and she responded that sometimes he was too nice and didn't say what he really wanted. As a flaw, that one is pretty minor!

The home study usually also includes a criminal record check and may require you to be fingerprinted at your local police station. You may have to provide financial information to show that you can support the child as well as medical reports to confirm that you have a normal life expectancy. It may feel like too much information gathering, but really, it's due diligence.

"The home study was nerve-racking, mostly because we were nervous wrecks," said Lorna, now adoptive mom to three grandsons. "And there was so much paperwork involved, I couldn't believe it! But it was all worth it to adopt our beautiful grandchildren."

THE CHILD'S NAME

You'll also be asked if you want to change all or part of your grandchildren's names. If the children are old enough, and you wish to, discuss possible name changes with them in advance. If the children's last name is different from yours, you may wish to legally change it—or you may not. Most people are less likely to change their grandchildren's first names, although some do make such changes. Some parents keep their grandchildren's middle names for some continuity, but you can change their entire name if you wish to. Let your caseworker know about the name change that you are seeking.

ADOPTION DAY: WHAT TO EXPECT AT THE HEARING

The adoption hearing is more or less a formality, albeit a necessary one; by this time, the adoption is pretty much a done deal. You will usually need an attorney to represent you, and if you are adopting your grandchild from foster care, the state may reimburse you for a portion of the attorney fees.

Find out first what is expected of you, and share with the child as appropriate; the child is usually welcome to come with you to the hearing and may be required to be present. The hearing may be held in the judge's chambers or in open court. You may be sworn in and must promise to tell the truth. Your attorney and the judge may each ask you several questions, which you will answer in a straightforward manner.

After the hearing, you will be given some preliminary papers granting your adoption; later you will receive the formal adoption decree. After making a few copies of the decree (to share with doctors, dentists, and others who may request it), place the original with your other very important papers. The court clerk will send a record of adoption to the state board of health or other agency so you will be issued a new birth certificate showing you as the parent and, if there's been a name change, the child's postadoption name.

Next on the agenda: Go celebrate! Throw an adoption party and invite the people you care about and who care about you. Share some special food, perhaps a cake, and make it a wonderful day for everyone. Because it *is* a wonderful day.

Adoption Day

Patty was thrilled: adoption day had finally come after three years of raising her grandsons. Patty's daughter Tanya, their birth mother, had fought the idea of adoption from the start. But Tanya was in and out of jail constantly and refused to comply with the case plan provisions that social services had created for her. The boys' fathers were unknown, so she had no backup. She hadn't held a job for more than a few days, she had declined parenting classes, and she refused free counseling sessions.

Finally, the judge decided that Tanya had had every opportunity. He terminated her parental rights, even though the caseworkers wanted to give her another six months to follow her case plan. The judge disagreed. Declaring the involuntary TPR, he said the children needed the security of a real home—which Patty had been giving them, based on his thorough review of the case.

There had been some tough times: Tanya had often told her mother she'd never forgive her for "stealing the children." But Patty had decided that her priority now was to give her grandchildren the best lives she could provide for them—no matter what.

And now here she was, in the courtroom, standing next to the smiling judge and the beaming boys, getting their picture taken. Patty promised the judge—and herself—that she would do her absolute best for the children.

244 I THE GRANDFAMILY GUIDEBOOK

AFTER THE ADOPTION

Now that the child is legally yours, you'll have a few important tasks to accomplish. For example, if you have decided to change the child's legal name, you'll also need to notify the Social Security Administration after you've received the child's postadoption birth certificate. You might also wish to request a new Social Security number, if you're concerned that the birth parents or others might try to use the original number to apply for benefits to which they're no longer entitled.

Tell your friends and relatives about the adoption. Most will be happy for you and your grandchild, but there may be some who do not like the idea, for their own reasons. Too bad! You're doing what's best for your family.

»

CHAPTER 8

Grandfamily Finance

When Bethany joined a local grandparent support group, she discovered that her three-year-old granddaughter Lizzie was eligible for Medicaid, the federal insurance program that covers many medical expenses. Bethany learned from her new friends that in a grandfamily like hers, the family income didn't "count" in determining eligibility. Lizzie could be a one-person case, and she had no income, so she was definitely eligible. What a relief! Lizzie had frequent ear infections and ongoing asthma, and sometimes the doctor and medication bills were pricey. Bethany filled out the necessary forms right away.

• • •

Most grandparents haven't budgeted for raising a second family. They might be living on a fixed income or earning just enough to make ends meet. Or maybe they're making a good income— but still, raising kids is expensive, probably more so than it was the first time around. Food, clothing, and school needs. Medical and dental care, and maybe prescription medicines. Counseling services for any or all of you and perhaps attorney fees. Daycare and babysitters when they're young. Boy, does it add up.

The good news is, financial help is available from a surprisingly wide range of sources: county, state, and federal. Are you thinking that if such resources were out there, you'd already know about them? Lots of grandparents think so at first. But wouldn't it be nice to be proven wrong in this case? Check out this overview of what you might be eligible for:

- Some resources come in the form of a **monthly check,** as with foster care payments, a guardianship or adoption subsidy, or child support received from the birth parents through a state agency.

- Other resources help you **reduce your expenses,** such as the Supplemental Nutrition Assistance Program (SNAP), formerly known as food stamps; other programs reduce your costs for child care or home heating fuel by paying the provider directly.

- Other programs offer **no-cost benefits** to those eligible. Examples:

  - Medicaid, a federal health insurance program for children and adults

  - free school lunch programs for children receiving Medicaid

  - Head Start, an educational program for children ages three to five (and Early Head Start for those even younger)

- If you adopt, you may be eligible for a **tax credit**: a one-time credit on your income taxes for expenses you incurred in the adoption or a one-time credit for adopting a child with special needs, whether you incurred any expenses or not.

Let's take a closer look at the specifics of some of these programs.

Use Your Resources!
Survey Shows Underuse of Programs
Benefiting Grandfamilies

American grandparents raising their grandchildren could be making much better use of the financial programs and benefits available to them. Of the more than seven hundred respondents to the Adesman Grandfamily Study in 2016, a surprisingly low fraction were using these benefits. For example:

- Only 35 percent received Medicaid benefits for the child: full coverage for the child's medical, dental, and prescription drug expenses.

- Only 21 percent received payments from social service agencies—the monthly payments made to grandparents in the foster parent or kinship care role.

- Only 17 percent received child-only TANF benefits, the monthly payments offered by the Temporary Assistance for Needy Families program. (And, as an additional value, TANF almost always adds child-only Medicaid to the package.)

- Only 16 percent used SNAP, the food-stamp benefit known as the Supplemental Nutritional Assistance Program.

If you've never applied for such benefits, hesitate no more. Use the resources in this chapter to check your eligibility. Then make use of them, for the good of your whole grandfamily.

Practical Help from Federal, State, and County Resources

"I'm not interested in those benefits. I'll provide for the kids myself without taking charity."

"My mother never applied for welfare, even after my dad died. I'll stand on my own two feet, like she did."

"There's too much red tape! Who knows if my grandfamily will even be eligible?"

Do you recognize those lines of thinking? If so, please think again. Raising a child is very expensive today. Because you're not the birth parent, you are not legally responsible for paying the costs of raising this child—unless you adopt, that is. (And even if you do adopt, you may be eligible for an adoption subsidy from the state.) By making use of the financial resources available to you, you can worry less about your future—and the future of your grandchildren. There's a lot to consider, whether you're raising your grandchild temporarily or permanently.

As to the red tape, you might be pleasantly surprised. Yes, you'll fill out application forms, but some states have "kinship navigator programs" to help grandparents and other relatives identify and apply for their state's financial and medical aid programs. Which states? See appendix 2 for a list of kinship navigator programs.

Programs That Provide Financial Assistance or Reduce Costs

Name of Program	Pays you directly?	Reduces your costs, rather than paying you?	Who may be eligible	Agency that runs program
Temporary Assistance to Needy Families (TANF)	Yes	No	Grandparents with custody of grandchildren	State or county social services
Foster care payments	Yes	No	Grandparents granted custody of grandchildren by state or county social services	State or county social services
Kinship care payments	Yes	No	Grandparents granted custody of grandchildren by state or county social services	State or county social services
Guardian subsidy	Yes	No	Grandparents who were given legal guardianship through the courts, as administered by state or county social services	State or county social services
Adoption subsidy	Yes	No	Grandparents who adopted their grand-children through state or county social services	State or county social services

continued

Name of Program	Pays you directly?	Reduces your costs, rather than paying you?	Who may be eligible	Agency that runs program
Supplemental Nutrition Assistance Program (SNAP), formerly known as the Food Stamp Program (FSP)	No	Yes	Individuals with low household income	State or county social services
Medicaid	No	Yes	Grandchildren with low or no income or assets in the custody of their grandparents	State or county social services
Free lunch program	No	Yes	Grandchildren with low or no income or who are receiving Medicaid	State or county social services
Head Start and Early Head Start	No	Yes *Limits need for child care*	Grandchildren who are in foster care; provides care primarily for children ages three to five years, although Early Head Start provides care for infants and toddlers	Local Head Start office
Child care assistance	No *Child care facility receives payment*	Yes	Grandparents who work and are income eligible	State or county social services

Name of Program	Pays you directly?	Reduces your costs, rather than paying you?	Who may be eligible	Agency that runs program
Low Income Home Energy Assistance Program (LIHEAP)	No *Utility company receives payment*	Yes	Grandparents who are income eligible	State agency
Social Security payment for children of retired adults	Yes	No	Grandparents who are retired and receiving monthly payments from the Social Security Administration	Social Security Administration
Supplemental Security Insurance (SSI)	Yes	No	Children who are severely disabled with cerebral palsy, epilepsy, and other disorders	Social Security Administration
IRS tax credits * *Reduces taxes or may provide payment if grandparents adopt a child with special needs from state foster care (see IRS Tax Topic 607 or check IRS Form 8839)*	It depends*	Yes	Grandparents who adopt their grandchildren	Internal Revenue Service
Special Supplemental Nutrition Program for Women, Infants, and Children (WIC)	No	Yes *Provides food or checks, cash-value vouchers, or debit cards*	Grandparents with children under age five	State agency

Cash Benefits: Programs That Make Direct Financial Payments

Let's start with the programs that provide actual monetary payments. On the chart shown here, they're the ones with a "Yes" in the second column: they make direct payments to you. Keep in mind that although you receive the check, the eligible person is the actual child. As the payee, you receive the check or other benefit because you are the child's caregiver and responsible for managing the money.

Temporary Assistance to Needy Families (TANF): "Child-Only" Payments

Often called TANF (pronounced "tan-if"), Temporary Assistance to Needy Families is a federal and state program that offers monthly payments to low-income families and children. You may not regard your family as needy, but don't let that word stop you; raising a grandchild is a big financial commitment. And "child-only" TANF benefits usually bring Medicaid coverage for the child—medical, dental, and prescription insurance— which is a big plus.[1]

TANF is a money payment program that was established in 1996 to replace Aid to Families with Dependent Children, or AFDC. Here we're discussing "child-only" TANF cases. That is, we assume that the adults in your household aren't eligible for payments themselves; it's the presence of the child that creates the need, and the adult files for the benefit on the child's behalf. Grandfamilies fall mostly in the first of three main "child-only" TANF categories:

- children who live with their relatives
- children of parents who receive Supplemental Security Income (SSI)

- US-born minor children whose immigration status makes their parents ineligible for TANF benefits[2]

How generous are TANF payments? Not very, in terms of actual cash. They are probably lower than the monthly foster care payments you'd receive for caring for your grandchild within that system or the subsidized guardianship payments some states offer to legal guardians. But remember to factor in the child's Medicaid enrollment, which comes along with child-only TANF. That's a very valuable benefit when you consider children's typical medical, dental, and prescription expenses.

Some researchers have found that more than 40 percent of all TANF cases in the United States are child-only, with no adult recipients. Yet child-only TANF payments are very underutilized, according to experts.[3] In the Adesman Grandfamily Study, only 17 percent of respondents said they received TANF for their grandchildren, and 20 percent said they did not know if they qualified. In addition, 5 percent said they did qualify but did not receive TANF—it is unknown why they didn't receive the benefit.

State eligibility requirements vary widely. For example:

- In some states, the grandparent must be a legal guardian.
- A few states consider the grandparents' income in determining eligibility.[4] If that income is low enough, the grandparents themselves may be eligible for a TANF monthly payment too.
- Some states place time limitations on collecting TANF benefits; many states have a four- or five-year cap for single parents.

- Some states require grandparents seeking child-only
  TANF to also seek child support from the birth parents.
  For some grandparents, the family dynamics might make
  that difficult.

Contact the agency that administers TANF in your state and find out the eligibility requirements. And, as with most government agencies, be prepared to fill out many forms. *Tip:* if you're filling out a hard-copy form, experts recommend writing "Child Only" or "Payee Only" at the top of the application form, clarifying that you're applying only on the child's behalf. Also, if your application is denied, appeal it. Explain your reasons for appeal, such as that you are seeking child-only TANF.

See appendix 3 for state-by-state information on payment amounts, information provided by the North American Council on Adoptable Children and published with that organization's permission.

Sometimes TANF is called by other names by a state, but the key principle—financial support for a child in need—is the same.

Payments for Foster Care or Kinship Care

Have your grandchildren been placed with you by the state or county because of abuse or neglect? If so, you may be eligible for monthly foster care payments. Some states call them kinship care payments if they are made to a child's caregiving relative. (You may also be eligible for TANF, but you cannot receive both, and TANF payments are likely to be smaller dollar amounts.)

Again, state systems vary. In some states, kinship care payments are lower than the amounts paid to nonrelatives who are foster parents. Some grandparents find that aggravating, especially when they're on fixed incomes themselves. Many states require grandparents to qualify as foster care parents, and in that case, you should be eligible to receive the same amount as other foster parents, although in some cases, grandparents may be paid at a lower rate. These payments are based on the number of foster children in your home, their ages, and other criteria.

Ask your caseworker how to apply for foster care benefits. In Dr. Adesman's Grandfamily Study, about one in five grandparents (21 percent) reported that they received payments from child services agencies. This low percentage may suggest that many of the children were placed with the grandparents by the birth parents, rather than through a child services system.

When you apply for foster care payments or kinship care benefits, the state or county may require you to seek child support from your grandchild's birth parents. This is a key reason that some grandparents do *not* seek any financial benefits—they do not wish to pursue child support from the birth parents, whether they feel they don't need it or they anticipate a negative reaction. But if you must apply (or you wish to apply) for child support from the birth parents, ask a caseworker to direct you to the right state agency for that. Each state has its own agency that handles child support. Don't worry if you don't know where the birth parents are living. In most cases, the state agency can find the birth parents through various agencies such as the Social Security Administration (if the birth parents have jobs) or other agencies. According to the National Conference of State Legislatures, child support may represent up to 40 percent of the income of poor custodial families.[5] Of course, you need not be "poor" to qualify for child support, because it is a general presumption that parents should support their children, whether in their custody or not.

Applying for child support from the birth parents won't cost you any money but will require you to fill out many forms. However, the real problem is likely to occur when your grandchild's parents discover that they are expected to pay child support. They may be upset and send some nasty comments your way, both in and out of the courtroom.

Guardianship Assistance Programs (GAP)

Are you a permanent legal guardian to your grandchildren? If you were appointed guardian by the court while your grandchild was in the foster care system, placed within your home for at least six months, you may become eligible to receive monthly subsidized legal guardianship payments.[6]

The point of subsidized guardianship is to offer stable support for children who have a close, loving relationship with their grandparents but for whom adoption doesn't seem like the best option. For example, the grandparents may believe that at some future point, the birth parents may be able to parent the children again.

Not all states have these Guardianship Assistance Programs (also known as GAP). The federal government makes them optional to states, and states with GAP have their own criteria for them. Subsidized guardianship programs are rarely, if ever, taxed by the federal government.[7] In addition, states may also reimburse grandparents for legal or other onetime expenses incurred to obtain the guardianship, up to a limit of about $2,000.[8] When the grandparents receive a GAP payment, the child is automatically eligible for Medicaid.[9]

A few states with subsidized guardianship programs may consider the child's income or other family income in determining eligibility. Check with your caseworker to determine how to apply for a GAP subsidy.

These payments may last until the child is eighteen (or sometimes older, such as age nineteen or twenty-one), depending on the state.[10] See appendix 3 for states that offer such payments.

Social Security Benefits for Retired Grandparents Who Adopt

Are you already retired and receiving Social Security payments? If so, and you've adopted your grandchild, you may be eligible to receive an additional monthly sum on the child's behalf, payable to you. Contact the Social Security Administration for details. You will need to provide verification of your relationship, such as a copy of the adoption decree. This benefit is not taxable.

Adoption Subsidies

If you've adopted your grandchild from within the foster care system, you're likely eligible for a monthly adoption subsidy, if your state has such a program. According to data from the Department of Health and Human Services, 92 percent of the 57,208 children adopted from foster care in 2016 were paired with an adoption subsidy.[11] These nontaxable payments are based on state adoption assistance programs. The amount varies widely from state to state (and sometimes from county to county), often scaling up with the age of the child and usually ending at eighteen.[12] The range is generally from several hundred dollars to a thousand dollars or more per month. As shown in appendix 3, Alaska had the highest adoption subsidy at $1,590 per month, Utah the lowest at $187. Keep in mind that these rates are subject to change but probably will not decrease.

Supplemental Security Insurance for Disabled Children and Adolescents

Do your grandchildren have a physical or mental impairment that will severely limit their functionality for at least a year?

If so, they may be eligible for a monthly payment through the Supplemental Security Insurance program, administered by the federal Social Security Administration.[13] This nontaxable benefit is paid to an adult caregiver for use on the child's behalf, and a child eligible for SSI is automatically also eligible for Medicaid. For a list of disorders covered, visit the "Childhood Listings"

Some Benefits Are Tied to Other Benefits

In some cases, eligibility for one benefit also makes you eligible for another. For example:

- If your grandchildren are eligible to receive state TANF or SSI program benefits through the Social Security Administration, then they are also eligible for state Medicaid.

- Further, if they are eligible for Medicaid, they may also be eligible for the free lunch program in school.

- Children receiving Medicaid may be eligible for other programs, such as child care subsidies paid directly to the facility.

Don't assume you'll be told when one program is linked to another. One grandmother declined the school free lunch program for years, although her grandson was on Medicaid, because she had assumed her family's income was too high. Eventually she was told that she would need to write a letter turning down the free lunch program for her grandson if she didn't want to receive it. That sounded silly to the grandmother, so she accepted the program benefits, now realizing that her grandson had been eligible all along. She wished she'd asked about eligibility earlier, instead of assuming that her income was too high.

page of the SSA's "Disability Evaluation" section: www.ssa.gov /disability/professionals/bluebook/ChildhoodListings.htm. You can also download a fact sheet as a PDF: www.ssa.gov/disability /Documents/Factsheet-CHLD.pdf.

To apply for SSI, you'll need to submit numerous forms and supporting documentation; some people seek help from an attorney for SSI applications.

Non-Money Benefits

Rather than cash payments, some programs provide services and other benefits for your grandfamily: Medicaid health care coverage for the child, help with grocery and home heating expenses, and day care and other child care programs, for example.

Child-Only Medicaid

Child-only Medicaid is government-funded health insurance for children, covering medical care, prescriptions, dental care, and other expenses, depending on the state. As noted earlier, it's a benefit that usually accompanies child-only TANF payments, but you can also apply for it separately, outside of TANF. In Dr. Adesman's study, slightly more than a third (35 percent) of the grandparents received Medicaid benefits for their grandchildren.

Not all pediatricians accept Medicaid, nor do many specialists, such as pediatric cardiologists. This means you may have to travel farther if the child needs to see a doctor who takes Medicaid. Most teaching hospitals associated with a medical school accept Medicaid, as do most major hospitals.

To learn more about Medicaid or low-cost health insurance, visit the Insure Kids Now website and use the interactive map: www.insurekidsnow.gov/.

State Programs and Benefits for Grandparents:
A Valuable Online Resource

To learn more about your state's benefits and programs, visit the "State Fact Sheets" page of the Grandfamilies.org website: www.grandfamilies.org/State-Fact-Sheets/. This site was jointly produced by Generations United, the Brookdale Foundation, American Association of Retired Persons (AARP), the American Bar Association Center on Children and the Law, Casey Family Programs, ChildFocus, Child Trends, the Children's Defense Fund, and the Dave Thomas Foundation for Adoption. We strongly recommend using this valuable resource!

Supplemental Nutrition Assistance Program, or SNAP

Although many people still refer to it by its former name, the Food Stamp Program, this federal and state program is named the Supplemental Nutrition Assistance Program, or SNAP. (Some states use a different name, such as the Florida Food Assistance Program or the New Hampshire Food Stamp Program.) Recipients can buy groceries for a reduced price using a special card that resembles a debit card. SNAP covers food items only, not body care items (toothpaste, toilet paper, diapers) or over-the-counter medications such as acetaminophen.

If you apply for SNAP, you need to know that your entire household income factors into your eligibility, meaning the income of everyone who lives in the home, whether they are related or not.

Of respondents to the Adesman Grandfamily Study, only 16 percent said that they received SNAP, while another 16 percent said they did not know if they qualified for it. Another 3 percent believed they were eligible but said they were not receiving it. Sometimes people may qualify for benefits but they do not apply for them, whether from not wishing to apply for government assistance or for other reasons.

Women, Infants, and Children (WIC) Program

Supporting children from birth until the age of five, the Special Supplemental Nutrition Program for Women, Infants, and Children provides nutritional screening and food assistance. WIC helps with infant formula—which can be pricey—and a broad array of other food items, such as milk and cheese. There are some income eligibility limits, but they may not be as stringent as with programs such as SNAP (food stamps). Grandparents raising babies or young children who are eligible for child-only TANF are also eligible for WIC. Learn more at the WIC website: www.fns.usda.gov/wic.

The Head Start Program

Your three- to five-year-old grandchildren may be eligible for free preschool and other assistance through your state's Head Start program. In fact, children are automatically eligible if they are in the foster care system, whether foster-parented by their grandparents or others.[14] Head Start is designed to help preschool children from low-income households. The Early Head Start program provides care for infants and toddlers up to age three years. Openings for the program may be very limited, but you may be able to get your grandchild on the waiting list. Income eligibility is based on the guidelines found on this page of the US Department of Health & Human Services website: https://aspe.hhs.gov/poverty-guidelines.

For more information and to find the administrative office nearest to you, go to the main Head Start website: www.acf.hhs.gov/ohs. You may also call for more information at this toll-free number: (866) 763-6481.

Free School Lunch Program

If your grandchildren receive Medicaid and are in public school, then they are automatically eligible for free school lunch. You will likely have to fill out forms when the children first enter school, but you need not reapply if they stay in the same school system. A school lunch costs a few dollars a day, and that amount adds up over time, so it's a good benefit. Your grandchildren may also receive free breakfast in public school as well. Some cities and counties offer summer day camp discounts to children on the free lunch program. You may need a letter from the school to provide verification to the day camp director.

Child Care Benefits

Child care can be very pricey, but grandparents who are raising their grandchildren and are also still working may qualify for some child care financial assistance from the state. That's particularly likely when the state or county child services department was the placing agency for the child. Another possibility: your child's school may have an after-school child care program for which the state would provide partial payments. The money is paid directly to the child care facility, and you pay the balance. Ask your caseworker for more information.

Many states have their own programs, administered by various agencies. In Montana, where an estimated 6,600 grandparents are raising their grandchildren, the Child Care for Working Caretaker Relatives Program helps pay for after-school child care while a grandparent continues to work.[15] In Arizona, where more than 76,000 children are being raised by relatives, the Department of Child Safety will pay for part-time or full-time child care if the caregiver is working or attending school. (Arizona's Department of Economic Security, Child

Care Administration determines the eligibility.)[16] In Oregon, where more than 51,000 relatives are raising children, working grandparents may be eligible for a child care subsidy through the Employment-Related Day Care program.[17]

To find affordable child care in your area, visit the Child Care Aware website at www.childcareaware.org, or call (800) 424-2246. The website also has an interactive map: www.child-careaware.org/resources/map.

Low-Income Heating and Energy Assistance

Wherever you live, you need energy in the form of electricity, gas, or other fuels, and your family may be eligible for heating or cooling assistance through the Low Income Home Energy Assistance program (LIHEAP). This is not a cash payment to you; instead, the program pays your utility company directly, thus reducing your bill. Keep in mind that air conditioning is no luxury if you live in states such as Arizona or Florida, just as families in chillier states need heating in the icy winters. To find out if you may be income eligible for the program in your state, visit the LIHEAP website: www.acf.hhs.gov/ocs/liheap-state-and-territory-contact-listing. Not everyone who applies to the program will be accepted, even if you do meet income requirements, but if you are not accepted the first time you apply, reapply later and you may be accepted at that time.

Other Benefits

Special situations may qualify you for some additional benefits, like the ones listed here.

Special-Needs Adoption Tax Credit

If you adopt your special-needs grandchild from the foster care system, you may be eligible for an adoption tax credit through the

Internal Revenue Service (IRS—3966). For adoptions in 2017, the maximum and onetime adoption tax credit was $13,570 per child.[18] (This benefit is reduced if you have claimed adoption expenses on prior tax returns. Also, this benefit begins to phase out for households with a modified adjusted gross income greater [MAGI] than $203,540 and is completely phased out for households with a MAGI greater than $243,540.) Thus, if you adopted two children with special needs in 2017 and your MAGI was less than $203,540, you may have been entitled to a one-time tax credit of up to $27,140. Note that the income limits for years after 2018 may change somewhat; however, most readers are unlikely to have adjusted gross incomes in the quarter-million dollar range. *Note:* You need not have expended this amount; the tax credit is not meant as a reimbursement for expenses. If you are receiving an adoption subsidy, this alone may be proof that the child has special needs. As mentioned elsewhere, 92 percent of children adopted from state or county foster care systems come with an adoption subsidy. For more information, go to this site online at the Internal Revenue Service: www.irs.gov /taxtopics/tc607.

Other Adoption Tax Credits

If you incur expenses in adopting your grandchild, such as legal fees, travel costs, or other related expenses, you may be able to use these expenses as a tax credit under the federal Adoption and Safe Families Act. You will need to itemize these expenses on IRS Form 8839, Qualified Adoption Expenses.[19]

Death Benefits for Children of Deceased Parents

Unfortunately, with the opioid addiction crisis today, far too many children are losing their parents to fatal drug overdoses. Whatever the reason for their parent's death, children may be

A Hot Topic at Tax Filing Time:
Who Claims the Children?

If you have been supporting your grandchildren for at least six months of the past calendar year, you may be able to claim them as dependents on your annual income tax return. Consult with an accountant or tax specialist.

Of course, a kinder approach would be to check with the child's birth parents first, when possible, to determine if they have claimed the child as a deduction for the past year. If they have, they may encounter legal problems related to tax fraud. To avoid such a problem, they could file an amended tax return. If you don't want to argue with the birth parents, you could warn them that next year, you *will* claim a deduction for the child. This income tax deduction is a major bone of contention among some families.

You might also consult with an Internal Revenue Service representative to find out whether the child's birth parents have filed for the same tax benefits—even though the child may have not lived with them for months or sometimes years. Not only is this unreasonable, but it also could be fraudulent. So consult an IRS rep *before* filing your claim, both to get needed information and to avoid any legal or tax confusion down the road.

Of course, if you have adopted your grandchildren, you are legally entitled to claim them as dependents.

You may be able to claim the Earned Income Credit on your federal income tax return if your income is less than a certain amount and you are raising one or more grandchildren. This benefit also applies when the child was placed with the grandparents by the foster care system. It may help you to reduce your taxes significantly and could also increase your income tax refund, according to information in IRS Publication 596 on the Earned Income Credit.[20]

eligible for benefits on their parent's behalf through the Social Security Administration or the parent's former employer. If the deceased parent was a retired veteran or disabled military veteran, ask the US Department of Veterans Affairs about survivor benefits. You may also wish to contact the local branch of the American Legion or the Disabled American Veterans for help in applying for such benefits for your grandchild.

The parent may also have had an employer-based life insurance policy naming the child as the beneficiary. If you have the opportunity to review the parent's important documents, you may find such a life insurance policy, or you might contact the human resources department of the parent's employer. If you do locate such a policy and your grandchild is a beneficiary, be sure to file a claim on behalf of your grandchild.

Don't leave yourself without financial resources. Especially if you are living on a fixed income, don't hesitate to apply for benefits for your grandchild. Your money may vanish more quickly than you think: the needs range from diapers, formula, toys, clothes, and shoes for infants and toddlers to backpacks, school supplies, and clothes for older children—not to mention ongoing expenses such as food and day care. Apply proudly for financial assistance if your grandchildren will benefit from it.

Finding Financial Aid: Three Resources

More help is at hand too. These three major resources can assist you in identifying and applying for financial benefits for you and your grandchildren: the federal Social Security Administration, your state social services offices, and grandparent support groups on every level, from local to national—with many online as well.

Social Security Administration

With offices throughout the country, the Social Security Administration is a large federal organization that determines eligibility and administers a variety of benefits programs for individuals throughout the United States and its territories. These include retirement benefits, health benefits through Medicare—not to be confused with Medicaid—and disability benefits. The SSA also issues Social Security numbers to children at birth as well as to other people. If you lose your Social Security card, you may apply for a new one through the SSA, although you will need specific types of documentation to verify your identity. *Note:* If you apply for benefits through the SSA on behalf of your grandchild, you will need to provide extensive documentation and can expect to wait months to learn if your claim has been accepted.

State Social Services

Called various names in different states, state social services offices administer programs such as TANF, Medicaid, and SNAP. Often individuals can apply online, although supporting documentation will be required at some point. In most states, social services organizations are located throughout the state in counties they serve.

Local and National Support Groups

Support groups provide fellowship as well as a wealth of information and experience. Those for grandparents include local groups, national support organizations, and online groups. All are focused on providing advice and assistance to grandparents and other relatives who are raising grandchildren. See appendix 1 for a partial listing of such groups.

When you contact a group for information, also ask for recommendations on other groups in your area that might help with that topic. Take notes and keep those notes! They may be very valuable to you later.

〉〉

PART 4

HEALTHY IN
BODY AND MIND

Do your best and don't blame yourself when troubles arise.

—*A parenting grandparent*

CHAPTER 9

Understanding Children's Behavioral Disorders and Mental Health

Connie and Hal, in their early sixties, are raising their two grand-children, who were recently placed with them after the horrifying discovery of abuse and neglect in their birth parents' home. Jared, age nine, has autism spectrum disorder, and Diane, age three, is an extremely anxious child who clings to Grandma Connie at every oppor-tunity. At home and in familiar settings, both children behave normally. But Jared often has disruptive and aggressive outbursts when the family is out in public, especially when he's unclear on what is expected or plans are changed even slightly. Diane doesn't have meltdowns, but she cringes if a stranger even looks at her.

It became clear the children needed extra help when one day Connie made an unscheduled stop at the supermarket on her way home with the children. Jared had a meltdown in the store, and Diane began sobbing hysterically. When other shoppers started looking sus-piciously at Connie, she burst into tears herself, shocking both children into silence.

After that experience, Connie asked her social services caseworker for help. The worker helped her arrange family therapy sessions so she and Hal could better integrate with the two troubled children. Connie also found a therapist who provided applied behavioral analysis (ABA) to help Jared deal with his autistic behaviors and another therapist who offered play therapy for Diane to help her deal with her issues. This sounds like a lot of therapy—and it is—but it was very helpful to the family.

• • •

Do you sometimes wonder whether your grandchild might have a diagnosable problem—maybe an emotional or behavior disorder? Many caretaking grandparents do. In fact, research has found that children in grandfamilies have a higher rate of psychological problems than those in intact families.[1] That higher rate isn't *because* of you, grandparent—it's despite you! But that research finding makes sense, because these grandchildren may have been exposed to abuse, neglect, and other trauma in their original homes. These factors—and sometimes prenatal drug or alcohol exposure—can lead to a wide range of symptoms, from anxiety to hyperactivity to depression or aggressive behaviors. You can help the children manage their disorders as best they can. Therapy and sometimes medications are options for many problems you'll learn about in this chapter.

But first the problem needs to be diagnosed. To do that, we suggest you observe your child in your daily interactions and look for any behavior patterns. You might want to write them down so you can describe these problems accurately to mental health professionals. It's easy to forget key points when you are in the doctor's office. Ask your grandchild's teacher for feedback about the child's behavior at school too.

Of course, plenty of children without traumatic backgrounds have these disorders, but early trauma can exacerbate them. In this chapter, we'll discuss these common issues:

- attention-deficit/hyperactivity disorder (ADHD sometimes still referred to as attention-deficit disorder, or ADD)

- autism spectrum disorder

- depression

- anxiety

- post-traumatic stress disorder

- disruptive behavior disorders, including oppositional defiant disorder (ODD) and conduct disorder (CD)

- prenatal substance exposure problems, such as fetal alcohol spectrum disorder (FASD)

We'll look at each in turn, discussing symptoms, diagnosis, and treatment. As you lead your children through this process, remember that you are their advocate. Forge ahead: make appointments, ask questions, and make sure you understand the answers (don't be shy). Ask your grandchildren how they feel, and keep an open mind. It's hard to predict the future, but do your best in the present. You have lots of company.

Understanding
Attention-Deficit/Hyperactivity Disorder

It might be more common than you think: In the United States, about 11 percent of all children ages four to seventeen have been diagnosed with ADHD, as of 2011—6.4 million children in all. And that number had jumped about 30 percent in the previous eight years.[2] It may be even greater today. (It's uncertain whether the increase is due to a higher incidence of ADHD or to more frequent assessment and diagnosis. Likely it is both.)

Symptoms and Signs

In general, a child with ADHD is distractible, forgetful, frequently loses items, and has difficulty staying on task. Some seem to be constantly in motion, as if driven by a motor, and may have trouble waiting their turn in line; they may often interrupt other people, including adults.[3] These impulsive symptoms show up in at least two settings, such as home and school.

Children with ADHD are usually diagnosed before the age of twelve. Many have other diagnoses too, such as depression or anxiety, auditory processing disorders (trouble making sense of what is heard in one or both ears), and learning disabilities. They're also more likely to be diagnosed with disruptive disorders, discussed later in this chapter.[4]

Could your grandchild have ADHD? If the child's attention span, behavior, or academic functioning gives you reason to wonder, talk with your pediatrician. If that doctor isn't comfortable assessing the child for ADHD, ask for a referral to a specialist, such as a developmental pediatrician, child neurologist, or child psychiatrist. Physicians experienced with ADHD will check (or should check) that the child's true underlying problem isn't depression, a learning disability, or another psychological issue. Note that although clinical psychologists aren't MDs, they are able to diagnose ADHD, but in most states, they cannot prescribe medication.

To help with the evaluation, the child's teacher is usually asked to fill out a rating scale on the child's behavior. You, the grandparent, will also be asked to fill out another scale regarding the child's behavior. The evaluator may ask to see the child's report cards and the results of any psychoeducational tests done at school or elsewhere. The professionals will use all this feedback and their own observations of the child to determine whether ADHD is present. The good news is that children with ADHD often qualify for classroom accommodations and educational services in the public school system.

Treatment Options

About half of all children diagnosed with ADHD are eventually treated with psychiatric medications. But especially for children under six, behavioral therapy may be a better first choice. This therapy rewards positive behavior while discouraging problem behavior, often by ignoring it.[5] For children between the ages of six and eleven, the American Academy of Pediatrics recommends behavior therapy and medication as two separate first-line treatment options. But families may find it difficult to afford behavioral therapy. Not surprisingly, only about half of children between the ages of two and five diagnosed with ADHD receive any form of psychotherapy.[6]

Especially for older children, medications can ease symptoms remarkably well. Although it might seem counterintuitive to treat hyperactivity with a stimulant, these medications have calming and focusing effects on children with ADHD. Additionally, three non-stimulant medications have been approved by the US Food and Drug Administration (FDA) for treatment of ADHD: atomoxetine (Strattera), extended-release guanfacine (Intuniv), and extended-release clonidine (Kapvay). For further information on medication, we recommend *ADHD: Parents Medication Guide*. Download it at the American Academy of Child & Adolescent Psychiatry website:

www.aacap.org/App_Themes/AACAP/Docs/resource_centers
/adhd/adhd_parents_medication_guide_201305.pdf.

Autism Spectrum Disorder: What Is It?

A developmental disorder with a wide range of variability, autism spectrum disorder includes the word "spectrum" in its name for just that reason: its signs include a spectrum of behaviors and symptoms, and each of them may range from mild to severe.

Children with ASD may be very bright or may have limited intelligence. They may display repetitive behaviors, have trouble communicating and socializing appropriately with others, and show other symptoms that impede functioning at home, school, work, or in other environments. Symptoms are often seen before a child is two years old, though most are not diagnosed until age four or later.

About one in every sixty-eight children in the United States is diagnosed with ASD, boys about five times more often than girls, although the reason for that is unknown.[7] The CDC says up to 12 percent of children with ASD were born too early, too small, or by a Cesarean delivery.[8]

You may have heard some widely spread but false information linking childhood vaccines to ASD. It's a myth, but it has caused many caregivers to be fearful about immunizations. Ignore this misinformation, which unfortunately persists in some circles, especially online. Children should be immunized on the schedule recommended by the American Academy of Pediatrics.[9] For more details, read the article "Vaccine Safety: Examine the Evidence," found at the AAP's Healthy Children website:

www.healthychildren.org/English/safety-prevention
/immunizations/Pages/Vaccine-Studies-Examine-the
-Evidence.aspx.

Some pediatricians deviate from AAP guidelines, so ask if your doctor follows the immunization schedule that AAP recommends. You can check guidelines yourself at this website:

www.aap.org/en-us/advocacy-and-policy/aap-health-initiatives
/immunizations/Pages/Immunization-Schedule.aspx.

Reactive Attachment Disorder

A rare disorder can sometimes develop in children who have been severely abused, neglected, or otherwise traumatized in infancy or their very early years, especially if they've had many changes in caregivers and environments. Children with reactive attachment disorder have not developed a bond with a parent or parental figure. Here are some of the key features of this disorder:

- rarely or minimally seeking comfort when distressed
- rarely or minimally responding to comfort when distressed
- minimal social and emotional responses to other people

Some of these features may also be seen in children with depressive disorders, intellectual disabilities, and with autism spectrum disorder, so care must be taken in making this diagnosis, especially because children with RAD may also have cognitive and language delays.[10] Not only can RAD be tricky to diagnose, but it is also considered very difficult to treat, and experts disagree on treatments.

Here are some online resources for more information and support:

- RAD support group on Facebook: www.facebook.com /Reactive-Attachment-Disorder-Support-Group-100800666670238/
- Association for Training on Trauma and Attachment in Children: www.attach.org
- Parenting Children and Teens with Reactive Attachment Disorder: www.reactiveattachment-disorder.com /2009/07/parenting-children-with-reactive.html

Symptoms and Signs

Children with ASD may fail to make eye contact with others, may not respond when called by name, and often have trouble interpreting social cues such as body language. For example, most children know that a person with a frowning face and with arms placed across their chest is not happy, but children with autism may not know this intuitively. They must learn the meanings of such expressions and gestures deliberately and learn to pay attention so they'll recognize them in others. Children with autism may also engage in repetitive behaviors such as flapping their hands, spinning, rocking, or jumping, and sometimes they exhibit self-harming habits such as banging their head against a wall.

About a third of children with autism behave seemingly "normal" for the first two years of life. Then they regress dramatically in their interactions and language skills, at which point they may be diagnosed with ASD.[11] The reasons for these regressions are unknown.

ASD has indicators in early childhood and in school-age children. But don't jump to conclusions—some of these signs also show up in a child with a developmental language disorder or an intellectual disability. Here are some early indicators of ASD, as listed by the National Institute of Neurological Disorders and Stroke:

- lack of babbling or pointing by age one
- no use of single words by sixteen months or two-word phrases by age two
- no response to the child's name, despite normal responses to other sounds
- loss of language or social skills that were previously acquired

- poor eye contact
- excessive lining up of toys or arranging other objects
- no smiling or social responsiveness

Later indicators of ASD include the following:

- an impaired ability to make friends with peers
- impaired ability to start or continue a conversation with others
- absence or impairment of imaginative and social play
- repetitive or unusual use of language
- abnormally intense or focused interest
- preoccupation with certain objects or subjects
- inflexible adherence to specific rituals or routines[12]

Early Intervention and Other Help

Some good news: free state-funded child evaluations are available for ASD or other developmental disorders, such as delays in speaking, crawling, or walking. You can call and request an early intervention assessment for children from birth to age three. For children three and older, the school district can provide assistance, even though most children don't begin school until age five. You should also discuss your concerns with your pediatrician. To learn more, read Barbara Smith's article "Does Your Child Need Early Intervention?" at the Parents.com website:

www.parents.com/toddlers-preschoolers/development /problems/early-intervention/.

Treatment Options

Treatment for children with ASD typically includes specialized psychological and educational approaches. These children also often qualify for occupational and speech-language therapy. Depending on severity, ASD can be treated with therapy, medication, or both. One common therapeutic approach, applied behavioral therapy, helps boost positive behaviors— such as greeting a caregiver at the beginning of the day—and helps minimize negative ones, such as unprovoked shrieking and running around a room. Depending on the age of the child, this therapy is often provided at the child's home or at school by ABA therapy specialists. Other proven treatment approaches include the Early Start Denver Model and Pivotal Response Treatment.[13] Medications may also be used for children with ASD who display significant symptoms of aggression, deliberate self-harm, temper tantrums, and quickly changing moods that have not improved with nonmedical approaches. Some medications are approved to treat aggression among children and adolescents with ASD, such as the antipsychotic medication risperidone (Risperdal).[14]

If the ASD is very mild, the child may be able to lead a relatively normal life, with or without assistance. (In some cases, mild ASD can even resolve itself with time.) If the ASD is moderate to severe, however, the child may always need assistance and may not be able to live independently as an adult.

When Your Grandchild May Be Depressed

Clinical, or serious, depression sometimes does occur in children. In fact, about 5 percent of all children and adolescents suffer from it, and the risk can be higher when children have other problems, such as ADHD, disruptive disorders, learning disorders, or anxiety.[15] Clinical depression may not be a problem you have dealt with before, but it's very important to get help for a depressed child or adolescent, just as you would make

Grandfamily Relationships Can Suffer
from Children's Early Trauma

If you sometimes clash with your grandchild, you're not alone. Research shows that relationships between adults and children in a grandfamily can be more conflicted if the child has had early exposure to violence or other trauma. Events such as birth complications, domestic violence, major accidents, or frequent moves are all risk factors for childhood psychological problems such as ADHD, oppositional defiant disorder, and conduct disorder,[16] and many children have experienced traumatic events prior to living with their grandparents. In a recent study of 251 grandfamilies, researchers found high rates of trauma with these children:

- Thirty percent had been emotionally or psychologically abused or maltreated.
- Twenty-seven percent had been neglected.
- Twenty-seven percent had former caregivers who were impaired by alcohol or drugs.
- Twenty-four percent had previously been exposed to domestic violence.
- Twenty-one percent had suffered a traumatic loss such as sudden death or separation.
- Twenty-one percent had been physically abused.
- Eighteen percent had been sexually abused or assaulted.[17]

In all, 181 of the 251 children had experienced at least one type of trauma; some had experienced more than one. A child's previous exposure to direct personal violence (such as sexual abuse, physical abuse, assault, or kidnapping) was predictive for more conflict with the grandparents, as was a greater number of traumatic events. The authors said the

continued

> trauma created a ripple effect, with a child's distress affecting the child-grandparent relationship: "Cumulative trauma exposure has a destabilizing effect on intra- and interpersonal functioning of the adults and children in these families, regardless of gender, race or age of the grandparent."[18]
>
> Traumatized children are likely to need extra help to support their psychological health and resilience, including individual or family counseling.

sure a child received help for serious physical ailments, such as a broken leg, bronchitis, or an ear infection. Start with your pediatrician, explaining that you think your grandchild may be depressed and why. The pediatrician may provide names of mental health professionals who treat children, such as child psychologists and psychiatrists. The doctor may find that the child has another medical or psychiatric problem instead—but you won't know until you ask for help.

Again, it's the long-term effects of the children's past experiences that may cause depression. In addition, as many grandparents can attest, there may be emotionally fraught aspects of grandfamily life—such as birth parent visits—that can end in moodiness or tears, perhaps exacerbating the depressive tendency.

Symptoms and Signs

Some indicators of childhood depression are crying, decreased interest in past activities, heightened irritability, poor concentration, marked changes in eating or sleeping patterns, talking about running away from home, low energy, extreme sensitivity, recurrent complaints of stomachaches or headaches, and social isolation. Be prepared to investigate further if you notice even one of these signs.[19] Some depressed children or teens may harm themselves. In extreme cases, they may become suicidal and you'll need to seek emergency treatment for them. If you are concerned that your grandchild may be suicidal, take the child to the emergency room at a children's hospital, if one is available, or to any hospital emergency room. Learn more about childhood depression at the National Institute of Mental Health website:

www.nimh.nih.gov/health/topics/depression/depression
-in-children-and-adolescents.shtml/american.

Treatment Options

Depression can be addressed through psychotherapy, medications, and lifestyle changes. Often a combination of two or more of these approaches is most effective.

PSYCHOTHERAPY

Depression in children and adolescents is generally treated with psychotherapy such as cognitive-behavioral therapy. With CBT, children learn to recognize and challenge their own negative thoughts and beliefs. For example, a child might assume that she somehow caused all the problems in her home of origin. (Many children blame themselves for their living situations—they think if only they had been smarter or better behaved, the problem would not have occurred.) The therapist can gently help a child recognize that assumption, then realize that it's not true.

For younger children, play therapy may help them express their true feelings as they play with toys and talk to them in the presence of a therapist trained in play therapy.

ANTIDEPRESSANT MEDICATIONS

In some cases, antidepressant medications are prescribed. The drugs known as selective serotonin reuptake inhibitors, or SSRIs, include fluoxetine (Prozac) and fluvoxamine (Luvox), which are FDA-approved for the treatment of depression in children ages eight years and older. In addition, the SSRI escitalopram (Lexapro) is approved for ages twelve to seventeen. Several older tricyclic antidepressants may also be used in children, including imipramine (Tofranil), desipramine (Norpramin), and amitriptyline (Elavil).

An antidepressant packaged for children or young adults includes a prominent warning that these drugs may increase the risk for suicidal behavior. Some adults worry about this "black box warning." But physicians are well aware of the risks and benefits of these drugs, and when they prescribe antidepressants, they believe that the benefits far outweigh the risks. According to the National Institute of Mental Health, a review of nearly 2,200 children treated with antidepressants revealed that none of the children died from suicide, although about 4 percent experienced suicidal thinking or behavior.[20] Still, remember that depressed children and adolescents who are *not* treated with antidepressants may be at risk for suicidal behavior as well.

Also note that while some medications in the SSRI class are approved by the FDA to treat childhood depression, others like sertraline (Zoloft) are not. But with regard to SSRIs, their similarities are greater than their differences, and it is reasonable for physicians to prescribe a specific SSRI to treat depression, even if it's not FDA-approved for use in children.

LIFESTYLE CHANGES

If your grandchildren suffer from depression, increased outdoor play, exercise, and participation in fun activities may help to elevate their mood, but never assume that these activities alone will be sufficient to treat their depression or that therapy or medications will not be needed.

Coping with Your Grandchild's Anxiety

Anxiety can take a variety of forms, from generalized anxiety to specific phobias. Let's look at some ways to identify and address them.

Symptoms and Signs

It's not surprising for children from unstable homes to develop anxiety. Children with generalized anxiety disorder might frequently worry about bad but vague things that could happen to them, and, understandably, they might have trouble paying attention in the classroom or elsewhere. Childhood anxiety might look like fear or worry to others, but it might also look like irritability and anger. Some children in a chronic state of anxiety have sleep difficulties, headaches, fatigue, or stomachaches. It's important to note that children with anxiety don't always cry somewhere off in a corner; they sometimes behave aggressively and act out.

Children with an anxiety disorder known as a phobia may have an extreme fear of a particular situation, such as doctor or dentist visits, or a particular object or aspect of their environment, such as dogs or spiders. Some young children may have separation issues that make them anxious about going to school.[21]

How can you help? Your grandchildren may tell you about their fears, or they might not tell you but exhibit symptoms of fears. For example, a child who is afraid of dogs may cringe, cry, and either freeze or run away every time she sees a dog. Watch your grandchildren and notice what seems to prompt their fear or anxiety. Offer reassurance or help them express how they feel and what prompts those feelings.

Treatment Options

Although antianxiety medications are available for children, it's best to avoid defaulting to those first. Instead, consider psychotherapy. Remember, when you're looking for a therapist, be patient and persistent. As with therapists for adults, success is partly a matter of good matchmaking and "chemistry." And, as with treatment for depression, CBT therapy, play therapy, or other approaches may help your grandchild. Exposure therapy may be used with phobias, where the child progressively learns to tolerate distress and deal with irrational fears while feeling safe.

Post-traumatic Stress Disorder in Children

Anyone who has witnessed or experienced extreme violence or other threats is at risk for developing post-traumatic stress disorder. And that includes children: read about Corey in the sidebar "The Aftermath of Abuse."

Trauma can result from either abuse or neglect. For a young child, neglect—being denied basic needs such as safety, shelter, food, or water—can mean the difference between life and death. It also carries the trauma of being ignored and uncared for. Verbal or physical abuse, while traumatic, at least involves attention from another—horrific as that attention may be. Both neglect and abuse are setups for possible PTSD.

Signs and Symptoms

Children who have directly experienced a traumatic event or seen others, such as a parent or caregiver, go through trauma may experience recurrent memories of the event—whether it was a single event or a repeated one—and may have dreams related to it. Sometimes, during waking hours, they feel like they are re-experiencing it again, in real time. Understandably, they may actively seek to avoid any reminders of it, including certain people, places, activities, or physical objects. In addition, traumatized children may become socially withdrawn or, alternatively, they may exhibit unwarranted anger toward others. They may also have an exaggerated startle response and be hypervigilant and watchful for danger. Having trouble falling asleep or staying asleep are other common symptoms of PTSD in children. Developmental regression such as bedwetting is also possible. Although the diagnosis is often made months after the traumatic event, sometimes years pass before the person is diagnosed.

PTSD must be distinguished from depression, anxiety disorders, ASD, psychotic disorders and traumatic brain injuries, because some of its symptoms may be similar. Children with PTSD are also more likely to have other mental disorders such as anxiety or depression.[22]

Treatment Options

The primary treatment for childhood PTSD is psychotherapy. Play therapy may be helpful to young children, while older children and adolescents may respond to approaches such as cognitive-behavioral therapy. Children with PTSD may also have other disorders, such as depression or anxiety, that may be treated with medications.

For children, how effective is psychotherapy at treating PTSD? The frequency and severity of symptoms can decrease by as much as 50 percent over six months, but a plateau may follow that progress: that was the finding of an analysis of twenty-seven studies of children ages five to eighteen with PTSD. Some children had a marked recovery, others a more moderate one.

But after six months, little changed. The researchers concluded that after this time, the natural improvement had reached its limit, and it was unlikely the child would fully recover from PTSD without further intervention.[23]

The Aftermath of Abuse: Post-traumatic Stress Disorder

"When you think of someone with PTSD, who comes to mind?" asked Marianne. "Probably a soldier coming back from Afghanistan or Iraq, right? But our grandson Corey, who's seven now, has PTSD because of the abuse he suffered from his mother." Marianne still has trouble believing that her daughter could have treated Corey so badly—but the daughter has admitted to it. Corey has been in therapy for three years, since Marianne was first awarded custody of him from the state protective services division.

"Corey is a very active boy and sometimes his behavior is still a true challenge to me and my husband," said Marianne. "His mother had anger issues and punished him to the point of physical abuse. Now we're dealing with behavior issues that stem from that." The abuse had come to light when Corey was four and his mom brought him to the hospital emergency room spiking a high fever. He had a severe ear infection, but the doctor was also concerned about some suspicious-looking bruises and the mother's angry and dismissive behavior when he mentioned them. She acted very differently from most moms with a sick child. On a hunch, the doctor ordered a skeletal survey—a series of X-rays of the major bones in the body. Corey's X-rays revealed evidence of several old, untreated fractures. The doctor called child protective services, and following an investigation, Corey was removed from his mother's care.

"Now that Corey is older, he is doing much better than he was at first," Marianne said. "He still sometimes wakes up in the night screaming. And he has displaced anger, which means sometimes he's mad at us instead of his mom, the one who abused him. But he's a strong little guy and he's going to be okay." She added with a shudder, "He would *not* have been okay if the state hadn't taken him away from his mother. In fact, he probably wouldn't even be alive. We are so fortunate that he survived and that we are able to help Corey overcome this trauma."

Disruptive Behavior Disorders

In contrast to many other psychiatric diagnoses, disruptive disorders are defined solely by behavioral features—the child's actions—rather than by how the child feels. Some children develop these disorders either because of past traumas, genetic influences, prenatal drug exposure, or a combination of factors. Oppositional defiant disorder (ODD) is the most common, followed by conduct disorder (CD).

When children with disruptive behavior disorders are not successfully treated, they are likely to continue this maladaptive behavior into adulthood. But before assuming that a child has a disruptive disorder, a psychotherapist should rule out other possible diagnoses, such as attention-deficit/hyperactivity disorder. It can be tricky to discern, however. One question to ask is, when the child misbehaves, is it impulsive or is it more intentional? A child with ADHD may impulsively shoplift a toy in a store, while a child with CD might steal it intentionally, having planned it in advance. But it's not always easy to determine.

Further complicating the issue, a child with ADHD is at a higher risk for ODD or CD. When children have co-occurring conduct disorder—that is, a conduct disorder alongside another psychiatric disorder—then both intentionality and impulsivity may be factors in their behavior.

Research shows that about 5 percent of all children ages three to seventeen years have a history of a disruptive behavior. Conduct disorder mostly affects older children and adolescents and is always preceded by ODD; about a third of children with ODD later develop CD. These disorders are about twice as likely among boys as girls, and the prevalence increases with age. The rate among children raised by their grandparents is not known.

Looking at Oppositional Defiant Disorder

ODD has a name that explains itself: children with oppositional defiant disorder take the opposing view to whatever others may think or wish. They are frequently resentful and angry, blame others for their own mistakes, are easily annoyed, and often argue with adults who try to direct them because they do not willingly accept authority. Children must show symptoms of ODD for at least six months before they can be diagnosed with the disorder.

SYMPTOMS AND SIGNS

Behavioral symptoms of ODD include frequent arguments with adults, temper tantrums, refusal to obey when asked to perform a task, and questioning rules. In general, the behaviors are centered on adult authority figures like grandparents, teachers, and coaches. Children with ODD do not exhibit delinquent behaviors, such as stealing or harming others.[24] Children with this disorder have no friends or only a few, largely because of their negative behavior. Learn more in *ODD: A Guide for*

Families, downloadable from the American Academy of Child & Adolescent Psychiatry website:

www.aacap.org/App_Themes/AACAP/docs/resource_centers /odd/odd_resource_center_odd_guide.pdf.

Important: When children enter your family for the first time, they may act out and "test" the family to see how other family members, particularly adults, will react. After the children accept their role in the family—within several months—most of the acting out will end. In contrast, children with ODD will continue with the angry, resentful, and authority-challenging behaviors.

Does your grandchild have attention-deficit/hyperactivity disorder? Up to 40 percent of children with ADHD may also have ODD, and the ADHD symptoms are typically visible first. Another danger area: compared to children with just one diagnosis, the risk for substance use and addiction is higher for children diagnosed with both ADHD and a disruptive behavioral disorder (either ODD or CD). Up to half of children with ODD also suffer from depression or anxiety, and 90 percent are diagnosed with another co-occurring psychiatric disorder at some point in their lives.[25] Other risk factors for ODD are a past experience of child abuse and harsh punishments.[26]

TREATMENT OPTIONS

Treatment for ODD includes behavioral therapy or cognitive behavioral therapy. Collaborative therapy, in which the child and the parent work together, may also help improve outcomes. In one study of children diagnosed with both ODD and depression, collaborative treatment significantly decreased the symptoms, both immediately after treatment and four months later.[27] Parent management training may also be helpful in families with children who have ODD. In this type of training, parents learn to back off on negative responses, such as harsh punishment, and to be more consistent with consequences when they are given.

Although there are no specific medications for treating this disorder, children with ODD may also have depression, ADHD, or anxiety, and those disorders may be treated with psychiatric medications. Most children with ODD who are treated (67 percent) have no symptoms three years later.[28]

Considering Conduct Disorder

Children with conduct disorder behave very aggressively toward other people and may also be cruel to animals, torturing or killing them. They have trouble getting along with their peers, may steal or damage property belonging to others, and may frequently lie. As they get older, they may commit crimes that lead to their arrest and detention.

SYMPTOMS AND SIGNS

Because this disorder is difficult to distinguish from other possible problems, a mental health professional should be the expert to diagnose the child. For example, the child who fails to follow rules in school might have ADHD rather than a disruptive behavior disorder.

TREATMENT OPTIONS

Conduct disorder is treated with psychotherapy. As with oppositional defiant disorder, there are no medications specifically approved by the FDA for treatment. However, if children with CD are depressed or anxious, they may be treated with antidepressants or antianxiety medications. Likewise, if children with CD also have ADHD, then treatment with medication for that disorder may be very helpful.

Prenatal Exposure to Alcohol or Other Drugs

Substance use during a mother's pregnancy may affect children over the long term. It is associated with many of the psychological issues discussed in this chapter, particularly ADHD, and learning disabilities or below-normal intelligence. Fetal alcohol spectrum disorders (FASD), caused by the pregnant mother's alcohol use, has its own constellation of effects. And babies who are born addicted to drugs must go through withdrawal and face possible developmental challenges.

Children Exposed to Illicit Drugs or Drugs of Abuse

For children born to drug-addicted mothers, the prenatal exposure may have serious long-term effects—including on intelligence.[29] They may also have developmental and neurological delays and should be carefully evaluated at birth and in the early years of childhood. One important caveat: we can't absolutely attribute all of these setbacks to prenatal drug exposure. Women who abuse drugs during pregnancy are also more likely to lack prenatal care and have unhealthy habits such as smoking and a poor diet. We can't single out the effects of opioids or other addictive drugs from these other factors that place a child at risk.

As a grandparent, you can't fix whatever damage was done to the child as a fetus. But you can arrange for therapy and regular physical exams, and you can follow the recommendations of your pediatrician and other medical specialists. In addition, for young children who need extra help, consider seeking services from the early intervention program in your state. For example, if your grandchild is not speaking or walking at about the expected age, an expert can perform an evaluation and offer recommendations. For details, visit the Early Childhood Technical Assistance Center at http://ectacenter.org/families.asp. As your grandchild grows up, do your best to find the right educational setting, services, and supports.

Effects of Prenatal Drug and Alcohol Exposure

If a pregnant woman uses alcohol or drugs—opioids, stimulants such as methamphetamine, or others—the stakes are high. During pregnancy, drugs of abuse readily cross through the placenta and may affect fetal brain development and the child's later abilities and behavior. For example, fetal exposure to methamphetamine is known to lead to a smaller head circumference, lower weight, growth problems, and abnormal brain development. As these meth-exposed children grow up, they may also have compromised long-term memory and attention spans. Some research has also found that prenatal meth exposure increased the risk for acting-out behaviors in children at age five and, as a result, parenting stress.[30] The same article, in considering prenatal exposure to cocaine, reported evidence of lower cognitive performance in language and behavior among affected children. Such drug exposure has also been linked to increased risk of aggression and delinquent behavior up to age ten.

Prenatal exposure to opioids—a rampant problem today—increases the risk for premature labor, low birth weight and smaller head circumferences, and symptoms of opioid withdrawal. In elementary school, children prenatally exposed to opioids struggle with significantly more cognitive and motor impairment compared to their peers, as well as an increased risk for inattention, hyperactivity, and ADHD.[31]

Fetal Alcohol Spectrum Disorders

Pregnant women should not drink any amount of alcohol, and women who might be pregnant should also avoid alcohol. The reason: women who drink during pregnancy may have children with fetal alcohol spectrum disorders. FASD refers to a range of effects that can occur in a child, such as abnormal facial features; a small head; poor memory; learning disabilities; hyperactive behavior; problems with the kidneys, heart, or bones; and other physical and mental disabilities. (Again, the word "spectrum" here points to the fact that the symptoms and severity can vary widely.) Children exposed to alcohol prenatally have a higher risk for developmental delays.[32]

In general, children who are diagnosed early with FASD are more likely to have a more severe form of the disorder, because the symptoms are more apparent. Children with FASD do better in loving and stable homes than in violent families.[33]

Four diagnoses fall under the umbrella of this disorder, including fetal alcohol spectrum disorder (FASD), the most severe disorder; partial FASD; static encephalopathy/alcohol exposed; and neurobehavioral disorder/alcohol exposed. Researchers at the University of Washington, at the forefront of FAS research, estimate that fetal alcohol syndrome is present in up to three in one thousand births, similar to the rate of Down syndrome.[34]

For further information on FASD, visit these websites:

• Healthline: Fetal Alcohol Syndrome:
www.healthline.com/health/fetal-alcohol-syndrome

• Centers for Disease Control and Prevention:
www.cdc.gov/ncbddd/fasd/facts.html

• Fetal Alcohol Syndrome Family Resource Institute:
www.fetalalcoholsyndrome.org/

• National Organization on Fetal Alcohol Syndrome:
www.nofas.org/

If your grandchild has one or more of the diagnoses discussed in this chapter, you will need to become a strong advocate. You may need to push hard for appointments with specialists such as neurologists, developmental pediatricians, and psychiatrists, particularly if your grandchild is receiving Medicaid. Sometimes you may find that experts discuss information at a level far above what you can understand. Be patient, and if you don't understand something, say so. Bring up your own subjects of concern and take notes.

■

Sometimes you may feel discouraged or even hopeless, but don't give up. Your grandchild is counting on you. Take a break, give yourself some "me time," and then come back to the problems later. You can do this! And remember that children nearly always have better outcomes when they are raised by people who love them and seek their best interests. Most grandparents fit that bill!

≫

CHAPTER 10

Raising a Healthy Child

Wanda was alarmed: Her granddaughter Rashonda, age two, had a fever of 103°F, and all evening she'd been fussy and restless. Should she give the child baby aspirin? That's what she'd done when Rashonda's father was a child and he came down with a fever. Or maybe she should place Rashonda in a tub filled with cold water to bring down that fever. Wanda remembered her own mother advising that remedy.

Wanda was conflicted, so she called her pediatrician. She was connected with the after-hours answering service, and the doctor called back quickly. When she asked about baby aspirin, his answer was a clear no. He explained that aspirin is dangerous for children, and what used to be called baby aspirin is now called low-dose aspirin. He also vetoed the cold bath, though he said a bath with tepid water was acceptable. The doctor suggested that Wanda buy some liquid children's acetaminophen (Tylenol), and give Rashonda the dosage recommended on the bottle. And he said she should call him in the morning.

• • •

If you raised your first family twenty or thirty years ago, you might be due for a child health care knowledge tune-up. As we see from Wanda's story, the conventional wisdom on medical care can change over the decades. How should I treat a high fever? How should I position a baby to sleep? Should I bandage that skinned knee, or let it heal in the open air? In this chapter, we'll examine some practices that may have changed since you last looked.

We'll also consider the possibility that your grandchildren have arrived in your care with neglected health. Their birth parents may have failed to get routine immunizations for the children or to treat common problems such as ear or throat infections. What do we do if a child arrives infested with lice, with a double ear infection, or with a mysterious rash? This chapter will help.

Of course, even with your good care, children still get sick sometimes, so we'll also cover common medical problems. We'll also discuss exercise, preventive care, including immunizations, and how to find a good pediatrician.

Dr. Adesman's Updated Child Health Care Tips for Grandparents

Let's begin by reexamining some practices that might have been common some years ago but for which pediatricians now have different recommendations.

TIP: *Update Your Knowledge on How to Treat a Fever*
If your child or toddler has a moderate fever (under 104°F) with no other symptoms, is relatively comfortable, and isn't seizure-prone, you can watch and wait a bit. Monitor the fever and give plenty of fluids to avoid dehydration. Use a clean, damp, lukewarm cloth on the forehead and body to soothe the child and help bring down the fever. If called for, such as when the child is clearly miserable and/or has a fever as described in the following section, then give children's acetaminophen or ibuprofen in liquid or chewable form, following the dosing instructions on the packaging.

When is medical attention called for?

For infants up to three months old, if the rectal temperature is 100.4°F or greater—with or without other symptoms—call the doctor right away or go to the hospital emergency room.

For older babies and children, seek medical care if they have:

- a fever of 104°F or greater, with or without symptoms OR
- a fever at any level, if accompanied by any of these symptoms:
  - drowsiness
  - lethargy
  - stiff neck or neck pain (could be meningitis, a serious illness requiring urgent treatment)
  - urinary pain
  - irritability
  - earache
  - headache
  - sore throat
  - rash

Again, some practices may have changed since you were last a parent. Many years ago, so-called baby aspirin was used to treat fever in children. But today doctors recommend against giving acetylsalicylic acid (ASA, also known as aspirin) to babies, children, and even adolescents because it can cause a potentially fatal condition known as Reye's syndrome. People also used to believe that immersing a feverish child in cold water could help, but doctors today don't recommend doing so: not only is it uncomfortable, it can cause hypothermia (below-normal body temperature) or shivering, which actually raises body temperature.

Also note that you shouldn't ignore a high fever if the child is teething. Yes, it's painful and can cause crankiness, but teething itself does *not* cause high fevers. Instead, the main causes are bacterial or viral infections—so follow the fever treatment guidelines mentioned here.

TIP: *Place Babies on Their Backs to Sleep*
Infants should be placed on their back to avoid the risk of sleep-related infant deaths, including sudden infant death syndrome (SIDS). Physicians used to urge parents to place babies on their stomachs, but this practice, as well as side sleeping, has been linked to an increased risk of suffocation.

TIP: *Take Allergies Seriously; They're More Common Than Ever Today*
Allergies may be annoying, causing runny noses and eyes as well as an outbreak of hives, a skin reaction, but they can also be life-threatening, as with a severe food allergy to peanuts or other substances. This severe reaction is known as anaphylaxis, and its early signs include fainting, low blood pressure, wheezing, and swelling. The child needs emergency treatment in this case.

The most common food allergies are to milk, fish, peanuts, eggs, tree nuts, shellfish, soy, and wheat. If your children have food allergies, inform their school, especially if they eat in the school cafeteria. Children with food allergies should have epinephrine (an EpiPen) available to them at all times, whether placed with the school nurse or to self-carry. It's not enough for a school to know about a food allergy if it doesn't have the training or medication to treat it in an emergency. Children with food allergies are also usually eligible for Section 504 Plans with the school, which outline precautions needed and steps to follow in an emergency. To learn more about food allergies and how to protect your grandchildren, go to the Food Allergy

Research and Education website: www.foodallergy.org. Even if your grandchildren bring their own lunch, make sure they are well aware of their own allergies and know when to turn down a snack offered by other children. And even if your grandchildren have gone to the same school for several years, at the start of each new school year, inform the school, the children's teachers, and the cafeteria director about the food allergies. Asthma is up to four times more common in children with food allergies; they may also have related problems such as eczema.[1] On the upside, some children outgrow their food allergies.

TIP: *Dairy Products Are Okay for a Child with Diarrhea*
Many people believe that dairy products are off-limits when children have diarrhea, but this is not true. The main point is to give plenty of fluids to avoid dehydration. If they want milk, yogurt, cheese, ice cream, or another dairy product, then go ahead and give it to them. It won't make their diarrhea any worse. This is a change from the conventional wisdom of a few decades ago. (When I did my pediatric residency in the 1980s, we told parents to hold off on dairy products until the diarrhea was resolved. Many people still believe this, including 81 percent of the Adesman Grandfamily Study respondents). You can also give the child water and other liquids, such as fruit juices. A healthy child doesn't need a lot of juice, but a sick child needs fluids, and juices often taste good to the child.

TIP: *Clean and Cover Any Wound with a Bandage—*
Even a Minor Scrape or Cut
Children often play hard and rough, and they skin their elbows and knees and develop other minor cuts all over their body. But even minor injuries should be cleaned with antiseptic and then covered with a bandage. Avoid cleaning wounds with hydrogen peroxide, as this is no longer recommended for cuts

and scrapes. Soap and water is better. If possible, run water on the wound and then use soap and water around it.

The myth that we should "let the air get to" a minor injury is still commonly held. Almost two-thirds of my study respondents (62 percent) thought so. Half that number correctly identified the statement "Scrapes and cuts heal better if they remain covered with a bandage" as being true, and 7 percent indicated they did not know.

TIP: *Babies and Toddlers Do Need Sunscreen, When Sun Exposure Can't Be Avoided*

It's a myth that infants and young children don't need sunscreen. The reality is that a child of any age, race, or ethnicity can develop a sunburn with exposure, so use sunscreen. And the younger the child, the more careful you should be about any sun exposure. It's best to keep babies under six months out of direct sunlight. For babies especially, avoid midday sun from 10 a.m. to 2 p.m., when ultraviolet rays are strongest.

If you are going to the beach or the lake, consider bringing a beach umbrella (which are handy in other settings too). Cover up the child as much as reasonably possible (try a wide-brim hat) and use sunscreen on unprotected areas. Buy a broad-spectrum product that protects against both UVA and UVB rays, with a sun protection factor (SPF) of at least 15.

Don't forget sunscreen for settings such as sports fields. Put sunscreen on your grandchild before you leave home, and bring the sunscreen with you so you can reapply later—at least every two hours, probably more if your child is swimming. No matter how "waterproof" the sunscreen label claims it is, it can still be washed off by an active child. It takes only a minute to slather more cream on the wiggliest of children. Put sunscreen on yourself too. All ages should avoid sunburn now to prevent later problems such as skin cancer.[2]

Tip: A Child's Excitability Often Has Causes Other Than Sugar
The myth that sugar makes kids hyper may be at least partially based on children's behavior at birthday parties or other occasions when they eat more sugary treats (as I covered in an earlier book, *Baby Facts*).[3] Many people are convinced that sugar causes hyperactivity, perhaps because of a "confirmation bias"—they see what they expect to see.

Doctors don't agree on how sugar affects behavior, and the research is mixed. This does not mean children should eat lots of sugary foods—that would be bad for their teeth and could lead to excess weight gain and diabetes. But don't assume a child is excitable because of eating too much sugar. Instead, look for other culprits.

Researchers Stephen Ray Flora and Courtney Allyn Polenick say in a review article that there is no evidence of sugar causing hyperactivity. In one study they cite, twenty-three school-age children whose parents said they were "sugar-sensitive" were given a diet high in sugar for three weeks followed by a diet low in sugar for three weeks. The researchers found no behavioral differences when compared to a control group of twenty-five children, and the researchers looked at thirty-nine different variables.[4] Moreover, they said research has also shown that sugar does not affect children with attention-deficit/hyperactivity disorder or even children previously identified as juvenile offenders—with one exception. In one study, juvenile criminal offenders who were given a sugar-filled breakfast showed *improved* behavior. Perhaps the troubled children perceived the sugary breakfast as a reward and behaved accordingly.[5]

Don't Forget the Child's Teeth

As your grandchildren grow, make sure they brush their teeth at least twice a day. At the age of one or two, children should have their first dental checkup, preferably with a pediatric dentist, as these professionals specialize in treating children.

Let's do a quick checkup on your own dental knowledge, correcting a few myths about caring for children's teeth. One study found that these four misconceptions were common among grandparents caring for four- to eight-year-olds.[6]

Myth: Any cavities or other problems with "baby" teeth won't affect the child's permanent teeth.

Fact: Such problems *can* harm the permanent teeth. Seeing the dentist regularly will help protect against such harm by identifying problems early.

Myth: Dental disease is not transmitted by sharing cups or utensils such as spoons.

Fact: Diseases causing cavities *can* be transmitted with these items, especially if an adult has dental decay and a child has new teeth that are erupting. If you want to taste a soup or other food to ensure it is not too hot, use one spoon to take one taste. Then, use a different spoon for the child.

Myth: It is okay to put a baby to sleep with a bottle.

Fact: This is an undesirable practice that could harm the child's teeth and interfere with healthy sleep habits.

Myth: Fluoride is not important.

Fact: Fluoride can prevent cavities. The American Academy of Pediatrics recommends using fluoride toothpaste from the sign of the very first tooth, usually at around six months of age.[7]

Common Medical Problems for Children

Now let's review some of the medical issues most children face at some point. You probably have experience with these conditions, but with a bit more background, you may be able to head them off at home by addressing early symptoms. The most common infections are those affecting the ears, gastrointestinal tract, and upper respiratory tract, ranging from the common cold to bronchitis. Other problems include flu (influenza), constipation, lice, and unusual rashes. Mild cases of all these problems can often be treated at home, but don't hesitate to visit a pediatrician, other doctor, or clinic in more serious cases.

Free and Low-Cost Medical Insurance for Children

Your grandchild may be eligible for child-only Medicaid or for the low-cost Children's Health Insurance Program (CHIP). To find programs in your state, go online and click on the map of the United States to your state at www.insurekidsnow.gov/state/index.html.

Ear Infections (Acute Otitis Media)

Although more common among babies and toddlers younger than age two and children attending day care, middle ear infections affect older kids too (and are known as acute otitis media by doctors). They can be painful. Young children with ear infections may be tired and irritable, possibly feverish, and may have trouble sleeping. They may constantly pull on and poke at their ears. Fits of fussiness and intense crying are seen in infants with such infections, while toddlers may clutch the ear while wincing with pain, and older children complain about feeling pain in the ear. Other symptoms of ear infections may include the following:

- crying and irritability (for babies, crying may be intense)
- complaint of ears feeling "full"
- headache
- neck pain
- fever
- sleeplessness
- vomiting or diarrhea
- impaired sense of balance

These infections are usually bacterial but could be viral in origin. Antibiotics are effective in treating only bacterial infections. Young children are especially prone to ear infections; fortunately, they're less frequent as children grow older and their eustachian tubes (the tube from the middle ear to the back of the nose) grows larger, allowing for better drainage. In most cases, ear infections will resolve on their own without antibiotics. Except for babies under six months, pediatricians no longer automatically order antibiotics for ear infections; this is an effort to help prevent the development of antibiotic-resistant bacteria. Of course, if an antibiotic is really needed, the doctor will order one.

Jason, age two, seemed to have one ear infection after another, characterized by crying, pulling on his ears, and a fever. One morning, Jason's grandmother noticed that he felt warm to the touch and seemed irritable. Was he coming down with yet another infection? She took his oral temperature and found he had a slight fever: 100.6°F. Because Jason was clearly feeling ill, she made an appointment with the doctor, who confirmed that yes, this was another ear infection. Jason's grandma said, "Doctor, how many is that? Is there anything we can do?"

Jason's doctor checked his records and found six ear infections in the past year. The doctor recommended she take Jason to an ear, nose, and throat specialist to see if Jason needed to have tubes inserted in his ears.

If an ear infection is suspected, the doctor will check the ear with a device known as an otoscope. If a child has three or more infections in six months or four or more in a year, the doctor may recommend that ear tubes be inserted: these allow for drainage into the external canal of the ear.

Flu (Influenza)

Commonly known as the flu, influenza is a viral infection. You can help prevent your grandchildren (six months or older) from getting it by making sure they get an annual flu shot, offered by your pediatrician or the health department. (Get the shot yourself too.) Each year, different strains of flu emerge. Some are more aggressive than others, so vigilance is needed.

Flu can cause a high fever and aching pain in the body, often with a sore throat, headache, and chills. It can lead to complications such as pneumonia, dehydration, and ear and sinus infections.[8] If your grandchild has symptoms of the flu, make an appointment for a doctor to determine if a flu test is needed. If the child is diagnosed with the flu (either with the test or clinically, by observing her symptoms), the doctor may prescribe an antiviral medication, especially if the child is under five or has an underlying severe, complicated, or progressive medical condition. Antivirals decrease the duration of the flu if given within the first forty-eight hours of infection. They're available as liquids, pills, or inhaled powders.[9]

Another reason for a doctor visit is to determine if the child has a bacterial infection rather than a viral infection like the flu. If the child has a sore throat, the doctor likely will do a throat culture or other test looking for evidence of streptococcus infection. Many primary care providers now do a "rapid strep" test, which gives immediate results, rather than the one- to two-day wait for the culture results. If the test is positive, the doctor will order oral antibiotics—either a liquid form that the pharmacy will mix up fresh for you or, if the child is old enough, a capsule.

Whether it's flu, strep, or something else, when your grandchildren have a fever, they need to stay home from school or day care for several days or until the doctor says it's safe to return. These infections can be contagious—especially the flu—so don't be surprised if you develop the infection.

Gastrointestinal Infections

Bouts of diarrhea, vomiting, or both at once: it's difficult for an adult to deal with these symptoms of stomach upset, and they can be very frightening for a child. The best thing to do when a child has diarrhea is to push fluids (water, juice, milk, popsicles) to prevent dehydration. Eventually the infection will clear up. If the problem becomes severe and the child seems to be losing weight or is in danger of dehydration, then you need to see the pediatrician. The child may have gastroenteritis requiring medication (and, in more severe cases with young children, hospitalization). Do *not* give a medication like loperamide (Imodium) to children younger than age six to stop the diarrhea unless recommended by the pediatrician.

Symptoms of dehydration include the following:

- less frequent urination than normal
- weakness
- no tears when crying
- tiredness
- irritability

Constipation

How often does the average child have a bowel movement? It's not necessary to have one each day. But if children age four or younger have only one or two bowel movements a week, or children over four have only two a week, then they may be constipated. Some children have occasional bouts of constipation (stools that are hard and difficult or painful to pass), while others have a chronic problem with it. "Functional constipation"—chronic constipation with no physiological or anatomic abnormalities—is a problem for many young children. One researcher reported that functional constipation affects 29 percent of children worldwide, and factors such as poor dietary habits, psychological stress, child maltreatment, and obesity may be key factors. Others might be problems at school or stress due to siblings who suffer from health problems.[10] Sometimes constipation occurs because children purposely "hold it in," not wanting to interrupt their activities, or maybe they don't want to use the toilet at school or daycare. (*Note:* Although it's counterintuitive, loose stools can sometimes signal constipation. Some children with hard stools that are partially blocking the gastrointestinal tract may leak loose stools, masking the fact that they are constipated.)

If you suspect your grandchildren are struggling with constipation, consult your pediatrician, because the constipation may indicate other health problems, such as diabetes, hypothyroidism, hypercalcemia (high blood levels of calcium), hyperkalemia (excess blood levels of potassium), or other diagnoses such as food sensitivities and allergies, which are increasingly common. Blood tests can rule some such diagnoses in or out.[11] In addition to blood tests, doctors may order abdominal X-rays to determine the severity of the constipation and to check for any masses. The doctor may also order tests to check the colon or a magnetic resonance imaging (MRI) test of the spine to detect any spinal abnormalities.[12] The doctor also is likely to recommend increasing the child's level of dietary fiber.

At the first signs of constipation, talk to the child. Remind him that it's normal for people to poop. Depending on the child's age, you might say, "It's good to get the poop out of our system so there's room for more poop to come down." You may wish to provide your grandchild some basics on how digestion works, starting with the mouth and the salivary system. Provide a wholesome diet with plenty of vegetables, fruits, and whole grains, and make sure the child gets enough exercise and drinks enough water.

Upper Respiratory Infections

Usually called "colds," upper respiratory infections are very common and highly infectious. They're often viral in origin, but sometimes upper respiratory infections are caused by bacteria, and they may lead to bronchitis or ear infections.

Often, no antibiotic is needed, even when an infection is bacterial. Many doctors overprescribe antibiotics for upper respiratory infections, according to the American Academy of Pediatrics, which says that one in five pediatrician visits result in a prescription for an antibiotic. The problem is that a child who takes antibiotics needlessly may have bacteria that build up a resistance to antibiotics over time. That makes it harder to address later needs, possibly more serious ones. Moreover, all drugs have some side effects, including antibiotics.[13]

It's impossible to prevent all upper respiratory infections, but there are a few ways to reduce their number by avoiding the transmission of germs. For example, teach your grandchildren to wash their hands before meals and to avoid sharing eating utensils or drinking glasses. Remind children to wash their hands if they sneeze into their hands or, better yet, to sneeze into their arm or a tissue.

Lice

Lice are very common in children who go to school or daycare. There's no shame in it—a case of lice does *not* mean that you keep a dirty house or that the child's friends in school or day care live in unsanitary conditions.

If you discover that your grandchild has lice or nits (immature lice), you can buy an over-the-counter medicated shampoo or gel containing pyrethrin or permethrin to eradicate the lice. Follow the directions on the container. Generally, you apply the shampoo or gel, wait for a given short period, rinse the hair and scalp with warm water, dry off with a towel that you immediately put into the washing machine, and then use a nit comb to get rid of the dead and dying lice. This should take care of the problem, or you may need to administer a second treatment within about nine days. If the lice are resistant to this over-the-counter treatment, which happens sometimes, then ask your pediatrician to prescribe a medication.[14]

Also note that there are a growing number of "lice salons" (also called lice bars) that specialize in removing and treating head lice. They are much pricier than buying a $20 package of lice treatment in a pharmacy, but the fee—several hundred dollars (or more)—may be worth it if you can afford it, because you won't have to remove the lice yourself. Some lice salons say their treatments are less harsh but just as effective as the lice treatments you can buy. Enter "lice salon" in your online search engine and include your city and state to find the nearest salon to you if this option interests you.

Check everyone else in the family for lice, including yourself, because lice spread within families. They can't jump like
fleas, but they can crawl. Look through the hair in multiple
locations on the scalp for anything that's moving. Wash the
child's bedding and pillows (and your own as well, if the child
ever comes into your bed), and soak the child's combs and
hairbrushes in bleach. You don't need to have the entire house
treated for insects or undergo an elaborate insect tenting proce-
dure—it's unnecessary. Lice die within about a day or so if they
have no human hair to attach themselves to. (Human lice don't
like cats and dogs, so don't worry about that if you have pets.)
It's also a good idea to teach your grandchildren to never share
hairbrushes, combs, or hats, to avoid a recurrence. But if it happens again, you know what to do.

Rashes

More than twelve million office visits per year are made because
of skin rashes and other skin-related ailments in children and
adolescents.[15] That's a lot of rashes, so let's look at the most
common ones and how to treat them.

DIAPER RASH

A rash in the diaper area is very common because a baby's skin
is delicate, easily irritated by urine and feces. To help prevent
it, change babies frequently and clean them thoroughly with
fragrance-free wipes. If diaper rash happens anyway, don't
panic. Use a zinc oxide diaper cream to treat the irritated area.
The American Academy of Dermatology recommends that you
layer on the rash cream as if you were frosting a cake—don't
skimp! Keep the cream on all day until you clean the baby in the
evening. If necessary, reapply more cream after the baby's bath.[16]
If the child has a fever, pus is present in the rash, or the rash

does not go away with treatment, take the baby to the doctor for diagnosis and treatment. A diaper rash composed of fine bumps is often a yeast rash and requires a prescription medicine (nystatin) to treat it.

OTHER TYPES OF RASHES

Skin rashes have many different causes. Some are caused by mosquito or other insect bites. A child with allergies may be exposed to an allergen and consequently develop a rash. Infections cause other rashes, such as roseola. An in-person visit to the doctor is the best way to determine if treatment is needed. The physician will ask you how long the rash has been present, if anyone else in the household has a similar rash, if the child is feverish (fever is present in roseola, for example), and whether the rash itches.

Allergic rashes are responses to common allergens, such as dust, medications, foods, or other substances to which the child is allergic. Hives from allergies are common and frequently ignored, but they may be an advance sign of a more severe allergic reaction such as asthma. Alert your grandchild's doctor if your child has an outbreak of hives.

Roseola, also known as sixth disease, is a common skin rash in children three and younger and is usually accompanied by a high fever. It may also be preceded by a cough, runny nose, and some diarrhea. The rash usually begins on the trunk of the body and then spreads outward. Roseola does not require antibiotics because it's a viral infection.

Scarlet fever is actually a type of rash, usually linked to a form of *streptococcus*. It causes a fever and sore throat before a rash appears on the upper trunk of the body. This infection is usually treated with antibiotics like penicillin.

Fifth disease, also known as *erythema infectiosum*, is a common infection that causes the child to have a low fever, lethargy, sore throat, headache, and nausea, followed by bright red color in the face on both cheeks. The child may be treated with non-steroidal anti-inflammatory drugs, if needed, as well as with antihistamines to control the itchiness.

Ringworm is another common skin infection, and it has nothing to do with worms. If present on the scalp, called tinea capitis, it leaves a characteristic patchy bald area. This infection can occur in many other parts of the body, called tinea corporis. It is usually treated with a topical (applied to the skin) antifungal medication.[17]

Daily Habits for Health

It's a good idea to help your grandchild develop some healthy basic daily habits. We've already covered teeth brushing, and it's also important for your grandchild to have a bath or shower every day or at least every other day. Here are a few more ways to help maintain good health in your grandchildren.

Exercise and Your Grandchild

A major part of good health is staying active. Most children love to run and play, and this natural inclination should be encouraged. Yet today many children are obsessed not just with television but also with video games and various other electronic devices and may spend hours with these activities, leading to a habit of sedentary behavior. Try to limit your grandchildren's recreational "screen time" and electronic activities to no more than an hour or two each day. Take them to the park on a regular basis or sign them up for soccer or softball. This will also commit you to taking them to practices and games, but the payoff in good health for your grandchildren makes it well worth the time

Safety in the Car Saves Lives

The use of a seatbelt or child safety seat in a vehicle can mean the difference between severe harm and little or no harm to a child. In addition, it's the law that many children sit in the back seat and in an approved car seat or booster seat. Old car seats your son or daughter used as a baby won't meet current regulations. Here are some basic recommendations:

- Children ages twelve years and younger should sit in the back seat.

- From birth to age two, children should be placed in a *rear-facing* car seat in the back seat of the vehicle, unless their weight or height indicates a forward-facing car seat is better. Secure the car seat with the seat belt. (And never place a rear-facing car seat in front of an active air bag.)

- From age two to at least age five, children should sit in a *forward-facing* car seat in the back seat (after they outgrow the rear-facing car seat).

- From about age five, a child should sit in a booster seat until seat belts fit properly.

- When too big for a booster seat, children should use a seat belt. The lap belt should lie across the upper thighs and not the stomach, while the shoulder belt lies across the chest, not the neck.[18]

Child safety seats reduce the risk for death by 71 percent in infants younger than age one and by 54 percent for children between the ages of one and four, reported the National Highway Traffic Safety Administration. In 2016 alone, seat belts saved the lives of nearly 14,668 people ages five years and older in the United States. Buckle up![19]

investment. There may be low-cost athletic options available at the local YMCA or community center. Taking walks around your neighborhood with your grandchildren is good exercise for all of you, as are activities such as biking or even dancing with the children to some "oldies" from your past.

Toll-Free Emergency Poison Control Number

What if a child consumes a substance that is or could be dangerous? Call the national Poison Control number at 1-800-222-1222 and follow the directions that the operator gives you. Post the number in a prominent place (such as the fridge) and add it to your cell phone contacts.

Basic Nutrition

Offer your grandchildren a variety of nutritious foods, with plenty of vegetables and fruits as well as grains and meats (or vegetable-based proteins). Limit nutritionally empty items such as chips and other junk food. For kids who resist vegetables, you may wish to read a cookbook by Jessica Seinfeld (wife of Jerry Seinfeld), who offers tips on putting kale in spaghetti, applesauce in muffins, and other suggestions for ensuring your grandchildren eat some vegetables (*Deceptively Delicious: Simple Secrets to Get Your Kids Eating Good Foods*). Limit the trips to hamburger and pizza joints—once a week is too much. Introduce salads to your grandchildren, and yes, some kids really do like salads!

The Facts about Immunizations

Immunizations are a cornerstone of the US public health system, helping protect the whole population from disease. When your grandchildren come to live with you, you may discover that they

Vaccine-Preventable Diseases and the Vaccines That Prevent Them[20]

Disease	Vaccine	How the disease spreads	Disease symptoms	Disease complications
Chicken pox	Varicella vaccine protects against chicken pox	Air, direct contact	Rash, tiredness, headache, fever	Infected blisters, bleeding disorders, encephalitis (brain swelling), pneumonia (infection in the lungs)
Diphtheria	DTaP* vaccine protects against diphtheria	Air, direct contact	Sore throat, mild fever, weakness, swollen glands in neck	Swelling of the heart muscle, heart failure, coma, paralysis, death
Haemophilus influenzae **type b (Hib)**	Hib vaccine protects against *Haemophilus influenzae* type b	Air, direct contact	May be no symptoms unless bacteria enter the blood	Meningitis (infection of the covering around the brain and spinal cord), intellectual disability, epiglottitis (a life-threatening infection that can block the windpipe and lead to serious breathing problems), pneumonia (infection in the lungs), death
Hepatitis A	HepA vaccine protects against hepatitis A	Direct contact, contaminated food or water	May be no symptoms, or may have stomach pain, loss of appetite, fatigue, vomiting, jaundice, (yellowing of skin and eyes), dark urine	Liver failure, arthralgia (joint pain), kidney, pancreatic, and blood disorders

* DTaP combines protection against diphtheria, tetanus, and pertussis   *continued*

Disease	Vaccine	How the disease spreads	Disease symptoms	Disease complications
Hepatitis B	HepB vaccine protects against hepatitis B	Contact with blood or bodily fluids	May have no symptoms, or may have fever, headache, weakness, vomiting, jaundice (yellowing of skin and eyes), joint pain	Chronic liver infection, liver failure, liver cancer
Influenza (Flu)	Flu vaccine protects against influenza	Air, direct contact	Fever, muscle pain, sore throat, cough, extreme fatigue	Pneumonia (infection in the lungs)
Measles	MMR** vaccine protects against measles	Air, direct contact	Rash, fever, cough, runny nose, pinkeye	Encephalitis (brain swelling), pneumonia (infection in the lungs), death
Mumps	MMR** vaccine protects against mumps	Air, direct contact	Swollen salivary glands (under the jaw), fever, headache, tiredness, muscle pain	Meningitis (infection of the covering around the brain and spinal cord), encephalitis (brain swelling), inflammation of testicles or ovaries, deafness
Pertussis	DTaP* vaccine protects against pertussis (whooping cough)	Air, direct contact	Severe cough, runny nose, apnea (a pause in breathing in infants)	Pneumonia (infection in the lung), death

* DTaP combines protection against diphtheria, tetanus, and pertussis
** MMR combines protection against measles, mumps, and rubella

Disease	Vaccine	How the disease spreads	Disease symptoms	Disease complications
Pneumococcal	PCV13 vaccine protects against pneumo-coccus	Air, direct contact	May have no symptoms or may have pneumonia (infection in the lungs)	Bacteremia (blood infection), meningitis (infection of the covering around the brain and spinal cord), death
Polio	IPV vaccine protects against polio	Air, direct contact, through the mouth	May have no symptoms, or a child may have sore throat, fever, nausea, headache	Paralysis, death
Rotavirus	RV vaccine protects against rotavirus	Through the mouth	Diarrhea, fever, vomiting	Severe diarrhea, dehydration
Rubella	MMR** vaccine protects against rubella	Air, direct contact	Sometimes a rash, fever, swollen lymph nodes	Very serious problem in pregnant women—can lead to miscarriage, stillbirth, premature delivery, or birth defects
Tetanus	DTaP* vaccine protects against tetanus	Exposure through cuts in skin	Stiffness in neck and abdominal muscles, difficulty swallowing, muscle spasms, fever	Broken bones, breathing difficulties, death

* DTaP combines protection against diphtheria, tetanus, and pertussis

** MMR combines protection against measles, mumps, and rubella

have not received all—or maybe any—of the vaccinations they should have. As soon as you can, talk to your pediatrician, who will advise you on a catch-up regimen. Many schools and child care centers require that enrolled children receive a certain number and type of vaccinations, and often this is based on state law.

Immunizations protect against serious diseases that, in the past, often killed or permanently harmed infants and children; this includes diseases such as whooping cough, rubella, measles, hepatitis, and tetanus. Vaccines also protect against highly contagious diseases like chicken pox that may come with major complications. A vaccine protects the body by prompting it to create antibodies that it will later use to fight a given disease, should the child become infected in the future. These antibodies are usually present in the body for many years. Most vaccines are injected in tiny amounts, but the polio vaccine is taken orally. See the Vaccine-Preventable Diseases chart for more details.

The Controversy over Immunizations

Despite their importance to public health, some people are opposed to immunizations, mistakenly believing that vaccines could be dangerous for children. Some parents have mixed feelings about immunizations because they can make their children fussy and ill for a few days, and children may also develop a low-grade fever. This is because their body is reacting to the vaccine and creating antibodies against it, which will help the child later. It may help to know that the American Academy of Pediatrics, the American Medical Association, the CDC, and many other respected organizations are all confident of the safety of vaccines and stress the importance of children receiving vaccines when recommended by their doctor. Yet despite assurances from these organizations, some parents and grandparents are still fearful of immunizations because some vocal celebrities are opposed to vaccines, taking an anti-vaccine position as a sort of personal cause they have adopted.

Medical Consent Laws for Grandparents

Most state laws allow non-custodial grandparents to obtain medical care for their grandchildren if they have a parent's consent. The type of consent needed varies by state but is usually a written and notarized document. States that do *not* directly provide for medical consent for grandparents (as of 2017) are the following: Alaska, Arkansas, Illinois, Iowa, Maine, Michigan, Minnesota, Nebraska, New Hampshire, New Jersey, Rhode Island, and West Virginia.[21]

List in the permission document the following information:

- the grandparent's name
- the child's name
- the name and policy number of the child's health insurance (whenever possible, obtain the child's health insurance card)
- the name of the child's pediatrician or family doctor
- the name of the birth parent granting permission
- the child's Social Security number

Make sure all information and signatures are clearly legible. The parent should sign and date the document in front of a notary. Most banks offer notary service free to their customers.

What if the child's birth parents are opposed to giving the child vaccines, convinced that the child may develop ADHD or autism? Try to assure the parents; however, if you have legal custody of the child, then you are the person who will make the decision about immunizations. Keep in mind that many states require immunizations before children may enter school, unless there is a valid reason for avoiding these vaccines.

Helpful Parenting Books on Babies and Toddlers

If your grandchild is an infant or toddler, we recommend two very helpful books: *Baby 411: Clear Answers and Smart Advice for Your Baby's First Year* and *Toddler 411*. Both books—written by pediatrician Ari Brown and Denise Fields and published by Windsor Peak Press—provide a wealth of important information and answers to common questions.

Finding a Good Pediatrician

Now that you're raising your grandchild, you need to find a good pediatrician. Even if you already have one, knowing how to identify a new doctor will prove helpful if your pediatrician retires or moves away. Try these sources:

- **Word of mouth: ask local friends and relatives** for recommendations, or go further, asking them for suggestions from trusted others. Tell them if you need a particular expertise: for example, a pediatrician experienced with developmental delays, behavior problems, or children with a background of abuse and neglect.

- **Ask your own primary care doctor** for a recommendation. Ask your doctor, "What pediatrician would you bring your own child to see?" Doctors frequently know about physicians in other specialties or can ask other doctors for their suggestions.

- **Check the American Academy of Pediatrics online.** This website can help you locate pediatricians in your area: www.healthychildren.org/English/tips-tools/find -pediatrician/Pages/Pediatrician-Referral-Service.aspx.

- **Ask the child's health insurer for a list.** If your grandchild is on Medicaid, the state will provide a list of local pediatricians who accept Medicaid coverage. If your grandchild has another form of health insurance, the provider will provide a list of pediatricians in its network, usually on its website.

- **Check other directories or affiliations.** For example, in many major cities, local city or county magazines will recognize "Best Doctors" based on the recommendations of other physicians. Or check the Castle Connolly Guide at this website: www.castleconnolly.com/. You may also wish to check for pediatricians who are affiliated with a children's hospital or a medical school.

Ideally, take your time with choosing a pediatrician for your grandchildren. It's always a good idea to meet with a doctor before making a commitment. If you're uncomfortable with that pediatrician, keep looking.

Don't base your decision about a physician based solely on ratings found on consumer websites. These ratings may be based more on convenience factors than quality: how quickly did they get an appointment, how long did they spend in the waiting room, and so on. Doctors whose patients are long-standing and loyal—for good reason—may not get reviewed at all on these sites. Sometimes good doctors are well worth the wait.

Finding Reliable Medical Websites

There are many good medical websites—and some very bad sites too. We recommend the American Academy of Pediatrics site (www.HealthyChildren.org). But you may be referred to others too, and you need some criteria to evaluate them. When you find a site and you're not sure if it's reliable, ask yourself these questions:

- **Does a medical doctor, group, or organization write the material** (or at least oversee it)? There are many medical writers who may write very good articles for the website, but it's important for a medical doctor to at least review them to make sure no major mistakes were made. If a doctor does review them, the doctor's name should appear prominently on the site or at the end of an article.

- **Is the material regularly updated?** The information you've found to help your grandchild may seem very useful, but check the end of the article for the date it was last revised. If the article was written in 1990 and never updated, do *not* rely on this old information. Don't make the common mistake of thinking that if it's on the internet, then the information is up-to-the-minute. Wrong!

- **Is the site free of dramatic or scary language?** If the website has inflammatory or frightening language, then its owners probably have a political or other lobbying position. Sometimes scare tactics are used to win over converts. A good medical site doesn't seek to unnerve or even terrify readers.

When You Have Little or No Medical Information on Your Grandchild

Sometimes when you gain custody, you have little or no medical information about the child. You don't know about any past illnesses, nor do you know about allergies, immunizations, or other important facts. If you can ask the child's parent for the information, do. But sometimes the parent is unavailable, uncooperative, or deceased. So, what do you do? Let's look at three possible avenues.

Ask the birth parents, other grandparents, and other relatives. If you are at least on speaking terms with the child's parent, ask for the name of the child's doctor. This doctor may be too far away for you to continue to see, but you can ask the new pediatrician for a consent form to obtain the child's medical records and then have the birth parent (usually the mother) sign this document. If you can go to the previous physician's office in person, you may be able to convince the staff to give you the information you need even without a parent's written consent. You will likely need to prove that your grandchild is not currently in the birth parent's custody (because the parent is in prison, in a rehabilitation facility, or some other reason) and that you are the grandparent. To prove this, show or send the doctor a copy of your adult child's birth certificate and, when possible, the child's birth certificate. This is all evidence of your direct link to the child.

Ask to see school health records. Many states allow grandparents to register their grandchildren for school, with written or sometimes verbal consent. If you have done so, ask the principal or the school nurse to release the child's health records to you, and explain that you need to provide this information to your grandchild's new doctor. School health records should reveal if the child has any allergies as well as past medical problems and surgeries. They should also include the name of your grandchild's most recent pediatrician. In addition, if the child previously attended a preschool or received early intervention in the public-school system (for children who had issues with speaking, walking, and so forth), then this source should also have health information on your grandchild. Privacy laws may impede you, but sometimes a convincing grandparent can gain the needed information. Keep in mind that if you act like you know what you are doing, most people will assume you do.

Contact the county health department where your grandchild last lived. If the child received immunization shots from the local health department, it will have these records. To see them, you may need to bring proof that you have custody of your grandchild, whether it's permission from the parent, court records, emergency custody papers, legal guardianship papers, or other documentation. (Read more about obtaining legal custody in chapter 7.)

■

In the next chapter, we offer information on keeping yourself healthy. It is important for you to stay as healthy as possible so that you can continue to care for your grandchild as long as possible. Of course, you are important as a person in your own right too!

〉〉

CHAPTER 11

Staying Healthy Yourself

Carla was just fifty-five, but she had an arthritic knee and used a cane. One day a social services caseworker called to tell Carla, a widow, that her daughter had just been arrested and jailed. She explained the story. Then she paused. Could Carla take in her five-year-old grandson? Carla had been afraid this day might come. Still, she wasn't sure she was up to handling an active little boy. But when the worker said that Donny would go into foster care otherwise, Carla said, "I'll do it!"

A year later Donny was still with her, probably for the long haul, and Carla had decided to get knee replacement surgery. Donny loved basketball, and she wanted to shoot baskets with him at the playground. Carla's sister offered to stay at home with her during the first week after surgery, and Carla's caseworker agreed to that plan. With physical therapy, Carla recovered quickly, and the next spring she was working on her jump shot while Donny clapped for her.

• • •

Some grandparents find themselves parenting again just as their own bodies are showing signs of wear and tear. They might even have some emerging health problems, such as arthritis, diabetes, or other serious issues such as heart disease or cancer. This chapter discusses these health challenges and suggests ways to keep as healthy as possible, bettering the odds for a long, vital life.

While parenting a child can sometimes take its toll on a grandparent's physical and/or emotional health, it can also motivate them to take better care of themselves. (Don't assume that heading up a grandfamily inevitably worsens your health: one study showed that of parenting grandparents with poor health, most had experienced their health problems *before* their grandchildren entered their lives.)[1] Even better, your own good health habits set a great example for your grandchildren. Actions speak louder than words.

Managing Common Health Conditions for Adults Fifty and Up

As you age, health problems usually become more frequent. But many medical problems can be managed and improved, especially if they're caught early. That's one reason why it's essential to have an annual checkup, even if you feel fine. Your doctor can help you address a variety of problems, such as type 2 diabetes, hypertension, obesity, arthritis, high blood cholesterol, and chronic heart disease. We'll look at each of these.

Type 2 Diabetes

If you've been diagnosed with type 2 diabetes, you have high blood sugar because your body is unable to use the insulin it produces. This disease is commonly diagnosed among those forty-five or older, and it represents about 95 percent of all the cases of diabetes in the United States. (In contrast, type 1 diabetes usually develops in childhood or young adulthood. With type 1, the body makes no insulin, so artificial insulin is needed to live.) More than a fourth of all Medicare beneficiaries (28 percent) have diabetes.[2]

Diabetes is often diagnosed during an annual physical exam, when the doctor is likely to order a fasting blood glucose test that will check for it. A urinalysis may sometimes be used: a simple dipstick of urine can detect glucose, which may suggest diabetes and the need for further testing. You could also have a precursor to type 2 diabetes called prediabetes—a condition of blood sugar that is higher than normal but not high enough for a diagnosis. An estimated 86 million people living in the United States have prediabetes, and 90 percent don't realize it.[3] Diet and exercise may also delay the diagnosis, so cut back on sugary and starchy foods and lose a few pounds if you are overweight.

If not diagnosed and treated, type 2 diabetes is dangerous and can lead to stroke, heart disease, kidney disease, blindness, and sometimes the need to amputate limbs. Even when it is treated, serious health consequences may result if blood sugar levels are not adequately controlled. In 2013, diabetes was the seventh leading cause of death in the United States.[4]

A Wake-Up Call—and a More Active Life

After Erica's three young grandsons came to live with her, her stress levels soared, even though she loved the boys. Not only was she managing their busy lives, she was still processing the crisis with their mother that had landed them there. On bad days, she blamed herself for her daughter's addiction. Erica began overeating to numb those feelings, and soon she'd gained twenty pounds.

At her next checkup, Erica's doctor diagnosed her with type 2 diabetes. She'd need to test her blood sugar level at least three times a day and regulate it carefully, and he also suggested weight loss and more exercise. Erica countered

continued

that she got plenty of exercise with three active boys, and besides, they loved the cookies and cakes she made for them. The doctor pointed out that they, too, would benefit from more fruits and vegetables, and Erica had to admit that although the boys were athletes, she was mostly watching from the sidelines.

Erica signed up for the clinic's course on managing type 2 diabetes. When she learned that diabetes could heighten her risk of blindness, nerve problems, and kidney disease, she was taken aback. *The heck with those kinds of problems!* she thought. *My boys need me!* She called her doctor. "If I lose the twenty pounds," she asked, "will the diabetes go away?" "There's a good chance it could go into remission," he answered. Certainly, her blood sugars would improve a lot.

Erica started walking every day, riding her bike with the boys, and cutting back on sweets and starchy foods. When she baked, she allowed herself just a small portion. Her blood sugar results improved, and within a few months she'd lost the extra weight. Not only that, her mood lifted, and she dwelled less on negative thoughts. Next time she saw her doctor, he told her she was in remission from diabetes and congratulated her. "I did it for me, but also for the boys," said Erica.

Type 2 diabetes is treated with medication; a modified diet and regular exercise is also recommended. You will also need to check your blood sugar several times every day. People with diabetes may develop low blood sugar, or hypoglycemia. If your blood sugar is too low, then you need to eat a small amount of a food with sugar in it. Conversely, if your blood sugar is too high, you need to cut back on carbs until the sugar level stabilizes. Your doctor or other health care provider may provide you with other recommendations. Weight loss is often recommended.

High Blood Pressure, or Hypertension
High blood pressure, also known as hypertension, is a common problem among older people. This condition needs to be treated because it increases risk for stroke, heart attack, diabetes, kidney disease, and other serious health problems. But most people with high blood pressure have no symptoms, and consequently, they may go for years without a diagnosis. Therefore, it's important to see a primary care doctor regularly—so such problems can be detected and treated. Weight loss and dietary changes, such as reducing salt intake, can help, but many people also need to take one or more prescribed medications.

Let's make sense of those blood pressure numbers. When you get a routine blood pressure cuff test at a doctor's office, the result appears as two numbers: 112/78 ("112 over 78"), for example. The 112 refers to "systolic" blood pressure, the maximum pressure that occurs when the heart is pumping blood. The 78 refers to "diastolic" pressure, when the heart is at rest between beats. A reading of 112/78 is within the healthy normal range, according to new criteria set by the American College of Cardiology in 2017.[5] See the "normal" numbers in the chart here.

There's a name for the just-above-normal range: elevated blood pressure, with systolic pressure of 120–129 and diastolic pressure of less than 80. Both numbers must fall within the "elevated" ranges shown on the chart. If you have diabetes and/or chronic kidney disease, try to keep your blood pressure no higher than this range.

Above the elevated range, though, either the systolic *or* the diastolic number alone can qualify you as having high blood pressure. High blood pressure has two stages, with greater health consequences at the higher end.

How's My Blood Pressure?[6]

	Systolic (top number)		Diastolic (bottom number)
Normal	Less than 120	*and*	Less than 80
Elevated	120–129	*and*	Less than 80
High blood pressure, stage 1	130–139	OR	80–89
High blood pressure, stage 2	140 or higher	OR	90 or higher

Overweight and Obesity

Excessive weight is linked to hypertension, type 2 diabetes, high blood cholesterol, and many other health problems. More than a third (36.5 percent) of adults in the United States are obese, with the highest rate among women between the ages of forty and fifty-nine: 42.1 percent.[7]

If you are overweight or obese, it's a very good idea to lose at least some weight to lower those health risks. If you already have diabetes or high blood pressure, weight loss may lead to remission from the disease, making medications unnecessary, although you should continue to monitor your condition. To discover where you should be, weight-wise, check the body-mass index calculator at this National Institute of Health website: www.nhlbi.nih.gov/health/educational/lose_wt/BMI/bmicalc.htm. Plug in your height and weight (be honest!) to see whether you are underweight, normal weight, overweight (BMI of 25–30), or obese (30 or above).

One benefit of raising your grandchildren is that you're likely to be more active. You may take the children to the park and other outings, bike or swim with them, and cheer them on at sports events. This extra activity may help take off the pounds and keep them off. To track your progress, try a Fitbit or other wrist-worn device that shows how many steps you have taken each day. Set your initial goal at a low number of steps and steadily increase.

Arthritis

Arthritis comes in many forms, such as osteoarthritis, rheumatoid arthritis, and gout. Nearly a third of Medicare beneficiaries (29 percent) suffer from some form of it.[8] In addition, about 54 million adults in the United States have arthritis, with risks for the disease increasing with age. Women are more likely to suffer from arthritis than men.[9] In a study comparing parenting grandparents with single parents, more than half (51 percent) of the grandparents had arthritis, compared to only 19 percent of the single parents. Of course, the single parents were considerably younger, and in general, arthritis is a problem connected with aging.[10]

If you're overweight or obese, weight loss can improve the pain of arthritis because your bones and muscles will have less weight to support. Regular physical activity may improve arthritic symptoms, particularly joint-friendly exercises such as biking, swimming, or walking. Some people need to take medications to control their arthritis, such as nonsteroidal anti-inflammatory drugs (NSAID), to decrease inflammation. There are both prescribed and over-the-counter (OTC) NSAIDs; for example, ibuprofen is an example of an OTC NSAID. However, such medications may have stomach upset as a side effect. Physical therapy may help with flare-ups of arthritis. Sometimes surgery may be needed, for example, severe arthritis pain in the knee, requiring a joint replacement.

High Blood Cholesterol

Keep an eye on your blood cholesterol: high levels of "bad" cholesterol are also often linked to diabetes, hypertension, and obesity and can raise the risk of heart and kidney disease and other serious ailments. Unfortunately, it's another common chronic health condition, and about 45 percent of Medicare beneficiaries in 2010 had high cholesterol.[11] As with high blood pressure, the person often has no symptoms.

Cholesterol is a waxy, fatty substance in the blood, and there are two main types, both measured by a blood test. The low-density lipoproteins (LDL), also known as "bad" cholesterol, should optimally measure less than 100 mg/dL (milligrams per deciliter of blood). The high-density lipoproteins (HDL), the "good" cholesterol, should be 60 mg/dL or greater. In addition, triglycerides, a fatty substance that is measured along with cholesterol levels, should be less than 150 mg/dL.

People age forty and up should have their cholesterol levels checked on a schedule recommended by their physicians, at least once every five years. Risk factors for high levels of bad cholesterol are a family history of high cholesterol or heart disease, hypertension and/or type 2 diabetes, being overweight or obese, a lack of exercise, and the use of certain medications. Behavioral risk factors are smoking; diets high in saturated fats, trans fat, and cholesterol; and inactivity. Some people of normal weight have high cholesterol readings largely because of an inherited genetic risk.

Weight loss and dietary changes may be enough to improve problematic cholesterol levels. It's best to eat more foods that are high in fiber (such as black beans or oatmeal) to help bring down your cholesterol. Also, consume foods that are low in saturated fat or trans fat, such as lean meat, whole grains, seafood, and yogurt. Sometimes medications are called for. These are known as "statins" (because their generic names end with "statin," such as at atorvastatin [Lipitor], pravastatin [Pravachol], rosuvastatin [Crestor], simvastatin [Zocor], and others). Patients are also urged to stop smoking and to exercise regularly.

Chronic Heart Disease

Aging hearts can become more stressed. In fact, nearly a third of Medicare beneficiaries have some form of heart disease.[12] For example, in one large study of parenting grandparents, 18 percent of the grandparents reported experiencing a heart attack, compared to less than 2 percent of the younger single parents. With regard to angina (heart pain) or coronary heart disease, 11 percent of the parenting grandparents had experienced one of these problems, compared to just 2 percent of the single parents.[13]

Nearly half of all people in the United States have at least one of the three key risk factors for heart disease: hypertension, high cholesterol, and smoking. Other risk factors for heart disease include diabetes, obesity, a poor diet, and insufficient exercise, as well as having a family member with heart disease. To live a more "heart-healthy" life, increase your physical activity, which should also help you lose weight, another recommendation. Don't have more than one alcoholic drink per day if you're a woman and two drinks daily if you're a man. Stop smoking! Smoking cigarettes damages the blood vessels of the heart and the heart itself.[14]

Take Steps to Help Prevent Serious Health Problems

People in their fifties, sixties, and beyond may develop more serious health conditions and illnesses. With aging, the risk grows for cancer, heart attack, and stroke, so be prepared with some knowledge.

Cancer

Many people with cancer are successfully treated and go on to live long lives, especially when the cancer is detected in its early stages. But for nearly all forms of cancer, the risks increase with age. Although a healthy lifestyle decreases the risk for cancer, it does not eliminate it altogether, because some cancer risks are genetic. This means that regular physical examinations with your doctor are important. Report any suspicious lumps, lesions, or dark spots anywhere in your body. A wound that does not heal may be a sign of cancer, as can black or tarry-looking stools or stools containing blood. A formal methodical monthly breast self-exam is no longer recommended; however, women should be familiar with their own breasts and should report any concerns or changes to their health care provider. Skin cancer is common, yet it is largely preventable. Use sunscreen, wear hats when you are in the sun, and put sunscreen on your grandchildren too.

Heart Attack

Heart disease is the leading cause of death in the United States, causing one of every four deaths.[15] Also known as a myocardial infarction, a heart attack occurs when part of the heart's muscle doesn't receive sufficient blood flow. A heart attack is a medical emergency. Here are some of the major symptoms of a heart attack:

- chest pain
- pain in the arms or shoulder

- pain in the jaw, neck, or back
- lightheadedness or weakness
- shortness of breath

Other symptoms may include pain in the upper abdomen, unexplained fatigue, and nausea and vomiting. Heart attack symptoms sometimes differ by gender. For women, chest pain may be less likely; instead, they may have shortness of breath, nausea and vomiting, severe fatigue, and pain in the shoulders, back, and jaw. Both men and women having heart attacks may notice one symptom or no symptoms at all. People with diabetes are more likely to experience only mild symptoms or no symptoms with a heart attack, although the reasons for this are unknown.[16]

If you or someone else has these symptoms, call 911 for an ambulance. Even if you live close to a hospital emergency room, an ambulance can nearly always get a patient to the hospital fastest, onboard treatments can be given, and ER staff are ready and waiting on arrival. Another recommendation: if you think you may be having a heart attack, if possible, chew and swallow one plain (non-coated) aspirin tablet that is equal to 325 mg—unless you are allergic to aspirin or your doctor has told you to not take aspirin.

Stroke

A stroke occurs when there is inadequate oxygen to the brain, just as a heart attack is prompted by inadequate blood oxygen to the heart. This is why a stroke is sometimes referred to as a "brain attack." A major stroke can lead to difficulty with movement, speaking, and other basic activities of life. Some individuals fully recover from a stroke while others partially recover. Stroke can also be fatal; it is the fifth leading cause of death in the United States. The risk for stroke increases with age. Even if people do not die from a stroke, they may become disabled, and about half of stroke survivors experience reduced mobility.[17]

A stroke is a medical emergency, with the following symptoms:

- sudden weakness or numbness in the face, leg, and/or arm, particularly on one side of the body
- sudden difficulty walking or the loss of balance
- difficulty seeing in one or both eyes
- sudden confusion and difficulty in understanding or speaking
- sudden severe headache with no identifiable cause[18]

The FAST test is a quick way to evaluate for possible stroke:

- "F" is for face. Ask the person to smile, and if one side of the face droops, this is a possible indicator of stroke.
- "A" is for arms. Ask the person to hold up both arms. Does one arm start to move downwards? This may be a sign of stroke.
- "S" is for speech. Ask the person to repeat a short phrase. Is the person's speech slurred?
- "T" is for time: that is, take quick action.[19]

If a person has these symptoms, call 911 for an ambulance, even if you live close to an ER. Quick action is important, ambulance staff will treat the patient on the way, and ER staff will be prepared on arrival.

Common risk factors for stroke are high "bad" cholesterol levels, hypertension, heart disease, diabetes, lack of exercise, obesity, excessive alcohol consumption, and tobacco use. In addition, a person who has had a stroke in the past is at a greater-than-usual risk for experiencing another stroke.

Preventive Care to Help You Live Longer

To help increase your longevity so you can care for your grandchildren as long as possible, take preventive actions to help identify any diseases or disorders in the early stages when they are most treatable. Do this by seeing your primary care doctor for annual physical examinations and go to your clinic for care when you are ill. Even if you haven't noticed any health problems, your doctor or routine tests may detect a health issue. And follow through with screening tests your doctor recommends! Do it for your grandchild and for yourself. If you're a woman, consider reading *The Smart Woman's Guide to Midlife and Beyond: A No-Nonsense Approach to Staying Healthy After 50* by Jane Horn, MD, and Robin Miller, MD, from New Harbinger Publications in 2008. If you're a man, check out this book by Edward H. Thompson Jr. and Leonard W. Kaye: *A Man's Guide to Healthy Aging: Stay Smart, Strong, and Active* from Johns Hopkins Press, in 2013.

Preventive Tests to Detect Medical Problems

An ounce of prevention: most doctors recommend basic screening tests to detect high blood cholesterol, a potential heart problem, breast cancer, prostate cancer, or colon cancer. Your doctor may order other screening examinations as well, but we'll discuss these five basic ones here.

BLOOD CHOLESTEROL SCREENING

Ask your primary care doctor whether you need a blood cholesterol screening test. (See the earlier discussion under "High Blood Cholesterol.") If your level of "bad" blood cholesterol is high, you may need to take cholesterol-lowering medications. Your doctor is also likely to recommend lifestyle changes, such as weight loss, dietary changes, and increased exercise. Follow-up screenings will reveal whether your levels are improving. It's worth careful attention, because lowering your cholesterol also lowers your risk of several serious illnesses.

EKG STRESS TEST

Coronary artery disease is heart disease in which plaque builds up in the arteries of the heart and may block the blood flow. To check for this condition, your doctor may order a "stress test": an electrocardiogram, also known as an EKG or ECG, that records the electrical activity in your heart through electrodes and special equipment. You'll walk or run on a treadmill or pedal a stationary bicycle, raising your heart rate and blood pressure. The EKG is monitored throughout the test by a physician or medical staff. The test is meant to detect any abnormal changes in your blood pressure or heart rate as well as any abnormal cardiac rhythms. Sometimes an imaging test such as a nuclear scan is done during the exercise stress test. Here a radioactive contrast material (dye) is injected into the bloodstream so that the doctor can observe the blood flow to the heart, both during exercise and when the heart is at rest.[20]

MAMMOGRAM

The mammogram is a radiographic screening test for breast cancer, which, if it occurs, is nearly always found in women, rather than men. (Men do not receive annual mammograms.) Because the risk for breast cancer increases with age, the annual mammogram is an important screening tool. It may be ordered by your primary care doctor or gynecologist.

Professional opinions differ over at what age annual mammogram screenings should start. For example, the American College of Obstetrics and Gynecologists recommends women begin annual exams at age forty.[21] But the American Cancer Society recommends yearly mammograms starting at age forty-five for women at average risk for breast cancer, then, starting at age fifty-four, decreasing to every other year.[22] Talk to your own physician about the need for a mammogram. Share if you've had any other form of cancer in the past and whether your mother, sister, or grandmother has had breast cancer, which could mean you have a genetic risk for the disease.

RECTAL EXAMINATION

It's embarrassing and annoying and nobody likes it, but the digital rectal examination is an important test. The doctor will use an inserted gloved finger to probe the rectum for any obvious signs of colon or rectal cancer. Sometimes prostate cancer in men is detected in this manner as well. If your primary care doctor thinks you may have colon or rectal cancer, you may need to see a specialist, such as a gastroenterologist, a physician who concentrates on diseases of the digestive system. If anything suspicious is found in your prostate, you will be sent to a urologist for further evaluation. If tests reveal that you do have cancer, your next step will be to see an oncologist, a cancer expert.

COLONOSCOPY

The risk for colorectal cancer increases with age. Ask your doctor if it is time for you to have a colonoscopy or another test used to help detect colorectal cancer. The preparation for a colonoscopy is inconvenient but necessary: a complete cleansing of the bowel. This means you will be given purgative medicine to drink that will completely empty your bowels. The actual test is done under moderate sedation. The doctor inserts a special scope into the rectum that extends up and into the colon. The colonoscopy will show if there are any precancerous polyps and if so, the doctor will remove them and send them for biopsy to test for cancer. The colonoscopy will also show the presence of any cancer in the colon. Colorectal cancer is a very common form of cancer, and early detection is often a lifesaver.

Act Now for a Longer, Healthier Life

To avoid or at least lessen the impact of any health problems you may face, work to make positive changes in your lifestyle. Not only will you improve your odds for a long life, you'll probably also feel a lot better: more energetic, more vital, more able to keep up with your grandchildren. So let's talk about some dos and don'ts. If you smoke, quit. If you drink, do so in moderation. Exercise regularly and eat healthily. The buddy system works well for most of these efforts: find others to support you and share the healthy times.

You're also setting a good example for your grandfamily. Your grandchildren will thank you, and so will everyone else who loves you.

End a Smoking Habit

Grandparents who smoke should stop as soon as possible, to protect their own health and to avoid inflicting passive smoke on others. ("Secondhand smoke" in the home is no fun for your grandfamily.) Do not increase your risk for lung cancer, emphysema, and other smoking-related diseases!

What's the best way to quit? There are many over-the-counter aids to help you cut back or end a smoking habit, in the form of nicotine replacement pills, gums, and so forth. You can also try prescription nicotine replacement products, available in lozenges, patches, nasal sprays, and inhalers. In addition, your doctor may prescribe medications to help curb your nicotine cravings, such as bupropion (Zyban) or varenicline tartrate (Chantix): ask your doctor about them. Some smokers quit with behavioral therapy, individual counseling, group counseling, or even hypnotherapy. If possible, convince one or more friends to quit smoking along with you, so you can boost each other up along the way with your own buddy system. Also, check out Freedom from Smoking, an interactive option from the American Lung Association that also will help you locate the nearest Freedom from Smoking support group. Go to www.lung.org /stop-smoking/join-freedom-from-smoking/.

Limit Alcohol Use

If you drink alcohol at all, it's wise to do so in moderation—now especially. You're responsible for a grandchild or maybe more than one. If you've gotten used to more than a couple of beers or glasses of wine with dinner, it's time to cut way back. What if your grandchild has an accident or other emergency that evening? You need to have a clear head so you can handle it.

There are medical reasons to limit alcohol too. Over time, alcohol damages many of the body's organs, especially the brain, liver, pancreas, and heart. It also increases the risk of several cancers, including mouth, liver, and breast cancer. Alcohol weakens the immune system, making you more vulnerable to disease and infection. And alcohol is high in calories, which undermines any weight loss you're trying to achieve. There's this too: by limiting your alcohol use, you're setting a very good example for your grandfamily.

344 | THE GRANDFAMILY GUIDEBOOK

Exercise

Many adults don't exercise enough—but it's essential to physical health, and it's a mental health booster too. Even walking around the block a few times a week can improve your overall health—and your mood. You may also wish to join a gym to get regular exercise. Many facilities offer reduced prices for seniors. Check out the gym before you join to see if it feels right for you. Also be aware that many gyms offer child care for young children, which is not an important feature for many older adults but may be very important to you. Also check out the local YMCA, which may offer swimming as well as yoga classes. You could also consider being active with the grandchildren, such as dancing with them to old songs that you love—and that they may come to love as well.

Improve Your Diet

Tell your physician you want to improve your diet, and your doctor will likely be thrilled to help you, either offering you pamphlets to read or steering you to local nutritional groups. Some medical groups have dietitians on staff. If you're also trying to lose weight, good nutrition will help. Avoid any fad diets or "miracle" supplements that promise to make you thin in a month. In many cases, these diets or drugs cause diarrhea and can be very dangerous to your health.

Eat fruits and vegetables daily unless your doctor advises against them. Increase your consumption of salads, which will also likely reduce any problems that you have had with constipation. And drink plenty of water. Water is the one substance that people cannot live without, so drink up! Don't get your water from diet soda or beer—drink tap water, or buy bottled water if you prefer to do that. Try to limit your caffeine consumption, whether in coffee, cola, or chocolate products. Too much caffeine can make you feel agitated, cause headaches, and make it hard to sleep at night.

■

You aren't going to live forever, and you can't control your genetic risks. But you can work with what you've got and improve on it. When you maintain your good health as much as possible, you can more fully enjoy parenting your grandchildren, and they also gain the benefits of your healthy interaction. It's a win-win!

>>

When *You* Are the Best Alternative

In this book, we've talked a lot about the feelings, problems, and coping strategies of grandparents and grandchildren, as well as legal, medical, and financial issues involved with becoming a grandfamily. We've tried to cram as much information as possible into this guidebook for one distinct reason: we've been where you are now, and through Dr. Adesman's research, we've met countless people just like you who were looking for a comprehensive resource. Maybe you can identify with some of the circumstances faced by the grandfamilies in our book. I (Dr. Adesman) spent many hours planning and creating my questionnaire for my study of grandparents, collecting the data, and then analyzing the results, much of which is shared in this book where it's relevant. We hope that you have found the information useful and interesting and that the book has been food for thought for you.

We also want to tell our readers who are grandparents raising their grandchildren to keep an important message in context across this long journey you are undertaking: there will be times you question yourself and your motivations. Family dynamics are complicated; they get more complicated in difficult situations. If you are faced with being involved in raising your grandchildren, it's more than likely some series of crises have affected your family. In the midst of all the "drama," try to remember that although no one is perfect, your intentions are clearly honorable. If you are stepping up to care for your family, you are "the good guy" in these family dramas, whether the cause for the birth parents' problems was a substance use disorder, a mental health disorder, incarceration, or emotional immaturity. Or all of the above. And remember that it is not your fault that your adult sons or daughters failed their children. Sure, you probably made some mistakes along the way when you were raising your own children—nobody's perfect. But when your grandchildren needed you, you stepped up and assumed responsibility—that is real love. That's the love that makes a grandfamily so special.

And consider the alternative: What would have happened if you had not agreed to raise your grandchildren? Many grandparents point out that they're older and can't do as many activities with their grandchildren as a younger parent could. They may think their grandchildren are deprived because they are not being raised by a much younger person. But what grandparents may forget to consider is this: Was that younger person an available alternative? Probably not.

Because when a birth parent cannot or will not raise a child, then someone else must take charge. Sometimes that "someone else" is another relative, but often that person is a stranger to the child. If there are no family members willing to raise the children, then they will likely go to a foster family or a group home. And there are many children in the US foster care system—437,465 as of 2016, based on statistics released in late 2017. This is about 10,000 more children than in 2015, and 40,000 more than in 2012.[1]

Many foster parents are wonderful and caring people—but it's pretty much the luck of the draw for children, who may get

Mr. and Mrs. Wonderful as foster parents. Or, they may be sent to live with Mr. and Mrs. Not So Nice. Also, if children have any developmental or psychiatric issues, or even something as common as ADHD, the foster family members may decide they don't want to cope with those children—they are just too difficult. Which means the children are sent to a different family, often confused and afraid, all over again. Sometimes it becomes a cycle—children act up because they are so angry about their life and their displacement, so they act even worse with the next foster family, who may reject them. And the next one, and so on. This can be a soul-crushing experience for children, who think, *No one wants me. No one loves me.*

With no other good alternatives, older children or adolescents may be sent to a group home with other unhappy confused children. Group homes do their best, but it's just not the same as living with a family.

So if you find yourself thinking, *Why me? Why do I have to be a parent all over again?* or *Maybe somebody else could do this better than me,* please consider our two answers.

Why not you? You may be the best available person for the job. As for somebody else doing a better job, sure, there are people out there who may be smarter or richer or more educated than you are. But they are not lining up around the block to love and raise children whose parents couldn't raise them. People who want to adopt nonrelative children usually want to adopt babies, and many will not go through the foster care system to adopt because they are afraid the children will be "sent back" to their birth family. The bottom line is, often you are the best choice to parent your grandchildren.

For those times when you are struggling to answer, "Is it all worth it?" we encourage you to think about who it would be, if not for you. Grandparents must decide for themselves, but in the Adesman Grandfamily Study, nearly all of them said that knowing what they know now, they would do it all over again. Or, as one grandmother put it, "It's a harder job than you can imagine but more rewarding than you'll ever know." Yes, with all the ups and downs and hundreds or thousands of daily tasks, they still think it's worth it. We admire them, and we admire you too.

Thank you, and best wishes to your grandfamily.

Resources

Social Media Resources

On Facebook:

- GrandsPlace—Grandparents Raising Grandchildren
- Kinship Parenting Group
- Grandparents Raising Grandchildren

On LinkedIn:

- The Addict's Mom—Grandparent to Grandparent (G2G) www.linkedin.com/pulse/addicts-mom-grandparent -g2g-barbara-theodosiou

National Organizations

- American Association of Retired Persons (AARP): www.aarp.org/grandparents
- American Bar Association, Center on Children and the Law: www.americanbar.org/groups/child_law.html
- Annie E. Casey Foundation: www.aecf.org
- The Brookdale Foundation Group: www.brookdalefoundation.org
- ChildFocus, Inc.: www.child-focus.org/
- Children's Defense Fund: www.childrensdefense.org
- Child Trends: www.childtrends.org
- Child Welfare Information Gateway: childwelfare.gov

- Child Welfare League of America: www.cwla.org
- Dave Thomas Foundation for Adoption: davethomasfoundation.org
- Generations United: www.gu.org
- GrandFamilies of America: www.grandfamiliesofamerica.org
- Grandfamilies.org: grandfamilies.org
- National Alliance for Public Charter Schools: www.publiccharters.org/our-work/charter-law-database /states
- National Kinship Alliance for Children: www.kinshipalliance.org
- North American Council on Adoptable Children (NACAC): www.nacac.org

Books and Other Publications

- *1-2-3 Magic: 3-Step Discipline for Calm, Effective, and Happy Parenting* by Thomas W. Phelan (Sourcebooks, 2016).

- *Baby 411: Clear Answers and Smart Advice for Your Baby's First Year, Eighth Edition* by Ari Brown and Denise Fields (Boulder, CO: Windsor Peak Press, 2017).

- *Baby Facts: The Truth about Your Child's Health from Newborn Through Preschool* by Andrew Adesman, MD (Hoboken, NJ: McGraw-Hill, 2009).

- *A Broken Heart Still Beats: After Your Child Dies* by Anne McCracken and Mary Semel (Center City, MN: Hazelden, 2000).

- *The Encyclopedia of Adoption, Third Edition* by Christine Adamec and Laurie C. Miller, MD (New York: Facts On File, 2007).

- *Everything Changes: Help for Families of Newly Recovering Addicts* by Beverly Conyers (Center City, MN: Hazelden, 2009).

- *Grandparents as Parents: A Survival Guide for Raising a Second Family* by Sylvie de Toledo and Deborah Edler Brown (New York: Guilford Press, 2013).

- *The Grief Club: The Secret to Getting Through All Kinds of Change* by Melody Beattie (Center City, MN: Hazelden, 2006).

- *Parenting Your Adopted Child: A Positive Approach to Building a Strong Family* by Andrew Adesman, MD, with Christine Adamec (New York: McGraw-Hill, 2004).

- *Raising Our Children's Children: Room in the Heart* by Deborah Doucette with Jeffrey R. LaCure (Lanham, MD: Taylor Trade/ Rowman and Littlefield, 2014).

- *Sometimes It's Grandmas and Grandpas: Not Mommies and Daddies* by Gayle Byrne (Abbeville Kids, 2009). (This is a children's book.)

- *Toddler 411: Clear Answers and Smart Advice for Your Toddler, Fifth Edition* by Ari Brown and Denise Fields (Boulder, CO: Windsor Peak Press, 2016).

- *When Your Adult Child Breaks Your Heart: Coping with Mental Illness, Substance Abuse, and the Problems That Tear Families Apart* by Joel L. Young, MD, with Christine Adamec (Guilford, CT: Lyons Press, 2013).

Kinship Navigator Programs
A State-by-State Directory

Some states have special programs to help grandparents and other family members who are raising children. Some programs cover the entire state while others cover only some counties within the state. These programs may help you determine what programs you may be eligible for in your state. They may also lead you to support groups in your area.

Arizona

Arizona Kinship Support Services
http://Arizonakinship.org

California

California Kinship
744 P St., MS 8-13-66
Sacramento, CA 95814
(800) KIN-0047
https://edgewood.org/kinship-support/

Community Coalition/Families Helping Families
8101 S. Vermont Ave.
Los Angeles, CA 90044
(323) 750-9087
http://cocosouthla.org/families-helping-families/

Lilliput Kinship Services
8391 Auburn Blvd.
Citrus Heights, CA 95610
(800) 325-5359
www.lilliput.org/parents/kinship-services

YMCA Kinship Services
(877) YMCA-4-KIN (9622-4546)
4080 Centre St., Suite 103
San Diego, CA 92103
www.ymca.org/community-support/ymca-youth-and-family
-services/family-support-and-preservation/kinship
-support-services

Florida

Children's Home Network
(888) 920-8761
For the following counties in Florida: Hillsborough, Osceola,
Orange, Pasco, and Pinellas

Iowa

Iowa Foster, Adoptive and Adoptive Parents Association
(800) 277-8145
www.ifapa.org/

Maine

Adoptive and Foster Families of Maine
34 Main St.
Orono, ME 04473
(207) 827-2331 or (800) 833-9786
www.affm.net/

Maryland

Family Navigator Services
St. Vincent's Villa
2600 Pot Spring Rd.
Timonium, MD 21093
(667) 600-3074

Massachusetts

Grandparents Raising Grandchildren of Massachusetts
Commission on the Status of Grandparents Raising Grandchildren
GRG Coordinator
600 Washington St., 6th Floor
Boston, MA 02111
(617) 748-2454
www.massgrg.com/

Minnesota

Lutheran Social Service of Minnesota
Kinship Family Support Services
2485 Como Ave.
St. Paul, MN 55108
(651) 642-5990 or (800) 582-5260
www.lssmn.org/kinshipcaregivers/

New Jersey

The Children's Home Society of New Jersey
169 Franklin Corner Rd.
Building 1, Suite 220
Lawrence, NJ 08648
(609) 895-0282, extension 131
www.chsofnj.org
Serves counties of Hunterdon, Mercer, Middlesex, Monmouth,
Ocean, Somerset, and Union

New York

New York State Kinship Navigator
87 N. Clinton Ave.
Rochester, NY 14604
(877) 454-6463
www.nysnavigator.org/

Ohio

Public Children Services Association of Ohio
37 W. Broad St., Suite 1100
Columbus, OH 43215
(614) 224-5802
www.pcsao.org/programs/kinship

Oklahoma

North Care of Oklahoma City
2617 General Pershing Blvd.
Oklahoma City, OK 73107
(405) 858-2700
www.northcare.com/programs/children-family/

Pennsylvania

Support for Kinship Care Families
http://extension.psu.edu/youth/intergenerational
/program-areas/kinship

Tennessee

Relative Caregiver Program
Kid Central TN
www.kidcentraltn.com/article/relative-caregiver-program

Vermont

Vermont Kin as Parents
(802) 871-5104
http://vermontkinasparents.org

Washington

Kinship Navigator
www.dshs.wa.gov/altsa/kinship-care-support-services

State Adoption Assistance and Subsidized Guardianship

Basic Facts

Grandparents who adopt their grandchildren, or serve as legal guardians, may be eligible for financial benefits from their state. These programs vary widely by state, so you'll need to do some local research for the latest information. With this chart, you'll have an idea of what to expect. Refer to chapter 7, "Child Custody Issues" to better understand your options.

State	Date Updated	Maximum Basic Rates (per month)			Subsidized Guardianship?	Subsidy after age 18?
		Age 2	Age 9	Age 16		
Alabama	2016	$462	$488	$501	Yes	Yes, in some circumstances
Alaska	2011	$746–$1,590	$746–$1,590	$746–$1,590	Yes, for children ages 10 and older	No, but resources may be available if child adopted after age 16
Arizona	2015	$590	$590	$652	Yes	Yes, in some circumstances
Arkansas	2014	$410	$440	$500	Yes	Yes, in some circumstances
California	2015	$688	$783	$859	Yes	Yes, in some circumstances
Colorado	2011	Varies by county	Varies by county	Varies by county	Yes	Yes, in some circumstances
Connecticut	2015	$779	$788	$856	Yes	Financial subsidy ends at 18, medical subsidy to age 21
Delaware	2012	$397	$397	$511	No	Yes, in some circumstances

State	Date Updated	Maximum Basic Rates (per month)			Subsidized Guardianship?	Subsidy after age 18?
		Age 2	Age 9	Age 16		
District of Columbia	2015	$1,011	$1,011	$1,138	Yes	To 21 if adopted after 5/7/2010, case by case if adopted before 5/7/2010
Florida	2015	$417	$417	$417	No, but Relative Caregiver Program with subsidy	No. Subsidy ends at 18
Georgia	2015	$441	$463	$486	No	Yes, in some circumstances
Hawaii	2014	$576	$650	$676	Yes	Yes, in some circumstances
Idaho	2014	$329	$366	$487	Yes	No
Illinois	2012	$384	$410	$445	Yes	To 19 if in high school, to 21 if disabled
Indiana	2010	$512	$512	$512	Yes	No, but part of federal program for children adopted after 16
Iowa	2012	$478	$497	$551	No	To 21 if disabled and a dependent

continued

State	Date Updated	Maximum Basic Rates (per month)			Subsidized Guardianship?	Subsidy after age 18?
		Age 2	Age 9	Age 16		
Kansas	2014	$500	$500	$500	Yes	May continue if still in high school; to 21 if disabled
Kentucky	2015	$690	$690	$751	No	To 19 or graduation if in high school, to 21 if disabled
Louisiana	2011	$330	$363	$406	Kinship only	No
Maine	2011	$797	$797	$797	Yes	Yes, in some circumstances
Maryland	2015	$835	$835	$850	Yes	Up to 21 if in school or disabled
Massachusetts	2012	$631	$710	$752	Yes	Up to 21 if in school or disabled
Michigan	2013	$534	$534	$637	No	Yes, in some circumstances
Minnesota	2015	$283	$670	$790	Kinship only	May extend to 21 if in school or disabled

State	Date Updated	Maximum Basic Rates (per month)			Subsidized Guardianship?	Subsidy after age 18?
		Age 2	Age 9	Age 16		
Mississippi	2013	$325	$355	$400	No	May extend to 21 if disabled
Missouri	2014	$232	$283	$313	Kinship only	May extend to 21 if disabled
Montana	2016	$550	$550	$658	Yes	May extend to 21 if disabled
Nebraska	2014	$597	$822	$1,047	Yes	No
Nevada	2014	$591	$591	$682	Kinship only (age 62+)	No
New Hampshire	2012	$480	$520	$619	No	No
New Jersey	2013	$738	$818	$877	Yes	May continue to 21 if enrolled in secondary ed
New Mexico	2014	$483	$516	$542	No	Until 21 if medically fragile

continued

State	Date Updated	Maximum Basic Rates (per month)			Subsidized Guardianship?	Subsidy after age 18?
		Age 2	Age 9	Age 16		
New York	2013	$497 metro; $453 upstate	$586 metro; $545 upstate	$678 metro; $631 upstate	No	Up to 21
North Carolina	2012	$475	$581	$634	No	No
North Dakota	2014	$752	$862	$945	Yes	May go to 21 if enrolled in secondary ed or disabled
Ohio	2014	Varies by county	Varies by county	Varies by county	No, very limited Kinship Permanency Incentive Program (KPIP)	Until 21 if disabled
Oklahoma	2015	$506	$583	$646	Kinship only, limited	Until 19 if in school or disabled
Oregon	2012	$575	$655	$741	Kinship only but inclusive definition	Yes, in some circumstances
Pennsylvania	2014	Varies by county	Varies by county	Varies by county	Yes	Yes, in some circumstances

State	Date Updated	Maximum Basic Rates (per month)			Subsidized Guardianship?	Subsidy after age 18?
		Age 2	Age 9	Age 16		
Rhode Island	2012	$436	$414	$479	Yes	Possibly until 21 if disabled
South Carolina	2015	$332	$359	$425	No	Possibly until 21 if disabled
South Dakota	2014	$518	$518	$622	Yes	May continue until school
Tennessee	2014	$731	$731	$831	Yes	Until 21 in some circumstances
Texas	2014	$400	$400	$400	Permanency Care Assistance for kinship	Until 21 in some circumstances
Utah	2014	$187	$199	$211	Yes, but some regions not funded	May continue to 21 if disabled
Vermont	2014	$522	$580	$640	Yes, kinship only	Until 21 if disabled, may continue beyond 18 if still in high school
Virginia	2015	$462	$541	$686	No	Until 21 if disabled

continued

State	Date Updated	Maximum Basic Rates (per month)			Subsidized Guardianship?	Subsidy after age 18?
		Age 2	Age 9	Age 16		
Washington	2016	$450	$546	$562	Yes, for kinship through Relative Guardianship Assistance Program	May continue to 21 if still in high school
West Virginia	2015	$600	$600	$600	Yes	May continue to 21 if in school or disabled
Wisconsin	2015	$384	$420	$499	Yes	Up to 19 if high school student; up to 21 if in high school or disabled
Wyoming	2014	$399	$399	$399	Yes	No, unless disabled

Adapted from table provided by the North American Council on Adoptable Children (NACAC), "Summary of State Adoption Assistance Programs," May 2016, www.nacac.org/adoptionsubsidy/summary.html, with permission from NACAC.

Notes

Chapter 1

1. Census Bureau, "Grandparents Living with Own Grandchildren Under 18 Years by Responsibility for Own Grandchildren by Length of Time Responsible for Own Grandchildren for the Population 30 Years and Over," 2012–2016 American Community Survey 5-Year Estimates, released in 2018, https://factfinder.census.gov/faces/tableservices/jsf/pages/productview.xhtml?pid=ACS_16_5YR_B10050&prodType=table.

2. The study focused on 1,309 children. David M. Rubin et al., "The Impact of Kinship Care on Behavioral Well-Being for Children in Out-of-Home Care," *Archives in Pediatric and Adolescent Medicine* 162, no. 6 (June 2008): 550–56.

3. Deborah Dowell, Tamara M. Haegerich, and Roger Chou, "CDC Guideline for Prescribing Opioids for Chronic Pain—United States, 2016," www.cdc.gov/mmwr/volumes/65/rr/rr6501e1.htm.

4. Centers for Disease Control and Prevention, "Today's Heroin Epidemic," July 7, 2015, www.cdc.gov/vitalsigns/heroin/index.html.

5. The Children's Bureau, "The AFCARS Report: 2016 Preliminary Estimates as of October 20, 2017," www.acf.hhs.gov/sites/default/files/cb/afcarsreport24.pdf.

6. Roberta G. Sands and Robin S. Goldberg-Glen, "Factors Associated with Stress among Grandparents Raising Their Grandchildren," *Family Relations* 49, 1 (January 2000): 97–105.

7. The Children's Bureau, "The AFCARS Report: 2016 Preliminary Estimates as of October 20, 2017," www.acf.hhs.gov/sites/default/files/cb/afcarsreport24.pdf.

8. US Department of Health & Human Services, Administration for Children and Families, Administration on Children, Youth and Families, Children's Bureau, 2018, *Child maltreatment 2016*, www.acf.hhs.gov/cb/research-data-technology/statistics-research/child-maltreatment.

9. National Conference of State Legislatures, "Child Support and Incarceration," February 10, 2016, www.ncsl.org/research/human-services/child-support-and-incarceration.aspx#Legislative%20 Considerations.

10. Tanja Rothrauff, University of Missouri Extension, "When a Child's Parent Is Incarcerated," undated, http://extension.missouri.edu /p/GH6202.

11. Rose A. Rudd et al., "Increases in Drug and Opioid Overdose Deaths— United States, 2000–2014," *Morbidity and Mortality Weekly Report* 64, nos. 50 and 51 (January 1, 2016): 1378–82.

12. Bethany L. Letiecq, Sandra J. Bailey, and Fonda Porterfield, "'We Have No Rights, We Get No Help': The Legal and Policy Dilemmas Facing Grandparent Caregivers," *Journal of Family Issues* 29, no. 8 (August 2008): 995–1012.

13. Megan Dolbin-MacNab and Burt Hayslip Jr., "Grandparents Raising Grandchildren," in ed. Joyce A. Arditti, *Family Problems: Stress, Risk, and Resilience*, p. 139.

14. Census Bureau, "Grandchildren Characteristics, 2016 American Community Survey 1-Year Estimates," https://factfinder.census.gov /faces/tableservices/jsf/pages/productview.xhtml?pid=ACS_16 _1YR_S1001&prodType=table.

15. Census Bureau, "Grandchildren Characteristics, 2016 American Community Survey 1-Year Estimates."

16. Renee R. Ellis and Tavia Simmons, *Coresident Grandparents and Their Grandchildren: 2012* (Suitland, MD: United States Census Bureau, October 2014), p. 17, www.census.gov/content/dam/Census /library/publications/2014/demo/p20-576.pdf.

17. Data derived from Centers for Disease Control and Prevention, "National Survey of Children in Nonparental Care," (Atlanta, GA: CDC, 2013) www.cdc.gov/nchs/slaits/nscnc.htm.

18. Camille L. Ryan and Kurt Bauman, "Educational Attainment in the United States: 2015," Census Bureau, March 2016, p. 2, www.census.gov /content/dam/Census/library/publications/2016/demo/p20-578.pdf.

19. Lesley Stahl, *Becoming Grandma: The Joys and Science of the New Grandparenting* (New York: Blue Rider Press/Penguin Random House, 2016).

20. Census Bureau, "Grandparents Still Work to Support Their Grandchildren," July 12, 2017, www.census.gov/library/visualizations /2017/comm/grandparents-support-grandchildren.html.

Chapter 2

1. Meredith Minkler et al., "Depression in Grandparents Raising Grand-children: Results of a National Longitudinal Study," *Archives of Family Medicine* 6, no. 5 (Sept/Oct 1997): 445–52.

2. Minkler, "Depression in Grandparents."

3. Denise Burnette, "Physical and Emotional Well-Being of Custodial Grandparents in Latino Families," *American Journal of Orthopsychiatry* 69, no. 3 (July 1999): 305–18.

4. Deborah Sampson and Katherine Hertlein, "The Experience of Grand-parents Raising Grandchildren," *Grandfamilies: The Contemporary Journal of Research, Practice and Policy* 2, no. 1 (2015): 75–96, http://scholarworks.wmich.edu/cgi/viewcontent.cgi?article=1020&context=grandfamilies.

5. Meredith Minkler et al., "Depression in Grandparents Raising Grand-children: Results of National Longitudinal Study," *Archives of Family Medicine* 6, no. 5 (Sept/Oct 1997): 445–52; Bethany L. Letiecq, Sandra J. Bailey, and Marcia A. Kurtz, "Depression Among Rural Native American and European American Grandparents Rearing Their Grand-children," *Journal of Family Issues* 29, no. 3 (August 2008): 334–56.

6. Roberta G. Sands and Robin S. Goldberg-Glen, "Factors Associated with Stress Among Grandparents Raising Their Grandchildren," *Family Relations* 49, no. 1 (2000): 97–105.

7. Reeves Wiedeman, "A Full Revolution," *The New Yorker*, May 30, 2016, www.newyorker.com/magazine/2016/05/30/simone-biles-is-the-best-gymnast-in-the-world.

8. Char Adams, "Simone Biles Breaks Down While Talking about the Year She Was Adopted: 'My Parents Saved Me,'" *People TV Watch*, April 10, 2017, http://people.com/tv/simone-biles-breaks-down-year-adopted-dancing-with-stars/.

9. Jan Backhouse and Anne Graham, "Grandparents Raising Their Grandchildren: Acknowledging the Experience of Grief," *Australian Social Work* 66, no. 3 (2013): 440–54.

10. American Psychological Association, "Idaho Becomes Fifth State to Allow Psychologists to Prescribe Medications," April 5, 2017, www.apa.org/news/press/releases/2017/04/idaho-psychologists-medications.aspx.

11. American Psychiatric Association, *Diagnostic and Statistical Manual of Mental Disorders, Fifth Edition (DSM-5)* (Arlington, VA: American Psychiatric Association, 2013), 286–87.

12. Michelle A. Emick and Bert Hayslip Jr., "Custodial Grandparenting: Stresses, Coping Skills, and Relationships with Grandchildren," *The International Journal of Aging and Human Development* 48, no. 1 (1999): 35–61.

Chapter 3

1. Unpublished data from a survey of 558 parenting grandparents. Centers for Disease Control and Prevention Grandparenting Sample subset, "National Survey of Children in Nonparental Care" (Atlanta, GA: CDC, 2013), www.cdc.gov/nchs/slaits/nscnc.htm.

2. Andrew Adesman, MD, Principal Investigator, Adesman Grandfamily Study raw data, 2017.

3. Timothy E. Wilens, et al., "Does Stimulant Therapy of Attention-Deficit/ Hyperactivity Disorder Beget Later Substance Abuse? A Meta-Analytic Review of the Literature," *Pediatrics* 111, no. 1 (January 2003): 179–185; Joseph Biederman et al., "Stimulant Therapy and Risk for Subsequent Substance Use Disorders in Male Adults with ADHD: A Naturalistic Controlled 10-Year Follow-Up Study," *American Journal of Psychiatry* 165, no. 5 (May 2008): 597–603.

4. Joel L. Young, with Christine Adamec, *When Your Adult Child Breaks Your Heart: Coping with Mental Illness, Substance Abuse, and the Problems that Tear Families Apart* (Guilford, CT: Lyons Press, 2013).

5. In a 2006 study of the children of incarcerated mothers and their caregivers (most of them grandmothers), researchers analyzed results for sixty-nine children ages six to twelve at a summer camp. The researchers found that 60 percent of the children with incarcerated parents had suffered from four or more additional life stressors in the past year. Those with the fewest stressors and who also said they felt supported by their caregivers had fewer incidents of externalizing ("acting out") behaviors. Virginia H. Mackintosh, Barbara J. Myers, and Suzanne S. Kennon, "Children of Incarcerated Mothers and Their Caregivers: Factors Affecting the Quality of Their Relationship," *Journal of Child and Family Studies* 15, no. 5 (October 2006): 581–96.

6. Malitta Engstrom, "Involving Caregiving Grandmothers in Family Interventions When Mothers with Substance Use Problems Are Incarcerated," *Family Process* 47, no. 3 (September 2008): 357–71.

7. Ann Adalist-Estrin, "Homecoming: Children's Adjustment to Parent's Parole," paper presented to the Child Welfare League in 1996 and updated in 2002, https://nrccfi.camden.rutgers.edu/files /Homecoming.pdf.

8. One reliable source of recovery information is the Hazelden Betty Ford Foundation: www.hazeldenbettyford.org.

Chapter 4

1. Betsy Keefer Smalley and Jayne E. Schooler, *Telling the Truth to Your Adopted or Foster Child: Making Sense of the Past*, 2nd ed. (Santa Barbara, CA: ABC-CLIO, 2015).

2. Keefer Smalley and Schooler, *Telling the Truth*.

3. Jim Haggerty, "Do People Inherit Schizophrenia?" July 17, 2016, https:// psychcentral.com/lib/do-people-inherit-schizophrenia/.

4. University of Georgia, Cooperative Extension, Grandparents Raising Grandchildren fact sheet series, "Helping Your Grandchild Deal with the Death of a Parent," July 2009, https://spock.fcs.uga.edu/ext/pubs /chfd/CHFD-E-59-04.pdf.

5. Robert Parisian, "Talking Stick: Grandparents Raising Grandchildren," *The ANA Messenger: Social Development Edition 2013*, September 26, 2013, www.acf.hhs.gov/ana/resource/the-ana-messenger-social-development-edition-2013?page=15.

6. Census Bureau, "Grandparents: 2012–2016 American Community Survey 5-Year Estimates," https://factfinder.census.gov/faces /tableservices/jsf/pages/productview.xhtml?pid=ACS_16_5YR _S1002&prodType=table.

7. Lynn Patmalnee, "In My Tribe: Kinship Care Among Native American Families," *News from OUR Foster Care Newsletter*, June 1, 2016, http:// foster-care-newsletter.com/tribe-kinship-care-among-native-american-families/; Ellen Wulfhorst, "Grandmothers Fill Void Left By Violence, Drugs on Native American Reservations," Thomson Reuters Foundation, May 19, 2016, https://oldbearblog.tumblr.com/post/144686133157 /grandmothers-fill-void-left-by-violence-drugs-on.

8. Andrew Adesman, with Christine Adamec, *Parenting Your Adopted Child: A Positive Approach to Building a Strong Family* (New York: McGraw-Hill, 2004).

9. Megan L. Dolbin-MacNab and Margaret K. Keiley, "Navigating Interdependence: How Adolescents Raised Solely by Grandparents Experience Their Family Relationships," *Family Relations* 58, no. 2 (April 2009): 162–75.

10. Dolbin-MacNab and Keiley, "Navigating Interdependence."

Chapter 5

1. Kevin A. Carter, Nathanael E. Hathaway, and Christine F. Lettieri, "Common Sleep Disorders in Children," *American Family Physician* 89, no. 5 (March 1, 2014): 368–77.

2. American Academy of Pediatrics, "American Academy of Pediatrics Supports Childhood Sleep Guidelines," June 13, 2016, www.aap.org/en-us/about-the-aap/aap-press-room/pages/American-Academy-of-Pediatrics-Supports-Childhood-Sleep-Guidelines.aspx.

3. Source: Adapted from American Academy of Pediatrics, "American Academy of Pediatrics Supports Childhood Sleep Guidelines," June 13, 2016, www.aap.org/en-us/about-the-aap/aap-press-room/pages/American-Academy-of-Pediatrics-Supports-Childhood-Sleep-Guidelines.aspx.

4. Nancy Fliesler, Boston Children's Hospital's Pediatric Health Blog, "Melatonin for Children—5 Things to Know," February 16, 2016, https://thriving.childrenshospital.org/melatonin-children-5-things-know/.

5. Irvin Janjua and Ran D. Goldman, "Sleep-Related Melatonin Use in Healthy Children," *Canadian Family Physician* 62, no. 4 (April 2016): 315–16. Canada's "off-label" drug use policy is comparable to the United States', with Health Canada the Canadian equivalent of the US Food and Drug Administration.

6. National Institute of Neurological Disorders and Stroke, "Brain Basics: Understanding Sleep," undated, www.ninds.nih.gov/Disorders/Patient-Caregiver-Education/Understanding-Sleep.

7. University of Washington, "What Is Sleep . . . and Why Do We Do It?" http://faculty.washington.edu/chudler/sleep.html.

8. Megan A. Moreno, "Sleep Terrors and Sleepwalking: Common Parasomnias of Childhood," undated, JAMA Pediatrics Patient page, July 2015, https://jamanetwork.com/journals/jamapediatrics/fullarticle/2337224.

9. Kevin A. Carter, Nathanael E. Hathaway, and Christine F. Lettieri, "Common Sleep Disorders in Children," *American Family Physician* 89, no. 5 (March 1, 2014): 368–77.

10. Helen M. Stallman and Mark Kohler, "Prevalence of Sleepwalking: A Systematic Review and Meta-Analysis," *PLOS One* 11, no. 11 (November 10, 2016), http://journals.plos.org/plosone/article/file?id=10.1371/journal.pone.0164769&type=printable.

11. National Association for Continence, "Pediatric Bedwetting," www.nafc.org/pediatric-bedwetting/.

12. National Association for Continence, "Pediatric Bedwetting."

13. Ersan Arda, Basri Cakiroglu, and David T. Thomas, "Primary Nocturnal Enuresis: A Review," *Nephro-Urology Monthly* 8, no. 4 (July 2016).

14. Arda, Cakiroglu, and Thomas, "Primary Nocturnal Enuresis."

15. Rajiv Sinha and Sumantra Raut, "Management of Nocturnal Enuresis—Myths and Facts," *World Journal of Nephrology* 5, no. 4 (July 6, 2016): 328–38, www.ncbi.nlm.nih.gov/pmc/articles/PMC4936340/.

16. Canadian Paediatric Society, "Management of Primary Nocturnal Enuresis," *Paediatrics Child Health* 10, no. 10 (December 2005): 611–14, www.cps.ca/en/documents/position/primary-nocturnal-enuresis.

17. Canadian Paediatric Society, "Management."

18. Kathryn Walton et al., "Time to Re-Think Picky Eating?: A Relational Approach to Understanding Picky Eating," *International Journal of Behavioral Nutrition and Physical Activity* 14, no. 62 (2017), https://ijbnpa.biomedcentral.com/articles/10.1186/s12966-017-0520-0.

19. Walton et al., "Time to Re-Think?"

20. Walton et al., "Time to Re-Think?"

21. Caroline M. Taylor et al., "Picky/Fussy Eating in Children: Review of Definitions, Assessment, Prevalence and Dietary Intakes," *Appetite* 95 (2015): 349–59, www.sciencedirect.com/science/article/pii/S0195666315003438?via%3Dihub.

22. US Department of Agriculture, "Food Security Status of U.S. Households in 2016," last updated October 4, 2017, www.ers.usda.gov /topics/food-nutrition-assistance/food-security-in-the-us/key-statistics -graphics.aspx.

23. Katja Rowell, "Healing from Food Insecurity: Beyond the Stash," *Adoptalk*, Winter 2013.

24. American Gastroenterological Association, "Prebiotics Reduce Body Fat in Overweight Children," *ScienceDaily*, June 7, 2017, www.sciencedaily .com/releases/2017/06/170607123949.htm.

25. Academy of Nutrition and Dietetics, "Water: How Much do Kids Need?" May 2, 2017, www.eatright.org/fitness/sports-and-performance /hydrate-right/water-go-with-the-flow.

26. American Academy of Pediatrics, "American Academy of Pediatrics Recommends No Fruit Juice for Children Under 1 Year," May 22, 2017, www.aap.org/en-us/about-the-aap/aap-press-room/Pages/American- Academy-of-Pediatrics-Recommends-No-Fruit-Juice-For-Children- Under-1-Year.aspx.

27. Based on a study of nearly 73,000 six- and seven-year-olds from seventeen countries: Irene Braithwaite et al., "Fast-Food Consumption and Body Mass Index in Children and Adolescents: An International Cross-Sectional Study," *BMJ Open* 2014, http://bmjopen.bmj.com /content/bmjopen/4/12/e005813.full.pdf.

28. Murray A. Straus, "Children Should Never, Ever, Be Spanked No Matter What the Circumstances," in eds. Donileen R. Loseke, Richard Gelles, and Mary M. Cavanaugh, *Current Controversies about Family Violence*, 2nd ed. (Thousand Oaks, CA: Sage, 2004).

29. Denise Continenza, "Time-Out or Time-In?" Penn State Extension, December 1, 2015. http://extension.psu.edu/youth/betterkidcare /news/2015/time-out-or-time-in.

30. Gina Shaw, "Disciplining Toddlers: Time In or Time Out?" Web MD, 2011, www.webmd.com/parenting/features/disciplining-toddlers#1.

31. Continenza, "Time-Out or Time-In?"

Chapter 6

1. National Conference of State Legislatures, "Educational and Medical Consent Laws," February 17, 2017, www.ncsl.org/research/human -services/educational-and-medical-consent-laws.aspx.

2. Barbara Coloroso, *The Bully, the Bullied, and the Bystander: From Preschool to High School—How Parents and Teachers Can Help Break the Cycle of Violence* (New York: Collins Living, 2008).

3. Laura Kann et al., "Youth Risk Behavior Surveillance—United States, 2015," *Morbidity and Mortality Weekly Report* 65, no. 6 (June 10, 2016), Center for Surveillance, Epidemiology, and Laboratory Services, Centers for Disease Control and Prevention, www.cdc.gov/healthy youth/data/yrbs/pdf/2015/ss6506_updated.pdf.

4. Kann et al., "Youth Risk Behavior."

5. "Technology and Preteens," Nobullying.com, April 10, 2017, https:// nobullying.com/technology-and-preteens/.

6. Stewart W. Twemlow et al., "Teachers Who Bully Students: A Hidden Trauma," *International Journal of Social Psychiatry* 52, no. 3 (June 2006): 187–98.

7. Kim Lachance Shandrow, "How to Protect Young Kids from Inappropriate Internet," NBCNews.com, July 9, 2012, www.nbcnews.com /id/48186441/ns/technology_and_science-back_to_school/t/how -protect-young-kids-inappropriate-internet/#.WXUQCE-WzmQ.

8. US Department of Education, "Every Student Succeeds Act (ESSA)," www.ed.gov/essa?src=rn.

9. ADDitude editors, "Every 504 Plan Should Include These Six Accommodations," www.additudemag.com/504-plan-adhd-accommodations/; National Resource Center on ADHD, "Section 504," 2017; www.chadd .org/Understanding-ADHD/For-Parents-Caregivers/Education/Section-504.aspx.

10. David Flink, *Thinking Differently: An Inspiring Guide for Parents of Children with Learning Disabilities* (New York: William Morrow, 2014).

11. National Center for Learning Disabilities, "Accommodations for Students with LD," 2006, www.ldonline.org/article/8022/.

12. "25 Famous People with Learning Disorders," Special Education Degrees, www.special-education-degree.net/25-famous-people -with-learning-disorders/.

Chapter 7

1. Telephone interview, Christine Adamec with Janice Ausburn, November 13, 2017. Also, written permission granted for this quotation.

2. Sources: Kathleen Meara, "What's in a Name? Defining and Granting a Legal Status to Grandparents Who Are Informal Primary Caregivers of Their Grandchildren," *Family Court Review* 52, no. 1 (2014): 128–41; *Hernandez v. Hernandez and Ausburn*, Supreme Court of the State of Idaho, Opinion No. 108 (2011), http://cases.justia.com/idaho/supreme-court-civil/37779.pdf?ts=1396120331; Matthew G. Bennett, "Idaho Custody Determinations: Limits on Standing," *Idaho Law Review* 50 (2013): 141–72, www.uidaho.edu/-/media/UIdaho-Responsive/Files/law/law-review/articles/volume-50/50-1-bennett-matthew-comments.ashx?la=en&hash=C5B6470926056EEBB060DE932C78567BB45 62E26.

3. Meara, "What's in a Name?"; *Hernandez v. Hernandez and Ausburn*, Supreme Court of the State of Idaho; Bennett, "Idaho Custody Determinations."

4. Allie Morris, "N.H. Becomes First State to Give Grandparents Preference in Guardianship Cases," *Concord Monitor*, June 27, 2017, www.concordmonitor.com/chris-sunni-signs-bills-for-foster-grandparents-10961736; Dave Solomon, "New Laws Foster Growth in N.H. 'Grandfamilies,'" *Union Leader*, June 27, 2017, www.unionleader.com/state-government/New-laws-foster-growth-in-NH-grandfamilies-06282017.

5. Daniel Pollack, "When Do Informal Parenting Arrangements Need Approval from the State?" *Policy & Practice* 74, no. 2 (April 2016): 25–29; quote is on page 29.

6. The Children's Bureau, "The AFCARS Report: 2016 Preliminary Estimates as of October 20, 2017," www.acf.hhs.gov/sites/default/files/cb/afcarsreport24.pdf.

7. The Children's Bureau, "The AFCARS Report."

8. National Conference of State Legislatures, "Supporting Relative Caregivers of Children," February 13, 2017, www.ncsl.org/research/human-services/relative-caretivers.aspx.

9. Melinda Perez-Porter and Margaret M. Flint, "Grandparent Caregiving: Legal Status Issues and State Policy," in ed. Carole B. Cox, *To Grandmother's House We Go and Stay: Perspectives on Custodial Grandparents* (New York: Springer Publishing Company, 2000), 132–48.

10. Christine A. Adamec and Laurie C. Miller, *The Encyclopedia of Adoption,* 3rd ed. (New York: Facts On File, 2007).

Chapter 8

1. Jane Mauldon et al., *TANF Child-Only Cases: Who Are They? What Policies Affect Them? What Is Being Done?* University of Chicago, December 11, 2012, www.chapinhall.org/sites/default/files/TANF%20Child-Only%20Cases%20--%20The%20Report%201-25-2013.pdf.

2. Mauldon et al., *TANF Child-Only* Cases.

3. Mauldon et al., *TANF Child-Only* Cases.

4. Mauldon et al., *TANF Child-Only* Cases.

5. National Conference on State Legislatures, "Child Support Overview," August 11, 2017, www.ncsl.org/research/human-services/child-support-homepage.aspx.

6. Children's Bureau, "Title IV-E Guardianship Assistance," June 28, 2017, www.acf.hhs.gov/cb/resource/title-iv-e-guardianship-assistance.

7. Information provided by email from Josh Kroll, project coordinator, Adoption Subsidy Resource Center of the North American Council on Adoptable Children (NACAC) to Christine Adamec, July 17, 2017.

8. Children's Bureau, Child Welfare Policy Manual, July 14, 2017, "8.5: Guardianship Assistance Program," www.acf.hhs.gov/cwpm/programs/cb/laws_policies/laws/cwpm/policy_dsp_pf.jsp?citID=370.

9. Children's Bureau, Child Welfare Policy Manual.

10. Children's Bureau, Child Welfare Policy Manual.

11. The Children's Bureau, "The AFCARS Report: 2016 Preliminary Estimates as of October 20, 2017," www.acf.hhs.gov/sites/default/files/cb/afcarsreport24.pdf.

12. Email from Mary Boo, executive director of the North American Council on Adoptable Children (NACAC) to Christine Adamec, July 14, 2017.

13. Social Security Administration, *Benefits for Children with Disabilities* (Baltimore, MD: Social Security Administration, 2017), www.ssa.gov/pubs/EN-05-10026.pdf.

14. Email to Christine Adamec from Head Start program officials, May 18, 2017.

15. Sandra J. Bailey, "Grandparents Raising Grandchildren: Parenting the Second Time Around," Montana State University, February 2016, https://dphhs.mt.gov/Portals/85/Documents/ProtectMontanaKids/PMK3.PDF.

16. Children's Action Alliance, "Help for Grandparents Raising Grandkids," 2016, http://azchildren.org/wp-content/uploads/2016/09/HELP-FOR-GRANDPARENTS-RAISING-GRANDKIDS-Resource-Document.pdf.

17. Oregon Department of Human Services, "Oregon's Legal Guide for Grandparents and Other Older Relatives Raising Children, 2016," January 2016, https://apps.state.or.us/Forms/Served/de9395.pdf.

18. Internal Revenue Service, "Adoption Credit and Adoption Assistance Program," www.irs.gov/taxtopics/tc607.html.

19. Internal Revenue Service, "Form 8839: Qualified Adoption Expenses," 2017, www.irs.gov/pub/irs-pdf/f8839.pdf.

20. Internal Revenue Service, "Earned Income Credit," Publication 596, December 21, 2016, www.irs.gov/pub/irs-pdf/p596.pdf.

Chapter 9

1. Gregory C. Smith and Patrick A. Palmieri, "Risk of Psychological Difficulties Among Children Raised by Custodial Grandparents," *Psychological Services* 58, no. 10 (October 2007): 1303–10.

2. Susanna N. Visser et al., "Trends in the Parent Report of Health Care Provider-Diagnosed and Medicated Attention-Deficit/Hyperactivity Disorder: United States, 2003-2011," *Journal of the American Academy of Child & Adolescent Psychiatry* 53, no. 1 (January 2014): 34–46.

3. Centers for Disease Control and Prevention, "ADHD: Symptoms and Diagnosis," October 5, 2016, www.cdc.gov/ncbddd/adjd/diagnosis.html.

4. American Psychiatric Association, *Diagnostic and Statistical Manual of Mental Disorders, Fifth Edition (DSM-5)* (Arlington, VA: American Psychiatric Association, 2013).

5. Centers for Disease Control and Prevention, "Behavior Therapy Is an Important First Step for Children Under 6 with ADHD," 2015, www.cdc.gov/ncbddd/adhd/documents/adhd-behavior-therapy-overview.pdf.

6. Centers for Disease Control and Prevention: State Medicaid Policies: Prescribing ADHD Medications for Children," 2016, www.cdc.gov /ncbddd/adhd/documents/fact-sheet-adhd-medicaid-policies.pdf.

7. National Institute of Mental Health, "Autism Spectrum Disorder," October 2016, www.nimh.nih.gov/health/topics/autism-spectrum -disorders-asd/index.shtml?utm_source=rss_readersutm_medium =rssutm_campaign=rss_full.

8. Centers for Disease Control and Prevention, "Key Findings: Population Attributable Fractions for Three Perinatal Risk Factors for Autism Spectrum Disorders, 2002 and 2008 Autism and Developmental Disabilities Monitoring Network," April 28, 2017, www.cdc.gov/ncbddd/autism /features/keyfindings-risk-factors.html.

9. See the immunization schedule provided by the American Academy of Pediatrics on its website: https://healthychildren.org/English/safety -prevention/immunizations/Pages/Recommended-Immunization -Schedules.aspx.

10. American Psychiatric Association, *Diagnostic and Statistical Manual of Mental Disorders*.

11. B. D. Barager, J. M. Campbell, and J. D. McDonough, "Prevalence and Onset of Regression within Autism Spectrum Disorders: A Meta-Analytic Review," *Journal of Autism and Developmental Disorders* 43, no. 4 (April 2013): 817–28.

12. National Institute of Neurological Disorders and Stroke, "Autism Spectrum Disorder Fact Sheet," September 2015, www.ninds.nih.gov /Disorders/Patient-Caregiver-Education/Fact-Sheets/Autism -Spectrum-Disorder-Fact-Sheet.

13. Autism Speaks, "Treatments and Therapies," undated, www.autism speaks.org/family-services/tool-kits/100-day-kit/treatments-therapies.

14. PsychCentral, "Medications for Autism," https://psychcentral.com/lib /medications-for-autism/, undated.

15. American Academy of Child and Adolescent Psychiatry, "Depression in Children and Teens," July 2013, www.aacap.org/AACAP/Families _and_Youth/Facts_for_Families/FFF-Guide/The-Depressed-Child -004.aspx.

16. Substance Abuse and Mental Health Services Administration, "Disruptive Behavior Disorders," April 5, 2017, www.samhsa.gov/ treatment/mental-disorders/disruptive-behavior-disorders#factors.

17. Ginny Sprang et al., "The Pathway to Grandparenting Stress: Trauma, Relational Conflict, and Emotional Well-Being," *Aging & Mental Health* 19, no. 4 (2015): 315–24.

18. Sprang et al., "Grandparenting Stress," 321.

19. AACAP, "Depression."

20. National Institute of Mental Health, "Antidepressant Medications for Children and Adolescents: Information for Parents and Caregivers," undated, www.nimh.nih.gov/health/topics/child-and-adolescent-mental-health/antidepressant-medications-for-children-and-adolescents-information-for-parents-and-caregivers.shtml.

21. Centers for Disease Control and Prevention, "Anxiety and Depression," November 16, 2016, www.cdc.gov/childrensmentalhealth/depression.html.

22. American Psychiatric Association, *Diagnostic and Statistical Manual of Mental Disorders, Fifth Edition (DSM-5)* (Arlington, VA: American Psychiatric Association, 2013).

23. Rachel M. Hiller et al., "Research Review: Changes in the Prevalence and Symptom Severity of Child Post-Traumatic Stress Disorder in the Year Following Trauma—A Meta-Analytic Study," *Journal of Child Psychology and Psychiatry* 57, no. 8 (2016): 884–98.

24. Hiller et al., "Research Review."

25. Margaret Riley, Sana Ahmed, and Amy Locke, "Common Questions about Oppositional Defiant Disorders," *American Family Physician* 93, no 7. (2016): 586–91.

26. Riley, Ahmed, and Locke, "Common Questions."

27. Ross W. Greene et al., "Effectiveness of Collaborative Problem Solving in Affectively Dysregulated Children with Oppositional-Defiant Disorder: Initial Findings," *Journal of Counseling and Clinical Psychology* (2015): 1–14.

28. American Academy of Child and Adolescent Psychiatry, "Oppositional Defiant Disorder," 2009, www.aacap.org/App_Themes/AACAP/docs/resource_centers/odd/odd_resource_center_odd_guide.pdf.

29. A 2015 study compared the cognition and intelligence levels of a group of children exposed to prenatal opioids and other drugs to a group of children with no known prenatal risks. The children were checked at ages 1, 2, 3, 4½, and 8½ years. The drug-exposed children had significantly lower intelligence scores—even those who had been

placed in stable adoptive or foster families at a young age. Egil Nygaard et al., "Longitudinal Development of Children Born to Mothers with Opioid and Polysubstance Use," *Pediatric Research* 78, no. 3 (September 2015): 330–35.

30. Emily J. Ross et al., "Developmental Consequences of Fetal Exposure to Drugs: What We Know and What We Still Must Learn," *Neuropsychopharmacology Reviews* 40, no. 1 (2015): 61–87.

31. Ross et al., "Developmental Consequences."

32. K. Nash et al., "Understanding Fetal Alcohol Spectrum Disorders (FASDs): Toward Identification of a Behavioral Phenotype," *Scientific World Journal* 8 (September 2008): 873–882.

33. Centers for Disease Control and Prevention, "Facts about FASDs," April 15, 2015, www.cdc.gov/ncbdd/fasd/facts.html.

34. University of Washington, FAS Diagnostic & Prevention Network, "The 4 Diagnoses under the FASD Umbrella," undated, http://depts.washington.edu/fasdpn/htmls/fasd-fas.htm.

Chapter 10

1. Amy M. Branum and Susan L. Lukacs, "Food Allergy among U.S. Children: Trends in Prevalence and Hospitalization," *National Center for Health Statistics Data Brief* 10 (October 2008): 1–7.

2. American Academy of Pediatrics, Healthychildren.org, "Sun Safety: Information for Parents about Sunburn and Sunscreen," April 1, 2014, www.healthychildren.org/English/safety-prevention/at-play/Pages/Sun-Safety.aspx.

3. Andrew Adesman, *Baby Facts: The Truth about Your Child's Health from Newborn Through Preschool* (Hoboken, NJ: McGraw Hill, 2009).

4. Stephen Ray Flora and Courtney Allyn Polenick, "Effects of Sugar Consumption on Human Behavior and Performance," *Psychological Record* 63 (2013): 1–12.

5. Flora and Allyn Polenick, "Effects of Sugar."

6. Jyoti Oberol et al., "Dental Knowledge and Awareness among Grandparents," *World Journal of Clinical Pediatrics* 5, no. 1 (February 8, 2016): 112–17.

7. American Academy of Pediatrics, "How to Prevent Tooth Decay in Your Baby," May 15, 2015, www.healthychildren.org/English/ages-stages /baby/teething-tooth-care/Pages/How-to-Prevent-Tooth-Decay-in -Your-Baby.aspx.

8. Centers for Disease Control and Prevention, "Protecting Against Influenza (Flu): Advice for Caregivers of Young Children," December 9, 2016, www.cec.gov/flu/protect/infantcare.htm.

9. Centers for Disease Control and Prevention, "Children and Flu Antiviral Drugs," January 25, 2017, www.cdc.gov/flu/children/antiviral.htm.

10. Shaman Rajindrajith et al., "Childhood Constipation as an Emerging Public Health Problem," *World Journal of Gastroenterology* 22, no. 30 (August 2016): 6864–6875.

11. Samuel Nurko and Lori A. Zimmerman, "Evaluation and Treatment of Constipation in Children and Adolescents," *American Family Physician* 90, 2 (July 15, 2014): 82–90.

12. M. M. Tabbers et al., "Evaluation and Treatment of Functional Constipation in Infants and Children: Evidence-Based Recommendations from ESPGHAN and NASPGHAN," *Journal of Pediatric Gastroenterology, Hepatology, and Nutrition* 58, 2 (February 2014): 258–74.

13. American Academy of Pediatrics, "Principles of Judicious Antibiotic Prescribing for Upper Respiratory Tract Infections in Pediatrics," *Pediatrics* 132, 6 (December 2013): 1146–54.

14. American Academy of Pediatrics, "AAP Updates Treatments for Head Lice," April 27, 2015, www.aap.org/en-us/about-the-aap/aap-press-room /pages/aap-updates-treatments-for-head-lice.aspx.

15. Amanda Allmon, Kristen Deane, and Kari L. Martin, "Common Skin Rashes in Children," *American Family Physician* 92, no. 3 (August 1, 2015): 211–16.

16. American Academy of Dermatology, "Diaper Rash: How to Treat," undated, www.aad.org/public/diseases/rashes/diaper-rash-how-to-treat.

17. Amanda Allmon, Kristen Deane, and Kari L. Martin, "Common Skin Rashes in Children," *American Family Physician* 92, no. 3 (August 1, 2015): 211–16.

18. Centers for Disease Control and Prevention, "Child Passenger Safety: Get the Facts," www.cdc.gov/features/passengersafety/index.html, September 18, 2017.

19. National Highway Traffic Safety Administration, "Lives Saved in 2016 by Restraint Use and Minimum-Drinking-Age Laws," *Traffic Safety Facts*, October 2017. https://crashstats.nhtsa.dot.gov/Api/Public/Publication/812454.

20. Source: Centers for Disease Control and Prevention, "Vaccine-Preventable Diseases and the Vaccines That Prevent Them," December 2017, www.cdc.gov/vaccines/parents/downloads/parent-ver-sch-0-6yrs.pdf.

21. National Conference of State Legislatures, "Educational and Medical Consent Laws," March 17, 2014, www.ncsl.org/research/human-services/educational-and-medical-consent-laws.aspx.

Chapter 11

1. Mary Elizabeth Hughes et al., "All in the Family: The Impact of Caring for Grandchildren on Grandparents' Health" *Journal of Gerontology Series B: Psychological Sciences and Social Sciences* 62, no. 2 (March 2007): S108–S119.

2. Centers for Medicare and Medicaid Services, *Chronic Conditions among Medicare Beneficiaries, Chartbook,* 2012 edition (Baltimore, MD: CMS, 2012).

3. Centers for Disease Control and Prevention, "At a Glance, 2016: Diabetes," www.cdc.gov/chronicdisease/resources/publications/aag/pdf/2016/diabetes-aag.pdf.

4. CDC, "At a Glance."

5. American College of Cardiology, "High Blood Pressure Redefined for First Time in 14 Years: 130 Is the New High," www.acc.org/about-acc/press-releases/2017/11/13/15/35/high-blood-pressure-redefined-for-first-time-in-14-years-130-is-the-new-high.

6. Source: American College of Cardiology

7. Cynthia L. Ogden et al., "Prevalence of Obesity among Adults and Youth: United States, 2011-2014," *NCHS Data Brief No. 219* (November 2015): 1–8.

8. Centers for Medicare and Medicaid Services, *Chronic Conditions among Medicare Beneficiaries.*

9. Centers for Disease Control and Prevention, "Arthritis: National Statistics," October 25, 2017, www/cdc/gpv/arthritis/data_statistics/national-statistics.html.

10. CDC, "Arthritis."

11. Centers for Medicare and Medicaid Services, *Chronic Conditions among Medicare Beneficiaries.*

12. CMMS, *Chronic Conditions.*

13. Deborah M. Whitley, Esme Fuller-Thomson, and Sarah Brennenstuhl, "Health Characteristics of Solo Grandparent Caregivers and Single Parents: A Comparative Profile Using the Behavior Risk Factor Surveillance Survey," *Current Gerontology and Geriatrics Research* (2015), www.hindawi.com/journals/cggr/2015/630717/.

14. Centers for Disease Control and Prevention, "Heart Disease Behavior," August 10, 2015, www.cdc.gov/heartdisease/behavior.htm.

15. Centers for Disease Control and Prevention, "Heart Disease Fact Sheet," August 23, 2017, www.cdc.gov/dhdsp/data_statistics/fact_sheets/fs_heart_disease.htm.

16. National Heart, Lung, and Blood Institute, "What Are the Symptoms of Heart Attack?" January 27, 2015, www.nhlbi.nih.gov/health/health-topics/topics/heartattack/signs.

17. Centers for Disease Control and Prevention, "Stroke Fact Sheet," undated, www.cdc.gov/dhdsp/data_statistics/fact_sheets/docs/fs_stroke.pdf.

18. Centers for Disease Control and Prevention, "Stroke Signs and Symptoms," January 17, 2017, www.cdc.gov/stroke/signs_symptoms.htm.

19. CDC, "Stroke Signs."

20. National Heart, Blood, and Lung Institute, "Stress Testing—Types of Stress Testing," www.nhlbi.nih.gov/book/expoert.html/4858.

21. American College of Obstetricians and Gynecologists, "ACOG Statement on Breast Cancer Screening Guidelines," January 11, 2016, www.acog.org/About-ACOG/News-Room/Statements/2016/ACOG-Statement-on-Breast-Cancer-Screening-Guidelines.

22. Kevin C. Oeffinger et al., "Breast Cancer Screening for Women at Average Risk 2015 Guideline Update from the American Cancer Society," *Journal of the American Medical Association* 314, no. 15 (April 5, 2016): 1599–1614, http://jamanetwork.com/journals/jama/fullarticle/2463262.

Conclusion

1. The Children's Bureau, "The AFCARS Report: 2016 Preliminary Estimates as of October 20, 2017," www.acf.hhs.gov/sites/default/files/cb/afcarsreport24.pdf.

Acknowledgments

Andrew Adesman, MD, and Christine Adamec would like to thank the hundreds of grandparents who responded to the Adesman Grandfamily Study in 2016 as well as the many other wonderful grandparents who are out there doing the often-challenging work of raising their children's children, sometimes under very difficult circumstances. You are our heroes!

We are extremely grateful to Dr. William Sears for his sincere and enthusiastic foreword, and we thank all of our kind colleagues and supporters for the endorsement of this work.

The authors also thank attorney Steven Kirsh of the law firm of Kirsh & Kirsh Adoptions, P.C. in Indianapolis for his review of and suggestions for chapter 7 regarding custody, guardianship, and adoption. The 2005 recipient of the Congressional "Angels in Adoption" award, Mr. Kirsh has more than thirty years of experience in family law and adoption and is a past president of the American Academy of Adoption Attorneys.

Thanks also to Mary Boo, the executive director of the North American Council on Adoptable Children (NACAC), for her gracious assistance in locating important information for our readers.

The authors also thank Tavia Simmons, social statistician and family demographer for the US Census Bureau, Fertility and Family Statistics Branch, who aided us in finding crucial data we would never have found otherwise and who also provided very helpful explanations.

Dr. Adesman would like to thank his wife, Dr. Angela Romano, for her enduring forbearance as loving partner, her sage counsel as parent and pediatrician, and her unflagging support for the past thirty years. He would also like to acknowledge his three children—Marisa, Danielle, and Jason. Although they are all now young adults, they continue to remind him that one's role as a parent never ends and that no parent is perfect. Thanks to them, his experiences as a parent have made him a better pediatrician (and, he hopes, *vice versa*). Last, Dr. Adesman thanks Dr. Charles Schleien and Mr. Jonathan Scheidt at Cohen Children's Medical Center of New York for their longstanding support, without which he could not have pursued research in this area and taken on an important writing project such as this. Dr. Adesman is grateful each and every day for the opportunities he has been provided to pursue so many different professional activities with the objective of helping parents and children in ways he never would have imagined thirty-seven years ago when he first decided to pursue a career in pediatrics.

Christine Adamec would like to thank her husband, John Adamec, for his unswerving support for this important book project.

Both Dr. Adesman and Christine Adamec thank our agent, Roger Williams, for helping us find the best publisher for this major undertaking: Hazelden Publishing.

Last, Dr. Adesman and Christine Adamec would like to thank Vanessa Torrado, editorial director of trade and consumer content at Hazelden Publishing, for strongly believing in our project and providing us with excellent ideas and assistance throughout the course of writing and producing this book. We also thank Mindy Keskinen, our developmental editor, for her word wizardry as well as excellent suggestions for organizing our book. Thanks also to the entire Hazelden team for their great work!

About the Authors

Andrew Adesman, MD, is a professor of pediatrics at the Donald and Barbara Zucker School of Medicine at Hofstra/Northwell in New York. He is also chief of developmental and behavioral pediatrics at the Steven & Alexandra Cohen Children's Medical Center of New York in New Hyde Park, New York. Dr. Adesman is board-certified in both developmental and behavioral pediatrics and in neurodevelopmental disabilities. Since 2016, Dr. Adesman has been named one of America's Top Doctors by Castle Connolly, an unusually prestigious honor for a developmental pediatrician. He has also been recognized repeatedly as a Top Doctor by New York magazine, Newsday, and other publications.

Dr. Adesman has authored and coauthored numerous research articles and review articles for medical journals on pediatric issues and problems. He recently wrote a book on parenting myths: *Baby Facts: The Truth about Your Child's Health from Newborn through Preschool.* In addition, Dr. Adesman coauthored *Parenting Your Adopted Child: A Positive Approach to Building a Strong Family* with Christine Adamec. Dr. Adesman is very proud of his 2016 study, the Adesman Grandfamily Study, a nationwide survey of grandparents serving as parents. This study provided not only important statistical information about grandfamilies, but the respondents also submitted comments conveying their heartfelt concerns and advice for other parenting grandparents. Dr. Adesman is married to a pediatrician, and they have three children. He hopes his grandfamily book will aid grandparents in their very important roles of being parents all over again as they raise their grandchildren, whether they have just stepped up to this crucial job or they have been raising their grandchildren for years.

Christine Adamec is a health and self-help writer whose coauthor credits include *When Your Adult Child Breaks Your Heart*; *The A to Z of Phobias, Fears and Anxieties*; and *Fibromyalgia for Dummies*. In addition, she has coauthored *Parenting Your Adopted Child: A Positive Approach to Building a Strong Family* with Dr. Adesman. Ms. Adamec and her husband are now raising a grandchild whom they adopted, which means they have a total of four children, including three adult children. Ms. Adamec likes to write books that may improve people's lives, and she also knows that parenting children—and grandchildren—can be extremely challenging at times and yet also a lot of fun on many occasions. Researching this book brought home to her the common struggles that many grandfamilies face today. One challenge is a lack of information, while another is feeling no one else understands what they are going through. She hopes those struggles are at least partially remedied by this book.

About Hazelden Publishing

As part of the Hazelden Betty Ford Foundation, Hazelden Publishing offers both cutting-edge educational resources and inspirational books. Our print and digital works help guide individuals in treatment and recovery, and their loved ones. Professionals who work to prevent and treat addiction also turn to Hazelden Publishing for evidence-based curricula, digital content solutions, and videos for use in schools, treatment programs, correction programs, and electronic health records systems. We also offer training for implementation of our curricula.

Through published and digital works, Hazelden Publishing extends the reach of healing and hope to individuals, families, and communities affected by addiction and related issues.

For more information about Hazelden publications,
please call **800-328-9000**
or visit us online at **hazelden.org/bookstore.**

ALSO OF INTEREST

Addict in the Family
Stories of Loss, Hope, and Recovery
BEVERLY CONYERS

In these gripping stories of fathers, mothers, sons, and daughters of addicts, you'll discover lessons on love, detachment, intervention, and self-care. Revised and updated edition.

Order No. 1018
ebook EB1018

Tending Dandelions
Honest Meditations for Mothers with Addicted Children
SANDRA SWENSON

Where love and addiction meet: this book offers wisdom and support to parents who find themselves tending to a life they didn't expect. In these pages, find empowering moments of recognition, confession, and healing.

Order No. 3481
ebook E3481

Codependent No More
How to Stop Controlling Others and Start Caring for Yourself
MELODIE BEATTIE

Have you lost sight of your own life in the drama of tending to someone else's? Use this book to chart a path to freedom. With personal stories, reflections, self-tests, and exercises, this modern classic serves as a healing touchstone for millions.

Order No. 5014
ebook EB5014

Take Good Care
Finding Your Joy in Compassionate Caregiving
CYNTHIA ORANGE

Are you caregiving or care-taking? Discern the subtle differences as you learn from a wide range of caregivers, leading experts in the field, and the author's own hard-won wisdom.

Order No. 3425
ebook EB3425

Hazelden Publishing books are available at fine bookstores everywhere. To order from Hazelden Publishing, call **800-328-9000** or visit **hazelden.org/bookstore**.